Clarinet FOR DUMMIES®

by **David Etheridge**
with **Joe Kraynak**

WILEY

Wiley Publishing, Inc.

Clarinet For Dummies®

Published by
Wiley Publishing, Inc.
111 River St.
Hoboken, NJ 07030-5774
www.wiley.com

Copyright © 2010 by Wiley Publishing, Inc., Indianapolis, Indiana

Published by Wiley Publishing, Inc., Indianapolis, Indiana

Published simultaneously in Canada

For general information on our other products and services, please contact our Customer Care Department within the U.S. at 877-762-2974, outside the U.S. at 317-572-3993, or fax 317-572-4002.

For technical support, please visit www.wiley.com/techsupport.

Wiley also publishes its books in a variety of electronic formats. Some content that appears in print may not be available in electronic books.

Library of Congress Control Number: 2010928468

ISBN: 978-0-470-58477-4

Manufactured in the United States of America

10 9 8 7 6 5 4 3 2 1

WILEY

About the Author

David Etheridge is David Ross Boyd Professor of Clarinet, Chair of the Woodwind Area, and a member of the Oklahoma Woodwind Quintet at the University of Oklahoma School of Music. He is also in demand as a recitalist and clinician across the United States and Europe. Etheridge is a former member of the Oklahoma City Philharmonic, having performed with them as both Principal Clarinetist and as a member of the clarinet section. Prior to his 35-year tenure at the University of Oklahoma, he served on the faculty of the Crane School of Music in Potsdam, New York, for 9 years. He holds degrees from the University of Colorado and the Eastman School of Music, where he completed his Doctor of Musical Arts in clarinet performance as a student of Stanley Hasty. Etheridge serves regularly on the faculty of the International Clarinet Camp in Hungary. He is also the founder of the internationally acclaimed University of Oklahoma Clarinet Symposium, which is now in its 35th year. His most recent publications include *A Practical Approach to the Clarinet for Beginning Clarinetists*, *A Practical Approach to the Clarinet for Intermediate Clarinetists*, the *Revised Edition of a Practical Approach to the Clarinet for Advanced Clarinetists*, and *Mozart's Clarinet Concerto: The Performers' View*. In addition to his David Ross Boyd Distinguished Professorship, his awards include the Amoco Foundation Award for Good Teaching and the University of Oklahoma Regents Award for Superior Teaching.

Dedication

To my wonderful wife, Cheryl, the love of my life, for her steadfast support of my career over the years and countless hours of assistance on this book. Also, to my parents, Eileen Etheridge and Ellis Etheridge, for the sacrifices they made to make my first clarinet lessons possible, and to my superb teachers, Jack Stevens, Richard Culver, Val P. Henrich, Jerry Neil Smith, and Stanley Hasty for instilling in me a love of teaching.

Author's Acknowledgments

Thanks to acquisitions editor Michael Lewis, who chose me to author this book and ironed out all the preliminary details to make this book possible.

Tim Gallan, my project editor, deserves a loud cheer for serving as a gifted and patient collaborator and editor — shuffling chapters back and forth, shepherding the text and graphics through production, making sure any technical issues were properly resolved, and serving as the unofficial quality control manager. Christy Pingleton and Krista Hansing, copy editors, earn editor of the year awards for ferreting out my typos, misspellings, grammatical errors, and other language foe paws (or is it faux pas?), in addition to assisting Tim as reader advocate. I also tip my hat to the production crew for doing such an outstanding job of transforming an enormous hodgepodge of text, photos, music, and fingering charts into such an attractive bound book.

I owe very special thanks to wizard wordsmith Joe Kraynak for asking questions to clarify challenging concepts and helping me capture in written form how I actually teach clarinet to eager beginners. I could not have completed this project without his excellent collaboration.

Also, many thanks to Carolyn Rossow for her superb photography; to Jessi Rodgriquez for her excellent modeling: to Patrick Conlon for his terrific music copying; to Leon Smith for his patience and expertise in engineering and recording the CD; to Matt Stock, Christina Giacona, Dr. Brad Benson, and Annette Luyben for their research assistance; to Jim and Kyle Pyne for their assistance with mouthpiece information; and to Glenn Kantor, Dr. Julianne Kirk, and Dr. Michael Raiber for carefully proofreading the manuscript and offering valuable input of their own.

Publisher's Acknowledgments

We're proud of this book; please send us your comments through our Dummies online registration form located at http://dummies.custhelp.com. For other comments, please contact our Customer Care Department within the U.S. at 877-762-2974, outside the U.S. at 317-572-3993, or fax 317-572-4002.

Some of the people who helped bring this book to market include the following:

Acquisitions, Editorial, and Media Development

Senior Project Editor: Tim Gallan

Senior Acquisitions Editor: Michael Lewis

Copy Editors: Christine Pingleton, Krista Hansing

Senior Editorial Assistant: David Lutton

Technical Editor: Dianna Davis

Editorial Manager: Michelle Hacker

Editorial Assistants: Jennette ElNaggar, Rachelle S. Amick

Art Coordinator: Alicia B. South

Photographer: Carolyn Rossow

Music Transcriptionist: Patrick Conlon

Cover Photo: © Getty Images / Comstock

Cartoons: Rich Tennant (www.the5thwave.com)

Composition Services

Project Coordinator: Sheree Montgomery

Layout and Graphics: Nikki Gately, SDJumper

Proofreaders: Melanie Hoffman, Shannon Ramsey

Indexer: Potomac Indexing, LLC

Publishing and Editorial for Consumer Dummies

> **Diane Graves Steele,** Vice President and Publisher, Consumer Dummies

> **Kristin Ferguson-Wagstaffe,** Product Development Director, Consumer Dummies

> **Ensley Eikenburg,** Associate Publisher, Travel

> **Kelly Regan,** Editorial Director, Travel

Publishing for Technology Dummies

> **Andy Cummings,** Vice President and Publisher, Dummies Technology/General User

Composition Services

> **Debbie Stailey,** Director of Composition Services

Contents at a Glance

Table of Contents

Part III: Above and Beyond: Essential Intermediate Techniques 179

Introduction

The clarinet is a remarkable instrument. With a single reed and only seven tone holes and 17 keys, a typical clarinet can play 48 notes — a pitch range greater than any of its fellow woodwind instruments. Of course, if you do the math, this can get downright scary. Ten fingers, 17 keys, seven holes, 48 notes — they all add up to the fact that, in order to play the clarinet, you need to blow in precisely the right manner while engaging your fingers in some incredibly challenging acrobatics.

Fear not. With a decent clarinet; a good, well-adjusted reed; this book; and a reasonable amount of persistence and practice; you'll soon be tooting your own horn about the amazing progress you've made in such a brief period of time.

About This Book

The late clairvoyant Edgar Cayce claimed he could sleep with a book under his head and wake up the next morning knowing everything it contained. I wish I could tell you that learning to play the clarinet is simply a matter of slipping this book into your pillowcase before dozing off. While I'm afraid it's not quite that easy, in *Clarinet For Dummies*, I make it as easy as possible to pick up the clarinet for the first time, start playing it, and quickly improve your sound.

This book covers everything you need to know to play the clarinet, and then play it even better. I guide you in selecting the right clarinet, show you how to put it together, present you with a primer on reading sheet music, and bring you up to speed on the basics of actually playing. I start you off with the very barest of basics and a mini-clarinet — only the mouthpiece and barrel, without all those formidable tone holes and keys — and build from there.

Because the clarinet is a fairly complicated piece of equipment, I present everything you need to know in nibbles, so you can develop the entire skill set required at your own pace. Sprinkled generously throughout the chapters in which you're actually learning notes, skills, and techniques, are hands-on exercises for experiencing everything you're learning and improving your retention of it.

To further assist you in developing at your own pace, this book includes parts titles, chapter titles, section headings, and a detailed table of contents and index, making it easy to maneuver through the book and find exactly what you're looking for.

Conventions Used in This Book

I use several conventions in this book to call your attention to certain items. For example:

- *Italics* highlight new, somewhat technical terms, such as *tonguing* and *glissando,* which I follow up with straightforward, easy-to-understand definitions, of course.

- **Boldface** text indicates key words and phrases in bulleted and numbered lists.

- Monofont highlights Web and e-mail addresses.

- When this book was printed, some Web addresses may have needed to break across two lines of text. If that happened, rest assured that we haven't put in any extra characters (such as hyphens) to indicate the break. So, when using one of these Web addresses, just type in exactly what you see in this book, pretending as though the line break doesn't exist.

What You're Not to Read

You can safely skip anything you see in a gray shaded box. We stuck this material in a box (actually called a *sidebar*) for the same reason that most people stick stuff in boxes — to get it out of the way, so you won't trip over it. However, you may find the brief asides in the sidebars engaging, entertaining, and perhaps even mildly informative.

Foolish Assumptions

In writing this book, I made a few foolish assumptions, mostly about your motivation and how much you already know about music in general and playing the clarinet:

✔ You have a strong desire to play the clarinet for whatever reason. Maybe you think it looks awesome, sounds incredible, or your parents are pushing you to join the band and you want an instrument they know absolutely nothing about. The reason doesn't matter, but you want to play badly enough to read this book and invest a reasonable amount of time and effort in practice.

✔ Although you may have had some music lessons, can read sheet music, and possibly even know how to play some other musical instrument, I'm working on the assumption that you're a rank beginner, a blank slate.

✔ Even though you may have a band director or music teacher, I'm assuming you're a do-it-yourselfer, a lone wolf picking up the clarinet with only this book as your guide.

✔ You have a clarinet, some money to buy or rent one, or someone who can provide you with a clarinet. In other words, you have a clarinet or you're going to get one soon.

How This Book Is Organized

This book is organized to facilitate two ways of using it: You can read it from cover-to-cover, which is what I recommend, or skip around to only those parts, chapters, or sections that capture your current fancy or serve your present needs. I've been teaching the clarinet for 45 years and playing it for 60 years and have developed my own unique approach that has been very successful for my students. This book follows that approach, presenting what you need to know in the order that tends to be most effective.

As you soon discover, however, developing the skills required for playing the clarinet and playing it well is not always a linear path. While learning new notes or techniques, you often must skip back to review what you thought you already knew. This book is optimized for skipping around to find exactly what you need whenever you happen to need it.

To further assist you in navigating the contents, I took the 20 chapters and two appendixes that comprise the book and divvied them up into five parts. The following sections provide a quick overview of what's covered in each part.

Part I: Tuning Up with the Basics

You can pick up a clarinet, slap it together, and start honking like a mad goose in a matter of minutes. To sound like you know what you're doing, however, you must establish a firm foundation. That's what this part is all about.

Chapter 1 gets you up to speed in a hurry, touching on all the key topics throughout the book, so you can wrap your brain around everything involved. The remaining chapters introduce the various types of clarinets, identify the parts of a clarinet, explain the fundamental physics of how the clarinet produces notes, guide you in choosing the right clarinet and putting it together, and show you how to read sheet music.

By the end of this part, the stage is set for the concert to commence.

Part II: And a One, and a Two, and a Three: Getting Started

In this part, you actually begin to play your clarinet. I start you out slowly by paring down the clarinet to the dimensions of an oversized duck call, so you can focus exclusively on the mouthpiece and reed, which team up to produce the raw sound. The focus here is on posture, breathing, and *embouchure* — how you form the parts of your mouth to deliver air as directly at the reed as possible.

Assuming you can coax some sounds out of the shortened clarinet, you're ready to piece together the rest of your instrument and get your fingers in the act. The remaining chapters in this part introduce a few basic notes; show you how to articulate notes to give them more definition; and add more notes to your repertoire, so you can play higher, lower, in between, and even above high C.

Part III: Above and Beyond: Essential Intermediate Techniques

A comedian can have the best jokes, but if his delivery is lousy, he's just not funny. This part starts with the foolish assumption that you can play most of the notes, but you're not yet ready to wow the audience with your very first clarinet solo.

The chapters in this part assist you in developing skills and techniques for refining your clarinet sound with fullness, color, and focus. I show you how to reach high and hit the top notes, tune up for the proper pitch, develop faster tonguing and fingering techniques, make your practice sessions more productive, produce some very cool special effects, and tweak your reed for optimum performance and sound.

This part also encourages you to take your clarinet playing to the next level by seeking guidance from an experienced teacher and getting involved in your local music community. The goal here is to play before live audiences as part of an ensemble or even as a solo performer. I offer some leads on where you can find performance opportunities and provide insight on how to overcome any lingering stage fright you may have.

Part IV: The Part of Tens

Every *For Dummies* book includes a Part of Tens — two to four chapters, each containing ten bite-sized, easily-digestible tips, tricks, or insights. Here I offer ten inside tips on how to improve your technique, and I name ten A-list clarinetists, past and present, who may help inspire you and influence your technique.

Part V: Appendixes

Tacked on to the end of this book, just before the index, are two appendixes (or "appendices," depending on which side of the track you happen to live on). One contains fingering charts, so your fingers know where they need to be to play each note. The other contains a list of everything on the CD.

Icons Used in This Book

Throughout this book, you'll spot icons in the margins that call your attention to different types of information. Here are the icons you'll see and a brief description of each.

Everything in this book is important (except for the stuff in the shaded boxes), but some information is even *more* important. When you see this icon, read the text next to it not once but two or three times to tattoo it on your cranium.

Tips provide insider insight from behind the scenes. When you're looking for a better, faster, safer, and/or cheaper way to do something, check out these tips.

This icon appears when you need to be extra vigilant or seek professional help before moving forward. Don't skip this important information — I'm warning you.

When you encounter the clarinet for the first time, you need to learn two new languages — the language of music and that of the parts, techniques, and concepts related to the clarinet. Whenever I explain something highly technical, which I do only on rare occasions, I flag it with this icon, so you know what's coming.

This icon indicates that a particular lesson or piece of music is on the accompanying CD for you to listen to.

Where to Go From Here

Clarinet For Dummies is designed to take beginners from ground zero upward to an intermediate level of play, but if you already know a few things, you don't have to start right at the beginning.

For the big-picture view of all that's involved, check out Chapter 1. If you don't have a clarinet to play, head to Chapters 2 and especially 3 for guidance in making the right selection. Can't read music? Head to Chapter 4. If your clarinet is sitting there all in pieces, Chapter 5 can help.

Chapter 6 is critical in establishing and maintaining proper embouchure, and Chapter 7 gets you started playing your very first notes. From there, the field is wide open. Forge ahead chapter by chapter or skip around to your heart's delight.

And don't forget to have fun. Enjoying music is just as important as playing it.

Part I
Tuning Up with the Basics

The 5th Wave   By Rich Tennant

"You said you wanted one with a beginner's mouthpiece."

In this part . . .

You can pick up any instrument and start playing it. Little kids do it all the time. They bang on the piano keys, strum the guitar, pound on the drums, blow into a trumpet or harmonica, you name it. Such an approach, however, can be counterproductive, resulting in a damaged instrument, the acquisition of bad habits, and time-consuming trial by error.

A better approach is to brush up on the basics first. By grasping the fundamentals, starting with the right clarinet, knowing how to read music, and knowing how to handle and care for your clarinet, you learn how to play much more efficiently without risking unnecessary damage to your clarinet.

Consider the chapters in this part your warm-up exercises. Here, I bring you up to speed on the basics; help you pick the right clarinet for your needs; show you how to read music; and reveal the proper techniques for assembling, cleaning, and caring for your clarinet.

Chapter 1

So You Want to Play the Clarinet

*W*henever you approach a totally new experience, the learning curve can seem incredibly steep. You may not know what to expect, and you have no similar experience to form the framework for organizing and processing all the new information you're about to encounter.

This chapter is designed to help with that — to get you past any lingering anxiety you may have over getting started, bring you up to speed on the basics, and assist you in wrapping your brain around what you're about to experience.

You are about to take your first step toward playing one of the most remarkable-sounding musical instruments ever invented. Congratulations!

So, without further ado . . . a one . . . and a two . . . and a three. . . .

Overcoming Tone Hole Anxiety

I love to watch a new clarinet player's face when he sees his clarinet for the first time. The expression is a mix of eagerness and terror — the eager anticipation of learning to play an instrument that sounds so absolutely cool and the terror of seeing all those holes and all that metal.

If you're feeling this way right now, please remain calm. Do not head for the exits. Admittedly, all those holes and all that metal may seem overwhelming at first, but as soon as you get your hands wrapped around your clarinet and your fingers in position, it all starts to make sense. Having a clear idea of the function of all those holes and metal may be enough to soothe your nerves.

What's with all the holes?

The clarinet is in the woodwind family, but in some ways it acts like it belongs in the string section. The clarinet sound is actually the result of a column of air vibrating inside the clarinet and some distance beyond the end of the instrument. By opening and closing various combinations of tone holes, you change the length of that column of air, just as a guitar player shortens a string on her guitar by pinching the string between her finger and a fret on the neck of the guitar. A change in the length of the vibrating column of air equates with a change in the pitch or frequency of the note. (For more about this column of air thing, check out Chapter 2.)

Thanks to all these tone holes and the register key and other keys, covered in the following section, the clarinet has one of the most extensive ranges of any of the wind instruments. This means the clarinet can play more notes, from low to high, than almost any other wind instrument.

How 'bout all that metal?

The clarinet has a lot of bling, which may appear somewhat intimidating at first. By knowing the purpose of all this metal, you gain a better appreciation of it, and it begins to feel less threatening. The following list accounts for most of the metal:

- ✔ The metal insert on the left thumb hole beneath the register key prevents wear and tear and makes a better seal when the thumb closes the hole.

- ✔ Keys put certain tone holes within closer reach. When you play the clarinet, your hands pretty much remain stationary as your fingers move. That is, you don't need to move your hands up or down the clarinet very far to reach the keys. This is due to the many keys on the clarinet. Instead of using your fingers to cover or uncover a tone hole, you press keys that are closer to where your hands are, and those keys happen to be metal.

- ✔ Metal rings around some keys make it possible to close more tone holes than you have fingers for. The rings are connected to pads that close additional tone holes adjacent to the open tone holes you see.

You may see other parts of the clarinet adorned with metal, too. The ligature that clamps the reed to the mouthpiece is typically made of metal, and you may see rings of metal around the bell (at the end of the clarinet) and near the joints where the parts of the clarinet connect to one another.

Clarinet trivia

Your clarinet is about to become one of your closest friends and companions, so you should know a little something about it — like where it came from, its favorite nickname, and the names of celebrities it has met throughout its existence. Brush up on the following clarinet trivia:

✔ The invention of the clarinet is commonly credited to Johann Christoph Denner, a renowned instrument maker from Germany in the early eighteenth century.

✔ The clarinet is the second newest member of the woodwind family. (The saxophone is the newest.)

✔ Back in her school days, actress Julia Roberts played clarinet in the band.

✔ Early in the movie *Jaws*, which he also directed, Steven Spielberg has a cameo appearance playing clarinet in an orchestra.

✔ Handel and Vivaldi are the first of the "great composers" credited with writing music for the clarinet.

✔ The most famous clarinet solo occurs at the beginning of George Gershwin's "Rhapsody in Blue."

✔ Musicians commonly call the clarinet by the nickname "the licorice stick."

✔ The clarinet can't play chords — it plays only one note at a time.

✔ Former Chairman of the Federal Reserve Alan Greenspan performed as a professional clarinet/saxophone player in dance bands.

Selecting a Clarinet and Putting it Together

Before you can even think about playing a clarinet, you have to get your hands on one and put it together. The first part is actually the more complicated of the two tasks, because the selection is so wide. You can purchase a new or used clarinet or rent one, and many different stores and individuals sell clarinets. Clarinets are sold at music stores online and off, at garage sales, at auctions, and via classifieds, to name a few of your options.

The following sections touch on these topics and refer you to other chapters in the book where you can find much more information and guidance.

Selecting a clarinet

When you're in the market for a clarinet, you have a lot to think about and many choices to make, as noted in the following list. (Chapter 3, the shopping chapter, covers most of these choices, except for the first one, which is covered in Chapter 2.) When shopping for a clarinet, take the following factors into consideration:

- ✔ **Type of clarinet:** Clarinets don't all sound alike. You can find them in A, B♭ (most common), C, E♭, and other keys. In Chapter 2, I describe the various types and which is likely to be best for someone who's just starting out. I also describe the two different fingering systems used on clarinets, so you don't get stuck with a clarinet you can't use.

- ✔ **Quality:** When shopping for a quality instrument, the choice usually falls into one of the following three ranges: starter-upper (for beginners), step up (for intermediate players), and "money is no object" (for professionals). Chapter 3 reveals the differences and trade-offs.

- ✔ **Material:** A major factor to consider is the material out of which the clarinet is made. The choices boil down to three: plastic, wood, or greenline (wood/resin composite). All three are good choices, depending on where you're playing, how gentle you are in handling the instrument, and the sound you're looking for. In Chapter 3, I show you how to sort out the material choices.

- ✔ **Buying versus renting:** The question of buying or renting a clarinet involves several factors, including budget, the likelihood that the person who's going to be playing it will stick with it, and the actual condition of the instrument. (Turn to Chapter 3 for additional guidance.)

- ✔ **New versus used:** A new clarinet is like a new car — as soon as you drive it off the lot, it loses some value — so you can often find good used clarinets at affordable prices. In Chapter 3, I show you where to look and provide guidance on selecting a new clarinet, as well.

- ✔ **Accessories:** You can purchase custom parts for your clarinet separately to improve its sound and how well it responds. In Chapter 2 I label the parts of the clarinet, and in Chapter 3 I reveal your options for swapping out parts.

Some assembly (and maintenance) required

The clarinet is not a one-piece instrument. It's comprised of several parts, and you need to put it together properly before you can play it. Putting all the pieces together is child's play (it's only six pieces), but doing it right without breaking something or causing unnecessary wear is a little more involved. Chapter 5 shows you how to assemble your clarinet properly and offers tips and tricks to make the process go as smoothly as possible.

In Chapter 5, you also discover the proper way to clean and store your clarinet, along with some maintenance tips and information on finding a repair technician to help correct wear and tear on the instrument and any damage to it.

Reading and Understanding Musical Notation

Even if you can play by ear, that won't help you much in performing the numerous exercises in this book, because they're all written in musical notation. In short, you must be able to read music. If the clarinet is your second, third, or fourth instrument, chances are good you can already decipher musical notation. You're one step ahead of the game. If you're unable to read music or need a refresher course, hop over to Chapter 4 for a quick primer.

When you're playing any wind instrument, you must be able to not only read music, but also read and interpret *fingering charts* — schematic illustrations that show you the tone holes that must be open and closed to play a particular note. In other words, a fingering chart shows you where to put your fingers. Chapter 7 introduces you to fingering charts and shows you how to finger your first notes. Appendix A provides fingering charts for all the notes in the clarinet's range.

Getting Physical with Your Clarinet

Playing the clarinet gives your entire body a workout, especially if you stand while playing. You must hold your body just so, breathe deeply, use just about every muscle in your mouth to direct airflow into the mouthpiece, use your tongue to launch and separate notes, and use your hands and fingers (and thumbs) to support the weight of the clarinet and play all the notes. I get tired just thinking about it.

Fortunately, with good equipment and proper technique, you won't be wrestling with the clarinet or yourself to play notes, and the physical activity will seem less of a burden and more of a joy. The following sections explain the basics of playing with proper technique. In Chapter 6, I fill in all the details and offer additional guidance and tips.

Assuming the proper posture

Most of what you need to do to assume the proper posture for playing the clarinet is to follow your mother's advice — stand up straight, don't slouch, and hold your shoulders back. Do all that in a natural and relaxed way, and you're halfway home.

To get all the way home, keep your chin up. This serves two purposes. First, it prevents you from looking like a mope. Second, it keeps your airway more open. Think of your airway as a garden hose. Bend that hose in half, and you cut the water flow to a trickle. Keep the hose straight, and water gushes out. To play the full range of notes on your clarinet, you need unrestricted airflow. You don't get that when your chin is down and your windpipe is pinched off.

Try it yourself. Breathe with your chin up and then try breathing with it down, almost touching your chest. Unless you're an anatomical anomaly, you breathe much more feely with your chin up.

To encourage good posture, raise your music stand so the top of the sheet music is at eye level. The music at the top is almost impossible to read if you let your chin drop or start slouching. You have to sit up (or stand up) straight!

Learning to breathe — correctly this time

As soon as you're born, the doctor flips you upside down and slaps you on the fanny, so you take a big, deep breath and start wailing like a fire truck. If that's how things went down after you were born, that was probably the deepest breath you ever took. Kids naturally breathe deeply. If you're like most people, from that point on your breathing has become more and more shallow. To play the clarinet well, you must break the bad breathing habits you've acquired over the years and rediscover how to breathe properly.

Breathing properly means breathing with your diaphragm rather than with your shoulders. Here's a quick way to check whether you're breathing properly:

1. **Lie flat on your back.**

2. **Lay this book on your stomach.**

3. **Breathe deeply, keeping an eye on the book and taking note of any other movement, such as in your shoulders.**

If the book moved up and down, and your back and shoulders remained stationary, you're in pretty good shape in terms of deep breathing, assuming you keep this up when you're standing or sitting. If the book didn't move but your back and shoulders did, don't worry. I show you how to fix this in Chapter 6, and how to breathe even more deeply if you happened to pass this preliminary test.

Holding your mouth just right

It looks soooo easy. You just stick the mouthpiece in your mouth and blow. Unfortunately, there's more to it than that. To get any sound to come out of a clarinet and to produce a quality sound, you must form and maintain proper *embouchure* — a fancy French word that describes how you form your mouth around the mouthpiece of a wind instrument. Proper embouchure forms a good seal around the mouthpiece, so no air leaks out when you blow, and it allows part of the reed to vibrate freely inside your mouth.

Here are the basics of proper embouchure for the clarinet:

- ✓ Your lower teeth and lip join forces to create a very narrow ledge on which the clarinet's reed rests. Smiling with your lower lip stretches the lip tightly against your lower teeth with only a fractional amount of your lower lip over your teeth. You don't talk with your lower lip inside your mouth, so don't play the clarinet that way either.

- ✓ You rotate your jaw forward so when you close your mouth around the mouthpiece you have about a half inch of reed inside your mouth. (In Chapter 6, I show you a trick to ensure you have the proper amount of reed in your mouth.)

- ✓ Your upper teeth press down on the top of the mouthpiece slightly farther back on the mouthpiece than your lower teeth. This creates a teeter-totter effect, resulting in pressure on the reed from the lower lip to commence reed vibration. See "Squeezing out notes by applying a little leverage," a little later in this chapter, for an explanation of how this works.

- ✓ Your lips seal around the mouthpiece to prevent air from escaping as you blow. Frowning with your upper lip helps make this seal.

Maintaining proper embouchure is crucial, so spend some time on this in Chapter 6.

Delivering fast air

Air is to the clarinet as gas is to a car engine. Fast-moving air makes the reed vibrate, which produces sound. No vibration, no sound. In addition, you use fast air to accent notes (make them louder) and create crescendos for transitioning from lower notes, which you can produce with slower air, to higher notes that require faster air. The speed of the air also contributes significantly to producing good tone (see the later section "Developing a Richer Tone").

Two components contribute to producing fast air — breath support and the shape of the inside of your mouth. You need to breathe deeply to supply a sufficient volume of air, and then position your tongue to drive a concentrated stream of air at the reed. With the front of your tongue raised up like someone lifted it up with a pencil, hiss like a snake to establish the proper tongue position. This pushes the air more forcefully at the reed.

Don't let your cheeks puff out. Your cheeks should press against your teeth.

Squeezing out notes by applying a little leverage

As explained earlier in the section "Holding your mouth just right," your lower lip functions as a narrow ledge on which the reed rests. This forms a teeter-totter with the clarinet. Your upper teeth sit on the very short end of the teeter-totter while the entire length of the clarinet extending beyond your lower teeth is on the other end.

If you hold the clarinet up, so it sticks straight out from your mouth, your lower lip applies very little upward pressure to the reed. If you blow, no sound comes out. As you lower the clarinet (bringing it closer to your body), while keeping your upper teeth and lower lip stationary, your lower lip applies more upward pressure to the reed, pushing it nearer to the mouthpiece. At a certain point, when the reed is close enough to the mouthpiece, physics takes over and the reed begins to vibrate. The sound is usually best when the clarinet is at about a 30-degree angle to your body.

You don't apply pressure to the reed by biting the mouthpiece. Your teeth remain stationary as you lower the clarinet. This gives you much more control over applying incremental changes in upward pressure (leverage) to the reed.

Getting your fingers into the action

Reed vibration vibrates the column of air inside the clarinet, producing sound but not producing individual notes. To play notes, you must get your fingers into the action. Your fingers press keys and seal off tone holes in various combinations to produce notes. As explained earlier, in the section "What's with all the holes?" opening tone holes changes the length of the vibrating column of air, which results in notes of different pitches.

Fingerings can be quite complex. On a piano, all you do is tap one key with a single, solitary finger to play any given note. On the clarinet, any number of fingers can be called into action to play a note. In addition, you can play some notes on the clarinet with different fingerings, which can come in handy when you're moving from one note to another — an alternate fingering may provide your fingers with a shorter or more convenient route to the next note.

Because fingerings on the clarinet are complex, I spread out their coverage. Chapter 7 presents basic fingerings for some mid-range notes. In Chapter 8, you add to your repertoire to significantly expand the range of notes you can play. In Chapter 10, you head higher with the altissimo notes and discover some alternate fingerings to help with awkward transitions between these higher notes. Chapter 13 reveals even more alternate fingerings.

Transitioning between notes: Slurring, tonguing, and more

You can play notes with or without spaces between them by slurring (no spaces) and tonguing (spaces). You also use tonguing to launch notes. In the following sections, you find out what slurring and tonguing are all about.

In language, *articulation* refers to using articulatory organs, including the tongue and lips, to shape sounds that make up words. In music, *articulation* is the shaping of notes, and includes tonguing, slurring, and accenting notes.

Slurring for smooth transitions

Slurring simply means running the notes together. Take a deep breath and then pronounce a string of vowels without stopping your flow of air: AyyyyEeeeeIyyyyOhhhh. You're clearly saying different letters, but without any space between them. That's slurring in a nutshell. Chapter 9 covers the topic in greater detail, and Chapter 4 shows you how to tell when to slur by looking at your sheet music.

Tonguing to launch notes

Tonguing consists of touching the tip of your tongue to the very tip of the reed, which either keeps the reed from starting to vibrate or, for a fleeting moment, stops its vibration. To launch notes with your tongue, you keep your tongue on the reed, supply some air, and release your tongue. It's just like saying the letter "T" followed by a hiss. Try it: Focusing on what your tongue does, say "T-heeee."

With tonguing, less is more. Slight upward pressure is all that's required to press the tip of the reed against the tip rail of the mouthpiece and stop vibration. Aiming your tongue at the tip rail rather than the reed, as explained in Chapter 9, is the best approach.

Tonguing to add space between notes

You create space between notes by tonguing to stop reed vibration, not by stopping airflow. Airflow should be constant as you move from note to note, speeding up or slowing down but never stopping except when you need to inhale. Tonguing comes in two styles:

- **Legato:** *Legato* (literally meaning "tied together") uses very little space between notes, giving a passage of music a sing-song quality.

- **Staccato:** *Staccato* (literally meaning "detached") is a style that gives more definition to each individual note by adding space between the notes.

To tongue faster, instead of "T-heeee," you use a D word, like "Deh" or "Dih," so your tongue spends less time on the reed, as explained in Chapter 14.

Adding accents and crescendos

Although you maintain airflow when transitioning between notes, you must often speed up the airflow to add accents and crescendos:

- ✔ **Accent:** An *accent* adds emphasis to a particular note, suddenly increasing its volume.

- ✔ **Crescendo:** A *crescendo* increases the speed of the airflow more gradually to ramp up to an accent or transition to a note of a higher pitch. (Higher notes require faster air.)

Developing a Richer Tone

To be a decent clarinet player, you must play in tune. To become an outstanding clarinet player, you must play in tune *and* produce a great *tone* — a full, rich sound. In the following sections, I introduce you to the four ingredients of great tone and discuss several additional topics that contribute to producing a quality sound.

Recognizing the four ingredients of great tone

All musicians, including clarinetists, are expected to play in tune, but each produces a unique tone that varies according to the type and quality of the instrument and what the musician adds through her skills, talent, and technique. Even though tone is unique to each individual and the clarinet she plays, great tone is always the result of mixing the following four ingredients, as explained in Chapter 11:

- ✔ **Amplitude:** Amplitude is a function of air volume and reed vibration. Without sufficient air volume, the reed remains still, and the clarinet silent.

- ✔ **Pitch:** Pitch is a function of leverage, discussed earlier in this chapter in the section "Squeezing out notes by applying a little leverage." As you apply leverage, you essentially shift the clarinet into gear and initiate reed vibration. To a large extent, how much leverage you apply controls the pitch, assuming your clarinet is in tune and your reed is in good working order. (See "Perfecting your reed," later in this chapter.)

✔ **Color:** Color adds brightness to the tone by enriching it with *overtones* — higher harmonics that resonate with the fundamental frequency (pitch) of the note. Adding color to your tone requires fast air to produce those overtones. If you're breathing properly and maintaining proper tongue position, delivering fast air is not a major challenge.

✔ **Focus:** Focus helps project the sound by keeping it narrowed to an intense beam. To focus the sound, you make very minor adjustments to your embouchure, shifting your top teeth back slightly and/or increasing your upper lip support.

Playing loudly, softly, and in between

You can play the clarinet in a soft whisper, something you can't do with most other wind instruments. As a result, many composers write music for the clarinet that includes passages that must be played *sotto voce* (very softly).

Contrary to what you may assume, playing soft requires more air, not less, so the clarinet can project that softer sound far enough out into the audience to be heard. In Chapter 11, I reveal techniques for playing in a whisper that everyone can hear.

Adding some special effects: Vibrato, glisses, and bends

Over the years, innovative clarinet players have developed ways to make the clarinet produce sounds it was never designed to produce. To add another dimension to your sound, consider adding these special effects to your repertoire, as discussed in Chapter 12:

✔ **Vibrato:** *Vibrato* is the undulating effect you often hear when listening to singers hit and hold a note. You can produce the same effect on the clarinet with jaw vibrato (sometimes called lip vibrato) or glottal vibrato. With *jaw vibrato,* the much more common of the two, you subtly move your lower jaw up and down quickly to change pressure on the reed. With *glottal vibrato,* you blow harder or more softly alternately to create the pulses within notes.

✔ **Glissandos and smears:** These are alternate ways of transitioning between notes. A typical *glissando* ("gliss" for short), consists of parts of scales with some chromatic notes added into the mix. (Chromatic notes are the sharps and flats between notes — the black keys on a piano.) A *smear* is a type of glissando in which you slide from one note to the next. The very beginning of Gershwin's "Rhapsody in Blue" best exemplifies the sound of a smear.

✔ **Bends and scoops:** A *bend* occurs inside a note, lowering its pitch and then raising it back up to pitch. A *scoop* occurs at the very beginning of a note, starting the note at a lower pitch and then raising it up to pitch.

Cranking up your tongue and finger speed

Clarinet music varies in tempo and may require you to play certain passages very quickly. To play such a passage well, you need to really know the music, practice it until your fingers and tongue know it, and engage your tongue and fingers in daily speed training exercises:

✔ **Speeding up your tongue:** Tonguing notes faster creates less space between them, resulting in faster play. Keeping the air flowing and your tongue relaxed are key. Check out Chapter 14 for additional suggestions.

✔ **Speeding up your fingers:** As you practice a piece, you can naturally play it faster and faster, because your fingers know where they need to be for each note. You can also increase your speed by improving finger strength and coordination, as explained in Chapter 14.

Devote a portion of every practice session to playing fast. This improves your ability to play well at any speed.

Tweaking your clarinet into tune

Whether you're playing alone, in a duet, or in an ensemble, keep your clarinet in tune. In addition to helping you blend in with the band, the process of tuning your clarinet trains your inner ear to recognize proper pitch.

Changing the pitch of a clarinet is relatively easy. All you do is pull out on the barrel while twisting it back and forth to widen the space between the barrel and the upper joint. You can make more minor adjustments by pulling the mouthpiece out from the barrel slightly or pulling the upper and lower joints apart ever so slightly. All of these adjustments increase the length of the clarinet, which changes its pitch.

The actual tuning process is fairly involved, so I spend an entire chapter on it. In Chapter 15, I show you how to warm up a cold clarinet before tuning it, tune it by ear or with an electronic tuner, make minor adjustments during a performance, and compensate for any quirky pitch tendencies your clarinet may have by using alternate fingerings and other tricks.

Perfecting your reed

Reed vibration generates the base sound the clarinet uses to produce various notes. No vibration, no sound. The reed is a very sensitive instrument, so minor problems with it can cause major problems for you and your sound. Fortunately, because the reed is made of cane (a wood-like material), you can make adjustments to it by removing tiny amounts of cane to bring the reed back into balance. Even brand new reeds require adjustments.

Repairing and refining a reed serves a dual purpose:

- ✔ **It makes the reed more responsive.** A well-tuned reed — like a well-tuned car engine — responds faster and with less effort when you give it gas. In the case of the clarinet, the gas happens to be the air you blow into the mouthpiece. With a responsive reed, you don't have to blow so hard to make it vibrate.

- ✔ **It improves the sound.** A defective or poorly adjusted reed produces a weak, wheezy sound, if it produces any sound at all. One or two very minor adjustments often result in major improvement in sound quality.

Chapter 17 shows you how to identify "talented" reeds — reeds that are good candidates you can make even better. You also discover how to test and diagnose a "sick" reed, gather the tools to fix it, and perform minor surgery to cure its ills.

Mastering the Two P's: Practice and Performance

This book contains everything you need to start playing the clarinet and to play it well. What it doesn't contain is the practice you must do to reinforce the skills and techniques presented in the book. Nor does it include an ensemble and a stage for your future performances. However, I've included the next best things — guidance on how to make your practice sessions most productive and suggestions on how to track down people to play with and places to perform.

Engaging in productive practice

Regular, well-focused practices — six days a week for at least a half hour each session — are crucial in learning specific pieces, retaining what you've learned in this book and elsewhere, and keeping yourself in shape to play your clarinet. Without practice, your fingers tend to become less limber and less coordinated, you're more likely to fall into shallow breathing practices, and you tend to forget stuff.

Chapter 16 assists you in establishing a practice routine that's not all work and no play. I provide guidance on the types of exercises and short pieces most valuable in honing your technique. And I provide a list of additional resources (mostly sheet music) designed specifically to help you maintain your enthusiasm for the clarinet while sharpening your skills.

Stepping up on stage

Music is a joyful pursuit to be shared, so when you feel ready, consider stepping on stage and sharing your music with a live audience. Nothing motivates or challenges you more than having to prepare a piece to play in front of others. In addition, performance puts you in contact with other musicians who can share everything they've learned in their musical careers.

If you're in school and your school has a music program complete with a band, you have ready opportunities to perform. If you're out of school, tracking down performance opportunities poses a more daunting challenge. In Chapter 18, I provide some leads, encourage you to take the stage, and assist you in overcoming any pre-performance anxiety.

Chapter 2

Getting to Know the Clarinet

*Y*ou don't *need* to know much about clarinets to start playing one. In fact, some accomplished clarinet players got their start by simply picking up a clarinet and fooling around with it, putting off the formal lessons for another day. By developing a general understanding of the clarinet, however, you have the framework in place to pick up new information quickly, retain it longer, and start out right — so you don't have to break so many bad habits later.

In this chapter, I provide that framework. I introduce you to the clarinet and its five basic parts, bring you up to speed on how the clarinet produces such a unique sound, let you in on the basic concepts of playing the clarinet, reveal the various types of clarinets you may encounter, and explain the two fingering systems you need to know about. By the end of this chapter, you have the foundation in place to start out right.

A Brief Lesson in Clarinet Anatomy

Until you can name the parts of a clarinet, you're limited to referring to them by pointing and grunting or using vague descriptions like "this little doo-hickey," "that thing you put in your mouth," and "those shiny gizmos." You won't know what I'm talking about when I lead you through the process of assembling the clarinet or mention the ligature — the liga-who?

In the following sections, I identify the five main parts of the clarinet (and some minor ones) and provide additional, fascinating information on how each part contributes to forming the unique sounds clarinets can make. If you're more of a visual learner, check out Figure 2-1, but read the text, too, for all the juicy details.

Figure 2-1: The parts of the clarinet.

The business end of the clarinet: The mouthpiece, reed, and ligature

The mouthpiece, reed, and ligature, together with your lungs, lips, tongue, and teeth, are the parts of the clarinet that produce the raw sound. Other parts of the clarinet contribute to modify that sound.

Mouthpiece

At the top of every clarinet is a *mouthpiece* — the part of the clarinet you stick in your mouth to play. Now you may think all mouthpieces are alike, but each mouthpiece can be very unique depending on the following characteristics (see Figure 2-2):

- **Size and shape:** Size and shape both contribute to the comfort and sound of the mouthpiece. Smaller is often better for younger players (who have smaller mouths). Shape can vary on the outside and inside, with the interior shape (the *bore*) contributing more to the tonal quality of the clarinet.

- **Material:** Most mouthpieces are made of plastic, but the better ones are made of hard rubber that can be machined.

- **Craftsmanship:** Generic mouthpieces are typically manufactured in an injection molding machine, while higher-quality models are molded and then machined by a skilled craftsman.

- **Window:** The *window* is the opening near the top of the mouthpiece in which the reed vibrates. The opening size and shape can also contribute to the tone.

- **Table:** The *table* is the flat area below the window that the reed clamps to.

- **Facing (or lay):** *Facing* is the area between the top of the table and the tip of the clarinet, where the reed vibrates. A mouthpiece with a longer facing increases the range but can be more difficult for beginners to control, because the reed has more room to vibrate.

- **Baffle:** The *baffle* is the surface inside the mouthpiece opposite the reed. Its depth can affect reed movement and help a player correct any irregularities in her tone.

- **Tonal chamber:** The *tonal chamber* is the hollowed-out inside of the mouthpiece that ultimately becomes part of the bore of the clarinet. The tonal chamber can vary in size and shape and is one of the most important factors contributing to the overall sound.

- **Bore:** The *bore* is the hole in the bottom of the mouthpiece that attaches to the barrel joint. A smaller bore produces a more compact, focused sound, whereas a larger bore produces a more mellow, darker sound.

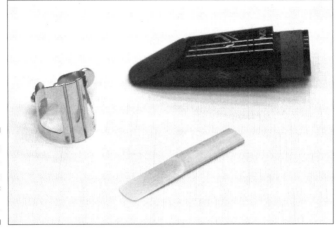

Figure 2-2:
The mouth-
piece has its
own set of
parts.

All characteristics of a mouthpiece contribute to producing its unique sound. Although the facing and tone chamber may be the two characteristics that contribute the most, the overall feel, comfort, and tone are the most important considerations.

In Chapter 3, I focus more on what to look for in a quality mouthpiece.

Reed

A clarinet without a reed would be like you without vocal cords. If you tried to say something, the air would rush out of your windpipe and through your larynx making nary a sound. Just as your vocal cords tighten and vibrate to produce sound as air passes over them, the *reed* vibrates as air passes over it, emitting a sound that the rest of the clarinet can then form into infinite variations.

Reeds are made from a special type of cane (actually from the grass family) that grows best in southern France and Spain. When harvested, it looks like long poles of bamboo. It's then carved up and sanded to make reeds, which look suspiciously similar to popsicle sticks, although they're quite a bit wider and somewhat thicker. And, like popsicle sticks, reeds are disposable.

A reed's cut and thickness determine how hard or soft it is, which influences both the clarinet's tone and the amount of air pressure necessary to make the reed vibrate — the harder the reed, the harder you need to blow to make a sound. For more about differences among reeds, check out Chapter 3.

Now that's mouthpiece loyalty!

Many clarinetists spend hundreds of dollars and many hours in their quest for the perfect mouthpiece — the one that feels just right and produces the tone they're looking for. If they're ever fortunate enough to discover the perfect mouthpiece, they tend to mate with it for life,

using the same mouthpiece throughout most or all of their clarinet-playing years.

Stanley Drucker, who recently retired as principal clarinetist of the New York Philharmonic, used the same mouthpiece for most of his 60-year tenure there.

Ligature

Ligature is a fancy word for "clamp." The ligature holds the reed firmly to the mouthpiece and allows the reed to act like a diving board. To understand the function of a ligature, hold a ruler on your desk with half of it hanging over the edge, press down on the half over the desk, twang the end that sticks out with your finger, and watch it vibrate. Next, relax your hand pressure on the desk side of the ruler and twang it again. Notice that it barely vibrates. This little experiment shows just how important a ligature is to reed vibration.

You're likely to encounter two types of ligature design: front-loading and back-loading. Front-loading ligatures, common on new clarinets, have screws on the reed side. Back-loading ligatures position the screws on the top of the mouthpiece for increased vibration and to allow the player to comfortably put more mouthpiece in his mouth. Which is best? Check out Chapter 3 for the answer to that question.

Pitching in to tune your clarinet: The barrel joint

The *barrel joint* is the connecting tissue between the mouthpiece and the upper joint. It's uniquely responsible for most tuning adjustments on the clarinet. Pulling out the barrel lowers the pitch, while pushing it in raises the pitch. Barrels can vary in respect to the following characteristics:

✔ **Length:** The standard length for B♭ clarinets (more about this later in the chapter) is 66 millimeters. Players in orchestras often opt for longer barrels, while clarinetists who are consistently flat may prefer a slightly shorter barrel (65 millimeters).

- ✔ **Bore dimensions:** The interior dimensions of the bore of the barrel can affect the sound of the instrument, the same way the mouthpiece is impacted by its bore dimensions.

- ✔ **Shape:** Barrels on early clarinets were primarily cylindrical. Present-day barrel joints have inverted cone shapes and poly-cylindrical interior shapes to give the clarinet a richer sound.

Accommodating your left hand: The upper joint

The upper joint is the clarinet's midsection. Above it are the barrel joint and mouthpiece. Below it are the lower joint and bell. The most important thing to remember about the upper joint is that it's where your left hand goes. On the upper joint, you find numerous keys and holes:

- ✔ **Tone holes** are covered (or uncovered as the case may be) by your fingers.

- ✔ **Trill keys,** the four small keys near the top of the upper joint, are all located on this joint and make many alternate fingerings possible.

- ✔ **The vent key** (otherwise known as the register key) can make the clarinet play higher or lower. Press this key, and the clarinet instantly plays 12 notes higher. Unlike saxophones, oboes, and bassoons, the clarinet is the only woodwind that isn't built in octaves, so it has no octave key.

Both the left thumb and first finger of the left hand do double duty, because they cover tone holes and operate additional keys.

Relying on your right hand: The lower joint

A short skip down from the upper joint is the lower joint, operated exclusively by your right hand. Like the upper joint, it has tone holes and keys, including keys you press with your little fingers. The keys are attached to levers that open and close pads over the tone holes. These key/lever mechanisms essentially perform the same function as your fingers do when they close the tone holes, but in this case, the tone holes are closed by default and open only when you press the keys.

At the back of the lower joint and towards the very top is the thumb rest, which supports the entire weight of the clarinet. This thumb rest sits on your right thumb, just above the knuckle.

Ringing in at the far end: The bell

Although it may sound nothing like a bell, due to its shape, the flared end of the clarinet is referred to as the *bell*. It serves two purposes:

- ✔ In part, the bell helps transfer the sound waves created by the clarinet to the surrounding atmosphere.
- ✔ The bell helps even out the notes on the instrument.

The interior shape of the bell is very important, as is the density of the materials from which it's made. In this regard, the bell has much in common with the barrel joint. I discuss this in greater detail in Chapter 3, where I show you clarinet upgrade options.

Exploring the Inner Workings of the Clarinet

You don't need to understand how an internal combustion engine operates in order to drive a car, but when you're first learning to play the clarinet, understanding how it produces sounds can make you more in tune with your instrument. After all, that clarinet doesn't make sounds all by itself. In a Zen-like way, you and your clarinet become one. Understanding a little about how the clarinet works can help you more effectively adapt to it and get it to make the sounds you want it to.

Getting the vibrations going

It all begins with you, primarily your lungs. Assuming you blow fast enough into the mouthpiece, the reed vibrates. As it vibrates, it opens and closes over the facing of the mouthpiece and creates high and low pressure zones that cause the air to vibrate inside the bore (the hole that runs through the inside of the clarinet). This makes the bore vibrate, just like a string vibrates on a guitar or violin. Of course, you can't see your clarinet vibrating, but the sound is proof that it happens.

Making notes

To produce different notes on the clarinet, you simply change its length. Change its length?! Sounds absurd, doesn't it? You've watched people play the clarinet before and never, ever have you seen them changing the length of their instrument. Maybe a trombone player, but never the clarinet players. However, you do, in fact, change the length of the instrument. When you cover more tone holes, the vibrating column of air inside the clarinet becomes longer. When you lift your fingers or press keys to let more air escape, that column of air becomes shorter.

These same principles apply when tuning a clarinet, but instead of covering or uncovering tone holes to make the column of air longer or shorter, you use the barrel joint to make the clarinet physically longer or shorter.

Grasping the Basic Concepts of Playing the Clarinet

One of the secrets of doing anything well is envisioning yourself doing it well. Long before Michael Jordan could fly through the air to execute one of his trademark slam-dunks, he had to imagine himself doing it. Use the same visioning technique to get your brain used to the idea that you can play the clarinet and play it well.

In the following sections, you get to step back and take a couple minutes to size up the instrument, without the pressure of making any sounds, and play a video clip inside your own mind of you playing the clarinet.

Blowing some hot air

The clarinet is a member of the woodwind family, with the accent on *wind*. Your lungs are the very source of the sound your clarinet makes. This means you need to learn how to breathe deeply and blow a fast, steady stream without making your cheeks bulge out.

The beauty of the sound depends on how well you can control the amount of air you expel at any one time. It's sort of like a car — just because you have a full tank of gas doesn't mean you use it all to run to the store and back.

Breathe in and out deeply, steadily, and forcefully, keeping your throat as open as possible — or just say "sheee."

Using the mouth as a plumbing device: The embouchure

Embouchure is how you shape your mouth to play wind instruments. The shape is very much like the one you likely make when putting lip balm on your bottom lip. Clarinet embouchure serves three functions:

- ✔ It connects your lungs — the source of wind — to the instrument.

- ✔ It helps close the reed against the mouthpiece facing, so the reed vibrates. According to the laws of physics, the reed must close half the distance between itself and the mouthpiece before it can vibrate. This is known as *blowing pressure* — the pressure necessary to bend the reed close enough to the facing of the mouthpiece to make the reed vibrate.

- ✔ It must create blowing pressure in a manner that allows free vibration of the reed. Instead of biting on the reed to close it, you use the leverage of the clarinet as discussed in the following section.

The reed is the sound generator. It must be allowed to do its thing. Don't let your mouth get in the way.

Using the clarinet as a lever (so to speak)

You should never use your clarinet as a crowbar, but in many ways, this is a good analogy for what you need to do to play it. You place your top teeth a short distance down from the tip of the mouthpiece and then place your bottom lip, slightly supported by your bottom teeth, about twice as far down the reed. Your lower lip functions as the fulcrum. As you lower the clarinet to play, your top teeth push down on the mouthpiece, pushing the reed down against your lower lip. This way, your embouchure doesn't have to squeeze so hard on the reed that it restricts its vibration.

For more about embouchure and using the clarinet as a lever, complete with illustrations, check out Chapter 6.

Fingering those notes

Although your lungs and mouth are the source of your clarinet's sound, your fingers aren't slouches when it comes to playing the clarinet. Their job, in addition to keeping the clarinet from falling out of your mouth, is to open and close tone holes to form the sound into various notes.

Even when some fingers are resting, they still need to be ready to spring into action — to cover a tone hole or press a key to uncover one. Think of your fingers as shortstops on a baseball team. A shortstop doesn't just stand on one base waiting for the ball to come to him. He has to be ready to cover second and third bases and everything in between. He may even need to step back into the outfield to field a short fly ball. In the same way, your fingers need to be ready to play the field, so to speak.

In Chapter 7, I illustrate the correct hand position, so you can get a grip on the basics.

Appreciating Clarinet Diversity

Here's a trivia question for you: Which family of instruments among the winds and strings is the largest? If you answered the clarinet family, you're absolutely right. The clarinet family boasts a membership of ten distinct types, many of which are pitched in different keys. Each member of this extended family has its own characteristic tone quality and projection level, as distinctive as a human voice.

The only characteristic shared by all members of the clarinet family is the range. All clarinets have an identical range: from E below the staff to G an octave above the G that's just above the staff.

The variations among the different members of the clarinet family can be attributed to the characteristics that distinguish each family member, including the following:

- ✔ **Length:** The longer the instrument, the lower the notes it can play. For example, bass clarinets often favor the lower notes of their range, which have the fullness and richness of baritone or bass singers.

- ✔ **Fingering systems:** Two fingering systems, French and German, result in clarinets that aren't fingered exactly the same. See "Exploring Two Unique Fingering Systems," later in this chapter, for details.

- ✔ **Materials:** The highest-quality clarinets are made from wood or a wood-resin combination. Less expensive instruments are constructed from a type of plastic.

- ✔ **Mouthpieces:** Most members of the clarinet family use mouthpieces and reeds of varying sizes.

Why so many lengths and types? Because the earliest clarinets had only two or three keys, orchestras needed clarinets of different lengths to play in all the keys that composers used.

Piccolo clarinet

The *piccolo clarinet*, also called the *octave* or *octavina clarinet*, is pitched in A♭ and sounds an octave and a seventh above the standard B♭ clarinet. The Piccolo clarinet in A♭ is the only surviving member of the piccolo clarinet group. Earlier instruments were also pitched in G, C, and B♭.

Because they often make a very shrill, cutting tone, piccolo clarinets find homes primarily in European military bands (except England) and in clarinet choirs around the world. They're constructed of wood and require their own type of mouthpiece and reed.

E♭ clarinet

E♭ clarinets are slightly longer than piccolo clarinets and are pitched in, you guessed it, E♭. In Italy, they go by the name *quartino clarinets.* E♭ clarinets sound a fourth higher than B♭ soprano clarinets and produce a high, brilliant, somewhat shrill sound. Composers use them when they want a garish, town-band sound. Consequently, they're usually played at the top of their range.

Earlier versions of the E♭ clarinet were pitched in G and D. The version in G was once very popular, and in England the D clarinet was a favorite of Richard Strauss. D clarinets were slightly longer and hence had a slightly warmer tone than their E♭ counterparts.

Soprano clarinets

Soprano clarinets are made in three pitch levels: C, B♭ (longer), and A (longest). The longer the instrument, the lower the relative range. Following are brief descriptions of each:

✔ **C clarinet:** As the shortest member of this group, the C clarinet makes a lighter but more cutting tone than its longer siblings. It's the only *non-transposing* member of the clarinet family, meaning it can play along with flutes, oboes, violins, or piano without having to transpose the music to another key. While many early clarinet sonatas, solo pieces, and chamber music were written for C clarinet, in modern times they're only used for performing orchestral music.

✔ **B♭ clarinet:** The B♭ soprano clarinet (somewhat longer than the C clarinet) is the most popular of the clarinet family. It's played in orchestras, bands, and jazz groups around the world. It's also a very popular folk instrument in Hungary and in Balkan regions as well as in Brazil. It's a frequent choice of bands, probably because it's pitched in the same key as trumpets and tubas.

✔ **A clarinet:** A clarinets (the longest of the group) are used in orchestral music, chamber music, and solo music. Because they're pitched in A, they sound a half step lower than B♭ clarinets when they play the very same note on the staff. They use the same mouthpiece and reed as B♭ clarinets. A clarinets have the same standard and extended range as B♭ clarinets, but because they're about an inch and a half longer, they sound slightly fuller and more mellow.

Basset horn

Basset "horn" is a misnomer, because this instrument isn't a horn. It's a clarinet. It probably owes its name to the fact that early curved or angled versions resembled the shape of a horn.

The basset horn is pitched in F and sounds a fourth below the B♭ clarinet. Its range extends downward to low C. Compared to the soprano clarinet, the basset horn's sound is richer in the very lowest notes and more haunting or somber in the notes above the staff. The basset horn's tone quality does not project as well as the soprano clarinet's, and consequently it has lost favor as orchestras have grown louder and performance venues larger. Newer hybrid-bore instruments project much better and produce a sound that's less stuffy or muffled.

Alto clarinet

The alto clarinet is pitched in E♭ and sounds a fourth below the B♭ soprano clarinet. It was invented in the early 1800s by Ivan Muller and Heinrich Grenser in an attempt to improve upon the basset horn. By 1809, Muller played on an alto clarinet that had 16 keys and was more mechanically sophisticated than the B♭ soprano clarinet of the time. The alto can play the standard clarinet range, and many altos have an added low E♭ key.

The alto clarinet produces the best-sounding notes below the staff, but the alto clarinet's sound doesn't project as well as that of the B soprano clarinet. Consequently, the alto clarinet is gradually falling out of fashion, and its voice range in the clarinet section of the band or clarinet choir is being replaced by soprano clarinets that are written for in the chalumeau register.

Bass clarinet

Bass clarinets are pitched in B♭ and sound an octave below the B♭ soprano clarinet. Their normal range is the standard clarinet range from E1 to G4, and most bass clarinets have an added low E♭ key. Professional models have additional keys for D, D♭, and C.

The bass clarinet is capable of producing many tonal colors and levels of projection. It can be dark and somber or haunting and distant, especially in its upper register, or more brash and present in its extreme upper range. Its lower register extends the richness and power of tone in the lower notes of the soprano clarinet farther downward to very low notes on the staff.

Bass clarinets are an important part of both orchestral and band clarinet sections. They're also used more and more frequently as a solo instrument by contemporary composers and as a jazz instrument.

Contra bass clarinets

Contra bass clarinets, sometimes referred to as pedal clarinets, sound best from the mid staff downward to the bottom of their respective ranges. They come in two flavors:

- ✔ The E♭ contra bass clarinet sounds an octave below the E♭ alto clarinet. It usually comes with the low E♭ key and is capable of playing the standard clarinet range. The E♭ contra has more high overtones and hence a more cutting, defined tone.

- ✔ The B♭ contra bass clarinet sounds an octave below the bass clarinet and always has added keys which extend its range down to low C. The B♭ contra has a less defined sound that adds fullness to the bass parts of larger ensembles.

Both types of contra bass clarinets are found in bands and occasionally in twentieth century orchestral scores and clarinet choirs. They're also popular for use in movies and musicals.

Exploring Two Unique Fingering Systems

Imagine that you've just discovered an incredible deal on a used clarinet — it's an older model, but it's half the cost of any comparable models you've come across. You jump at the deal, fork over your hard-earned cash, and proudly tote your clarinet to your first lesson. As soon as you see the look on your music teacher's face when you pull the clarinet out of its case, you know something's wrong, but what is it? It's probably the wrong fingering system.

Garage sale and Internet bargain hunters should be aware that fingering systems can be as different as the English and metric systems. In this case, the two fingering systems are Boehm (French) and Oehler (German), and they get along about as well as they did in World War II. By the 1920s, almost all

Americans were playing on the Boehm fingering system, but a few clarinets are still floating around that use the Oehler (pronounced "uh-ler") system.

The two have very different keywork systems and sound somewhat different due to their different bore sizes. (The bore is the hole that runs through the center of the instrument from the mouthpiece through the bell.) Your choice fingering system hinges on where you live. If you live in Germany or Austria, go with the Oehler. If you live and play anywhere else, you want the Boehm.

Before buying a used clarinet, check the fingering system. What may seem like a great deal on a used clarinet could be an expensive disaster when little Mary goes to her first band class. An easy way to tell the difference is to count. A Boehm clarinet has 17 keys plus seven open tone holes and six ring keys. An Oehler clarinet has at least 22 keys along with only five ring keys.

The Boehm system

The Boehm system was invented between 1839 and 1843 by Hyacinthe Klose and Auguste Buffet, who set out to improve the 12-key clarinet by using a system inspired by flute maker Theobald Boehm. They added additional tone holes covered by pads that were attached to ringed keys surrounding the tone holes. The keys make it possible to cover (and uncover, when necessary) additional tone holes with the same nine fingers used to play earlier clarinets.

The additional covered tone holes greatly improve the intonation of the instrument and, along with their addition of duplicate keys activated by the little fingers, make fingerings much less complicated. The Boehm clarinet has remained essentially the same to the present day.

The Oehler system

The Oehler system, invented by Oskar Oehler (1904-1973), was also the result of an attempt to improve Iwan Mueller's 12-key clarinet. Oehler clarinets have 22 keys and five rings, which work in a similar fashion as those found on Boehm clarinets, but make them a little more complicated than Boehm system clarinets. Oehler clarinets also have a different bore size than Boehm clarinets, which gives them a slightly different tone quality.

Chapter 3

Picking the Right Clarinet for You

· ·

In This Chapter

▶ Shopping for a clarinet in your price/proficiency range

▶ Comparing materials — plastic, wood, and resin or greenline

▶ Searching for the perfect mouthpiece

▶ Picking the right reed

▶ Accessorizing your purchase

· ·

*B*uying a clarinet means answering questions and making trade-offs. New or used? Buy or rent? Plastic, wood, greenline or resin? Music store, Amazon, eBay, garage sale, or classifieds? Buy on a budget or take out a second mortgage? The list goes on.

If you're struggling to find answers to these questions, you've come to the right place. In this chapter I serve as your helpful, friendly shopping guide. I reveal your options and provide guidance based on your situation, so you buy the right clarinet for your needs and budget and steer clear of the most common and costly pitfalls.

Looking at Clarinets for Beginners and Beyond

Clarinets can be divided into one of three groups that are generally geared toward players of a particular level of proficiency: starter-upper (or student) models, step-up (or intermediate) models, and conservatory (or professional) models. Not surprisingly, the price increases incrementally with each level of proficiency — the more advanced the clarinet, the bigger the price tag.

In the following sections, I offer some advice regarding budget considerations and then tell you what factors to consider at each price/proficiency level. I also describe the characteristics of each type of clarinet, and compare some of the most popular brands in each category.

Shaking your piggybank: How much clarinet can you afford?

Quality clarinets can range in price from a few hundred to a few thousand dollars, less if you buy used, and even less per month if you rent. You also have to figure in the cost of accessories — between $50 and $100 for a music stand, reeds, method books, a cleaning swab, key oil, cork grease, and perhaps a more suitable mouthpiece.

Consider your budget in the context of your situation and clarinet-playing goals. If you're just starting out, a quality beginner model may be sufficient. On the other hand, if you're determined to go pro by year's end, an upscale model may be the better choice.

Starter-upper models vary in price from $500 to $700. Step-up models range from $900 to $1,500, and professional models command from $2,700 to $5,800.

Affordable doesn't mean cheap. A poorly made or worn-out instrument can frustrate a beginner into giving up. A quality instrument is essential for success at all levels.

Starter-uppers (student models)

At some point in time, just about everyone decides to learn how to play a musical instrument. Over half of those who start ultimately give it up for one reason or another, and then the instrument ends up in the attic, the next garage sale, or in an online auction. The moral of the story is that if you're just starting out, don't invest a great deal in a fancy new clarinet.

When shopping for a student model, consider price, durability, and climate: price for obvious reasons; durability because "student" usually means "youngster," which means the clarinet is going to be riding the school bus, getting dropped, and experiencing all sorts of other unforeseen accidents; and climate because dry air and cold winters are more likely to crack wooden clarinets.

Here are some more specific considerations to make when shopping for a student model:

- ✔ **Material:** Plastic is usually the material of choice for beginners. It's fairly durable in all climates and less apt to get scratched or dented than wood. For more about differences in materials, see "Sorting Out Material Choices," later in this chapter.

- ✔ **Keywork:** All beginner-level clarinets have nickel-plated metal keys, but some have keys that bend more easily than others, which is not a good thing.

- ✔ **Mouthpiece and ligature:** All clarinets come complete with a mouthpiece, cap, and ligature, but some are better quality than others. See "Checking Out the All-Important Mouthpiece," later in this chapter, for details.

- ✔ **Ease of response:** All beginner clarinets are designed to respond easily to the player's breath, but some have too little resistance and don't sound as full as others.

- ✔ **Case:** A solid case does a better job of protecting the clarinet when the case is dropped and may provide more insulation from cold or dry air. Some cases even have a backpack style that's easier to carry.

- ✔ **Warranty:** Most new clarinets come with a one-year limited warranty; check to make sure.

Table 3-1 provides a comparison chart for the most popular brands of beginner clarinets.

Table 3-1		Beginner Clarinets			
Brand	**Model #**	**Body**	**Pads**	**Keywork**	**Description**
Buffet Crampon B12	BC2540-5-0	Resonite	Double fish-skin	Nickel-plated	Excellent beginner clarinet, very durable, lightweight, and easy for young clarinetists to maintain.
Leblanc by Backun "Bliss"	LB320	High-tech synthetic	Black Valentino	Black or gray nickel-plated	Features even intonation and professional-feeling keywork.

(continued)

Table 3-1 _(continued)_

Brand	_Model #_	_Body_	_Pads_	_Keywork_	_Description_
Leblanc/Bliss	LB210	Aged Grenadilla	Valentino	Black nickel-plated	An excellent first wooden instrument; popular among teachers and students who prefer a wooden instrument.
Conn Selmer Prelude	CL711	Resin	Bladder pad	Nickel-plated	Intended for beginners, value priced.
Yamaha	YCL-250Y	Matte resin	Valentino	Nickel-plated	Standard student-model clarinet.

Step-up (intermediate) models

While student models are suitable for the uninitiated and relatively unde-cided players, players with more experience or a higher level of commitment are wise to consider a step-up model:

✔ School-age players who are entering their final year of junior high or their first year of high school band have usually proven their interest in the clarinet and are old enough to appreciate a more expensive, higher-quality instrument.

✔ Adult beginners should start on an instrument of this level, because intermediate-quality clarinets serve their purposes very well for many years and may be the only clarinet they ever have to purchase.

Well-cared-for clarinets have a longevity of at least 20 years. The only factors limiting the life of a clarinet are the metal parts of the keys that move against one another. Just as even a well-lubricated car engine can wear out, so can these key parts, because that's what metal does.

When you feel ready to step up to a more expensive, higher-quality clarinet, look for the following qualities:

✔ **Material:** Look for a clarinet with a body made of wood or greenline composite, which produce the most resonant tone quality. See "Sorting Out Material Choices," later in this chapter.

✔ **Keywork:** While nickel-plated metal is actually preferred by some play-ers, silver-plated keys feel totally different and are worth considering.

✔ **Mouthpiece and ligature:** Whereas the type of mouthpiece and ligature included is important for adult beginners who choose to start out with a step-up model, more experienced players, including high school stu-dents, prefer to choose their own mouthpiece and ligature brand. See "Checking Out the All-Important Mouthpiece," later in this chapter, for more information.

✔ **Ease of response:** Step-up models should have good intonation on all pitches of the scale and a good, even sound throughout their range. *Intonation* is how well in tune the clarinet is. A clarinet with poor intonation has two or three (or more) notes that sound either too low (flat) or too high (sharp) compared to the notes around them when you play a scale. Singers with poor intonation sound off-key. Experienced players eliminate instruments with poor intonation.

✔ **Case quality and durability:** Case quality is important regardless of your stage of play. Look for a sturdy case that has a good closing mechanism and provides sufficient protection against the elements. A backpack-style case or one with a shoulder strap may be easier to carry.

✔ **Warranty:** Most new clarinets come with a one-year limited warranty; check to make sure.

Table 3-2 provides a comparison chart for the most popular brands of intermediate or step-up clarinets.

Table 3-2		Intermediate Clarinets			
Brand	*Model #*	*Body*	*Pads*	*Keywork*	*Description*
Buffet Crampon Ell France	BC2501F-2-0	Unstained, aged African Blackwood (Mpingo)	Double fish-skin	Silver-plated	*The* best step-up clarinet for advancing student clarinetists; made in the tradition of Buffet Crampon craftsmanship.
Leblanc by Backun Cadenza	LB130B	Aged Grenadilla	White Valentino	Silver-plated	An excellent, easy-to-play clarinet with a mature tone.
Lablanc Symphonie B♭	LB120B	Grenadilla, two barrels Grenadilla and Cocobolo, barrel is Cocobolo	Valentino	Nickel silver, silver-plated	Includes many adjustment screws and an alternate C♯/G♯ trill key, in addition to two Backun barrels and one Backun cocobolo bell.
Selmer USA	CL201/211	Unstained Grenadilla	Bladder	Silver	Easy to play; the design is ideal for small fingers.
Yamaha	YCL-450N	Grenadilla	Bladder	Nickel	Intermediate-model wooden clarinet.

Conservatory or professional models with not-so-conservative price tags

If you're serious about playing the clarinet at a high level, whether you're a high school or college student or a dedicated hobbyist who wants to play well, consider stepping up to a professional model.

When you're in the market for a professional model, consider the following:

- **Material:** When you step up, you leave the plastic models behind. Limit your selection to wooden and greenline models.

- **Keywork:** The choice here is still between nickel- or silver-plated keys, which pretty much hinges on your preference. You also have the choice of added keys, including the left-hand pinkie E♭ key and the alternate low F key.

- **Mouthpiece and ligature:** The quality of the mouthpiece and ligature is less of a factor, because most players at this level prefer to purchase a customized mouthpiece and ligature separately.

- **Richness and resonance of tone quality:** More experienced players actually prefer a little more resistance when they blow and often choose a clarinet that beginners would avoid. The resistance of the clarinet often affects the evenness of its tone throughout the entire range of the clarinet, and evenness is extremely important.

- **Intonation:** Look to see whether the clarinet has undercut tone holes, because these greatly improve both the intonation of individual notes and also the overall tone quality of the clarinet. (You may need to have an expert look for you.)

- **Case quality and durability:** The type of case is important but not a deal-breaker at this level, because many players purchase custom cases.

- **Warranty:** Most new professional models come with a comparable warranty – longer than the standard one-year warranty.

It's very important to have an experienced player test a professional-quality clarinet before you make the purchase. As with all handmade items, there's a great deal of variance among the respective clarinets, and one must have a baseline to judge the differences.

Table 3-3 provides a comparison chart for the most popular brands of professional-quality clarinets.

Competition makes the world go 'round

The old saying that "competition makes the world go 'round" couldn't be truer than in the world of top-line clarinets. The race began in the early 1970s when Yamaha of Japan produced a professional-model clarinet that seriously challenged the long-standing Buffet, Leblanc, and Selmer instruments.

Each of the four predominant clarinet manufacturers, including Yamaha, have made wonderful improvements over the clarinets from the '40s, '50s, and '60s. So many improvements have been made in tone quality and intonation and in the keywork of recent upper-level clarinets that very often the earlier, less improved top-line clarinets are now sold as step-up or intermediate level clarinets.

The real winners in this game of one-upmanship have been clarinet players around the world.

Table 3-3		Professional Clarinets			
Brand	*Model #*	*Body*	*Pads*	*Keywork*	*Description*
Buffet Crampon R13	BC1131-2-0	Aged African Blackwood (Mpingo)	Double fish-skin	Silver-plated	"The Legendary Choice of Professionals" is the most popular clarinet in the world — the gold standard for professional clarinets in most major orchestras and universities/ conservatories.
Buffet Crampon R13	BC1131-5-0	Aged African Blackwood (Mpingo)	Double fish-skin	Nickel-plated	Same description as preceding entry.
Buffet Crampon R13 Green Line	BC1131G-2-0	African Blackwood and carbon fiber	Double fish-skin	Silver-plated	Same description as first entry.
Buffet Crampon Tosca B♭	BC1150L-2-0	Premium, unstained African Blackwood (Mpingo)	GT and cork pads	Silver-plated	Produces a full, rich, dark sound. Chosen by many professional musicians, professors, and advanced students worldwide.

(continued)

Table 3-3 *(continued)*

Brand	Model #	Body	Pads	Keywork	Description
Buffet Crampon RC Prestige B♭	BC1106L-2-0	Premium, unstained African Blackwood (Mpingo)	GT and cork pads	Silver-plated	Features a left-hand E♭/A♭ key and a bell with an egg-shaped inner contour for projection, low-end response, and a remarkable tone.
Leblanc by Backun, Symphonie, B♭	LB120B	Aged Grenadilla	White Valentino	Silver-plated	Features many adjustment screws, an alternate C♯/G♯ trill key, two Backun barrels, and one Backun cocobolo bell.
Leblanc 11915 Opus II	L11915	Aged, unstained Grenadilla	Bladder Pisoni	Silver-plated	Features adjustable bridge mechanism and E/B and F♯/C♯ keys; ergonomically designed keywork.
Selmer Paris Recital	B1610R	Grenadilla	Bladder Pisoni	Silver-plated or nickel-silver keys (Go with nickel-plated)	Features a warm, rich, round tone; very vivid, it attracts those who seek "a sound."
Yamaha YCL-CSV Series Professional	YCL-CSVN	Grenadilla	Bladder	Nickel-plated	Designed to produce a rich, dark sound. Many new features contribute to the added resonance and ease of play.
Yamaha YCL-CSV Custom B♭	YCL-CSV	Grenadilla	Bladder	Silver-plated	Custom-level, hand-crafted clarinet.

Sorting Out Material Choices

The predominant portion of the clarinet — its body — is typically made of plastic, wood, resin, including greenline, or, on rare occasions, metal. Which is best depends on your level of play, budget, and climate, as I explain in the following sections.

Saving your pennies with a plastic model

Plastic sounds cheap, but in the world of clarinets, plastic models have one big advantage over their wooden counterparts — you can take a plastic clarinet outside. So, if you're planning on playing your clarinet in the marching band, plastic is the way to go. Sun and cold devastate wooden instruments.

For all you trivia experts out there, plastic clarinets were introduced in the early 1950s by the Selmer/Bundy company, using a plastic called *resonite*. They became an instant hit and quickly replaced metal clarinets.

If you're in a marching band, keep your plastic or composite model if you're trading up to a fancier wood model, so you have an instrument you can play outside.

Sticking with the classics: Wooden models

If you're shopping in the intermediate to advanced range, you're likely to be looking at plenty of wood clarinets. Many clarinetists favor African Blackwood (Mpingo), because it has the most resonant sound. Although wood is generally better than plastic, it does require more TLC (tender loving care):

- ✔ Always warm the upper joint to room temperature if the instrument has been in the cold.
- ✔ After playing your clarinet, always swab it out.

The best way to warm the upper joint is to hold it in your armpit, where it absorbs your body heat.

Checking out resin-made (greenline) clarinets

Greenline clarinets combine the best of both plastic and wood. They sound like wood clarinets and, like plastic clarinets, are less susceptible to cracking. This makes them an excellent choice for dry or cold climates. The bodies of greenline clarinets are made of ground-up African Blackwood (about 95 percent) mixed with resin (about 5 percent).

Greenline clarinets offer one additional advantage over wooden models — the *bore* (the hole that runs through the middle of the clarinet) retains its shape for the life of the instrument. With wooden clarinets, the bore tends to swell slightly from condensation, adversely affecting the sound of the instrument over time. A greenline clarinet will sound just as good 20 years down the road.

The scarcity of metal models

Although metal clarinets do exist, they're pretty much an endangered species. Some manufacturers, including Conn, produced them during World War I and II when getting a wooden model made in Europe was next to impossible.

A lack of metal clarinets is no great loss. These instruments were never able to achieve the tone quality found in wooden or composite clarinets. Many hobbyists make them into lamps, which is probably the very best use for them.

The Buffet Company in France was first to include greenline clarinets among its professional models. More and more clarinetists are using greenline instruments, and more and more manufacturers are building composite instruments.

Checking Out the All-Important Mouthpiece

As a clarinet player, you'll develop an intimate relationship with your mouthpiece, so don't skimp. In the following sections, I show you how to evaluate a mouthpiece based on its five most important characteristics: size, material, craftsmanship, facing, and tone chamber. I then take you on a shopping trip to check out the two types — beginner and professional — and help you decide between mouthpieces that are more conducive to either jazz or classical music.

For details about the parts that make up a mouthpiece, complete with a diagram identifying the parts, visit Chapter 2.

If you just shelled out several hundred dollars for a clarinet, you're probably wondering whether you now have to toss the mouthpiece that came with it and pay for a replacement. Well, you may not need to. Many of the major clarinet manufacturers, including Buffet, are reacting to the need for better beginner mouthpieces and include them with the instruments they sell. Some music stores may also provide this service, encouraged by local teachers to do so. Check Table 3-4 to determine which new clarinets are more likely to include a better mouthpiece, or ask at the music store.

Evaluating mouthpiece characteristics

Mouthpieces vary by size, material, craftsmanship, facing, and tone chamber. Keep these characteristics in mind when comparing mouthpieces and ultimately selecting one.

Overall size

When choosing a mouthpiece, bigger is not necessarily better. In fact, smaller is usually better for beginners, who are usually younger and have smaller mouths. A mouthpiece with a smaller profile allows you to take the proper amount of the mouthpiece into your mouth, and this is why many experienced players prefer them as well.

I recommend Profile 88 mouthpieces manufactured by Vandoren. The Pyne/ Clarion and Lomax Classic mouthpieces, which many professionals prefer, also have smaller profiles.

Materials

When selecting a mouthpiece by the material it's made of, you have two choices: plastic or rubber. Both generally involve some sort of molding process, but the better-quality mouthpieces are made of hard rubber, through a combination of molding and machining.

The least expensive models are sold nearly as is . . . the way they are immediately after being ejected from the injection mold. With higher-quality mouthpieces, an artisan mouthpiece craftsman customizes the dimensions of the facing and tone chamber for optimum performance.

Craftsmanship

Injection molding and automated machining processes can combine to produce a quality mouthpiece, but craftsmanship is required to hone a mouthpiece to perfection. An experienced craftsman can adjust a mouthpiece to fit an individual player's preferences. For more about the modifications a craftsman can make, see "Stepping up to professional-quality mouthpieces," later in this chapter.

Facing

The area in which the reed vibrates is the facing, and it has a great effect on the response and tone of the mouthpiece. Facings can vary in size but generally fall into one of the following three categories:

- **Close:** 1 millimeter
- **Medium:** 1.15 millimeters
- **Open:** 1.2 millimeters or more

Most players, including professional clarinetists, play on medium-close to medium-open facings, which allow for more range but tend to be more difficult to control.

On very old mouthpieces, the tip rail and side rails were very narrow. Now they're much wider, which makes them sound darker and more mellow.

Tone chamber

The size and shape of the tone chamber, inside the mouthpiece, contributes significantly to its tone quality. The interior shape of most present-day mouthpieces is patterned after mouthpieces constructed in France in the late 1930s. On higher-quality mouthpieces, the baffle and bore are both adjusted by hand.

Getting started with a beginner mouthpiece

If you've settled on a beginner clarinet, get it a matching beginner mouthpiece. As with the clarinet itself, a beginner mouthpiece comes with a smaller price tag, making it less costly to replace if the beginner breaks it. But remember that less expensive doesn't mean inferior. You can get a quality mouthpiece at an affordable price.

Don't buy a big-beaked mouthpiece for a small-mouthed player. Unless the player can take enough of the mouthpiece into his mouth, he's going to have a difficult time hitting the high notes. Furthermore, because humans are creatures of habit, they often continue to take in too little of the mouthpiece when they move up to a better-quality mouthpiece. As a result, they may end up always struggling to get a full sound and good response from their clarinet.

Prices for good beginner mouthpieces range from $38 to $95. I recommend the following:

- ✔ **The PolyCrystal from Pyne/Clarion:** Hand-faced and play-tested before shipping; $46 (www.pyne-clarion.com)
- ✔ **The Prelude from Lomax Classic Mouthpieces:** Made of polycarbonite with some hand finishing; $38 (www.lomaxclassic.com)
- ✔ **The Profile 88, M30, or M15 from Vandoren:** Some hand-facing; $95 (www.vandoren.com)

All of these mouthpieces have medium-open facings, which are best for beginners.

Stepping up to professional-quality mouthpieces

Not all dental structures or facial features are identical, so custom-crafted mouthpieces make sense. With higher-quality mouthpieces, the craftsman can modify the mouthpiece to adjust for individual physical characteristics and player preferences. For example, the craftsman can adjust the length of the mouthpiece facing according to the player's natural overbite and the amount of flesh on the lower lip. Craftsmen can also adjust mouthpieces so that they respond and sound to the personal preference of the individual player by trimming the facing, the rails, the tip, the sides of the baffle, and the inside walls.

Prices of intermediate and professional mouthpieces range from $95 to $650. This is cheap compared to violin bows that can cost many thousands of dollars.

Mouthpiece makers of note include Pyne/Clarion (www.pyne-clarion.com), Lomax Classic (www.lomaxclassic.com), Dan Johnston, Backun-Morales (www.backunmusical.com), Vandoren (www.vandoren.com), Redwine-Jazz (www.redwinejazz.com), Brad Behn (www.behnmouthpieces.com), and David McClune (www.mcclunemouthpiece.com). Each of these companies crafts a wide variety of quality mouthpieces. See Table 3-4 to compare some of the top models.

Table 3-4	Top Mouthpiece Models	
Brand	*Material*	*Machine or Handmade*
Backun Musical Services Camerata Legend (Intermediate)	Hard rubber	Combination of machine and handmade
Morales Backun (Professional)	Hard rubber	Combination of machine and handmade
Behn Mouthpieces International Overture Collection (Intermediate)	Acrylic	Machined and hand-finished
Behn Mouthpieces International Artist (Professional)	Hard rubber	Machined and hand-finished
Behn Mouthpieces International Vintage (Professional)	Behn proprietary rod rubber	Machined and hand-finished
Behn Mouthpieces International Signature (Professional)	Behn proprietary rod rubber	Machined and hand-finished
Dan Johnston	Hard rubber	Custom mouthpieces made by appointment only
Lomax Classic Prelude (Beginner)	Polycarbonate	Hand-finished
Lomax Classic "New" Symphonie (Intermediate)	Hard rubber	Hand-finished
Lomax Classic Elite (Professional)	Hard rubber and ebonite blend	Hand-finished
Pyne/Clarion Polycrystal (Beginner)	Clear polycrystal	Hand-finished

(continued)

Table 3-4 *(continued)*

Brand	Material	Machine or Handmade
Pyne/Clarion Symphonies (Intermediate)	Hard rubber	Hand-finished
Pyne/Clarion Bel Canto (Professional)	Hard rubber	Hand-finished
McClune Plato (Beginner and Intermediate)	Plastic	Hand-finished
McClune Lyceum (Intermediate and Professional)	Hard rubber	Hand-finished
McClune SP and SPE (Professional)	Hard rubber	Hand-finished
Redwine Jazz	Hard Rubber	Some hand finishing
Vandoren M30	Hard rubber	Some hand finishing
Vandoren B40	Hard rubber	Some hand finishing
Vandoren M13	Hard rubber	Some hand finishing

Comparing jazz to classical mouthpieces

When you're shopping for a mouthpiece, consider the style of music you intend to play. If you're leaning toward playing classical music, you may want to lean toward close-medium tip models. Jazz players often prefer open facings, which have the largest amount of space between the tip of the reed and the mouthpiece, because they allow the greatest amount of flexibility in bending the tone.

Doublers (people who play two or more instruments) often prefer mouthpieces with a more open tip, because they more closely resemble saxophone mouthpieces.

Wading through the Reeds: The Tone Generators

Without a reed, your clarinet is just an oversized straw — a conduit for wind. Slap a reed on it, and suddenly you have a clarinet. Because the reed plays such a key role in producing sound, select your reed carefully. Pick a reed that's too hard, and it may not vibrate at all. Too soft, and it may vibrate too much. Like Goldilocks, you want one that's just right.

In the following sections, I tell you what to look for in a reed, whether you're a beginner or a more experienced player, and I give you a chart for brand comparison purposes.

Reed cuts: Numbers aren't everything

When you start shopping for reeds, you may get the feeling that you're playing a numbers game. A reed's hardness (or stiffness) is ranked by numbers ranging from 1.5 (soft) to 5 (hard). However, hardness is only one factor, and not the most important one at that. When selecting a reed, consider the following factors:

- ✔ **Cane:** Even more important than a reed's hardness is the cane it's cut from. Ultimately, reeds are just like wine. Exquisite wine starts with exquisite grapes. The most vibrant, longest-lasting reeds start with excellent cane.

- ✔ **Player level/age:** Beginners and young players may not be able to blow hard enough to make a hard reed vibrate, so they may want to start with a softer reed — 3.0 hardness or less (4 or higher is considered hard).

- ✔ **Mouthpiece tip opening:** Mouthpiece facings with close tip openings require harder reeds because softer reeds close on them too easily. Very open mouthpieces, like those preferred by doublers, can use softer reeds.

- ✔ **Thickness:** Reeds are manufactured from three sizes of blanks: traditional thickness, thick, and very thick. The thicker the reed blank, the harder the reed is to close with lip pressure.

Beginner reeds

When you're in the market for a beginner reed, look for the following:

- ✓ **Standard thickness:** Reeds with a standard or traditional thickness are best.

- ✓ **Medium hardness:** While beginners may not have the embouchure strength and air support to play very hard reeds, don't go too soft. Beginners need to train themselves to use more air.

- ✓ **Durability:** Younger players tend to be harder on equipment and are more likely to break or chip their reeds. You want a reed that's likely to last at least a few weeks.

- ✓ **Price:** Medium-priced reeds are less expensive to replace and still of high-enough quality.

Reeds for more advanced players

If you're an intermediate or advanced player, look for thicker, harder reeds made of higher-quality cane:

- ✓ **Intermediate:** Look for a 3 to 3.5 hardness, cut from thick blanks with filed cuts. A *filed cut* means the cane has been removed from the back of the reed (its *spine*) with an added process. They're usually more expensive but more resonant in the lower register.

- ✓ **Advanced:** Consider a 3.5 to 4.5 hardness, cut from thick or the thickest blanks. These reeds have the most pronounced spine down the center, and require the most lip leverage to close and the most air support to blow. Experienced players rotate their reeds and expect the average reed to last at least a month.

To compare reeds (both beginner and advanced), take a look at Table 3-5.

Table 3-5	Reed Brands and Types for All Player Levels				
Brand	*Traditional*	*Thick*	*Thickest*	*Unfiled*	*Filed*
LaVoz	X			X	
Mitchell Lurie	X			X	
Rico: Grand Concert Select		X		X	

Brand	Traditional	Thick	Thickest	Unfiled	Filed
Rico: Reserve			X	X	
Rico: Reserve Classic		X		X	
Vandoren: Blue Box	X				X
Vandoren: V12		X			X
Vandoren: 56 Rue Le Pic		X			X

Saving Some Dough: Buying Used or Renting

That fancy new greenline clarinet is mighty nice, but it's going to set you back some serious greenbacks, and maybe you're not so sure you're willing to make that much of a commitment at this point. You can save a considerable amount of money by purchasing a used clarinet or renting one from the music store. The following sections give you the lowdown on these two options.

Buying a used clarinet

Plenty of used clarinets are looking for good homes. You can find these orphans at garage sales or flea markets, in the classifieds (including Craigslist and Facebook's Marketplace), on eBay, at local music stores, and even through a school's music department. But be careful. You don't want to get stuck with someone else's problem. You want an instrument that plays well or can be restored for a reasonable amount of money — typically $150 to $350.

Play before you pay. If possible, have an experienced player test the clarinet for you before you hand over your money. In addition, inspect the clarinet carefully for the following warning signs:

- ✔ **Clarinet hasn't been played for several years:** Regardless of the source, beware of instruments that have just been sitting in a case, especially wooden models, because the wood gets dried out. If you play a dried-out clarinet for more than a few minutes a day for a month, it absorbs too much condensation too quickly and splits like a rail.

✔ **Leaks:** Any leaks prevent you from playing all the notes. Check for leaks one joint at a time. Cover all the tone holes of the joint you're checking with the fingers of one hand, and use the palm of the other hand to seal the bottom end of the joint. Place the top end of the joint in your mouth and either suck or blow air through it. Repeat with the other joint. If you're blowing air, listen for air escaping. If you're sucking air, you should feel the suction on the palm of your hand and the fingertips covering the tone holes. Leaks may indicate a minor problem (a leaking pad or cork, for example) or a major problem (cracks in the body).

✔ **Frayed or waterlogged pads:** Pads that are frayed around the edges or appear waterlogged must be replaced, which isn't a huge cost. Another way to test the seal on pads is to place a piece of cigarette paper under the suspicious pad, close the pad with the fingers on one hand and gently tug against the cigarette paper. If it slips out easily, chances are the pad isn't sealing.

✔ **Cracks from trill keys to the top of the upper joint:** This is the place where a wooden instrument is most susceptible to cracking, because many of the drilled-out tone holes in this area weaken the instrument.

✔ **Chipped tone holes:** Inspect the tops of the tone holes for chips on the inside. Chipped tone holes are just the same as tone holes that have been drilled with improper measurements. Good repair technicians can fix chipped holes, but you should avoid the instrument anyway because it's a sign of general abuse.

✔ **Gummed-up tone holes:** Tone-hole dimensions are critical to good intonation. You can clean out the dirt or grease around tone holes by using a pipe cleaner. (Experienced players carry a pipe cleaner in their clarinet case and use it once a week.) However, the dirt and grease may be covering up the chips.

When negotiating a price, consider the cost of a new mouthpiece. Regardless of the mouthpiece's condition, replace it for sanitary reasons if nothing else.

Renting versus buying

Renting rather than buying a clarinet is often a smart move, especially for young children who want to try an instrument but aren't quite sure they'll stick with it. It's also a good choice if you want to take an instrument for a test drive for a few weeks before purchasing a new one just like it. Rentals offer the following benefits:

- ✔ They're less expensive to walk away from if you change your mind.

- ✔ The instruments are usually well maintained and in good working condition.

- ✔ Most repairs are included in the cost.

- ✔ Some stores offer rent-to-own programs, so if you do decide to purchase the instrument, you haven't completely lost your rental fees.

Swapping Out the Barrel or Bell

The fact that your clarinet comes in five parts (see Chapter 2), enables you to customize it by swapping out parts. I show you in the previous sections how to customize a stock clarinet by changing the mouthpiece and reed, but if you're looking to customize in a more substantial way, consider upgrading the barrel joint or bell — or both!

Barrels: Tubular, dude!

Stock barrels with a standard cylindrical shape can't possibly accommodate the wide variety of mouthpieces available. When the mouthpiece bore fails to work well with a clarinet, a custom barrel can significantly improve both tuning and tone quality. Clarinet craftsmen can adjust barrels in numerous ways. They can

- ✔ Customize the interior dimensions, including tapering the barrel from wide at the top to narrower at the bottom.

- ✔ Adjust the barrel length to accommodate pitch idiosyncrasies of mouthpieces. Mouthpieces that play on the sharp side should be accompanied by barrels that are longer than the 66-millimeter standard length.

- ✔ Use a different material. The material makes a big difference in the sound of the clarinet. Barrels are constructed from both African Blackwood and many other exotic woods.

For details relating to various brands of custom clarinet barrels, see Table 3-6.

Table 3-6	Compare Custom Clarinet Barrels	
Brand	*Model*	*Material*
Muncy Winds	MB	African Blackwood or Cocobolo
Muncy Winds	MA	African Blackwood or Cocobolo
Backun Musical Services	Traditional	African Blackwood or Cocobolo
Taplin-Weir	Custom	Custom

Bells that'll make your ears ring

The bell is more than just a convenient stand for your clarinet when you're not using it. It performs two main functions: It helps form the standing wave that vibrates inside the clarinet, and it transmits the clarinet's sound to the surrounding air. When it does its job properly, it enhances the richness of the sound and the quality of the tone.

Clarinet manufacturers are constantly trying to improve their own products and have made many excellent innovations in bells. As with barrels, the materials used for bells can make a lot of difference in the way they function. They range from African Blackwood to more exotic woods.

For recommended makes, models, and materials from the two most prominent makers of custom bells, check out Table 3-7.

Table 3-7	Recommended Bell Makes, Models, and Materials	
Maker	*Model*	*Materials*
Backun Musical Services	Traditional	Grenadilla (African Blackwood) or Cocobolo
Taplin-Weir	Custom	African Blackwood or Cocobolo

Tossing in a Few Accessories

Even with a custom mouthpiece, barrel, and bell, your shopping cart is looking a little empty. Besides, you need a few extra items to have a complete clarinet starter kit. The following sections make sure you're equipped with all the essentials.

Cleaning cloth

Assuming you use one regularly and properly, a cleaning cloth prolongs the life of the keywork and maintains the beauty of the clarinet. By wiping off the keys regularly, you prevent your hands' slightly acidic perspiration from corroding the keys' nickel or silver plating and prevent silver keys from tarnishing. BG and Muncy Winds make excellent polishing cloths.

Place your cleaning cloth over the keys to avoid touching them when assembling your instrument.

Reed case

Unlike guitar picks, your reeds need to be handled with care. Don't just toss them in your clarinet case when you're done playing. For best results, store your reeds in a reed case to prevent breakage and warping.

A good reed case must have a well-ventilated surface and be humidified so that it dries properly and retains some of its moisture. Rico, Vandoren, and Muncy Winds produce excellent, inexpensive reed cases.

When you're done playing, always remove the reed from the mouthpiece. Most experienced players rotate their reeds and save their best reeds for performances.

Cork grease

Corks tend to dry out over time. When they do, they crack and crumble. To prevent the corks on your clarinet from drying out and ensure proper seals, grease the corks once every ten times you assemble your clarinet. Grease the corks even more frequently if your clarinet is brand new. Dry corks wear faster and, in the case of new clarinets, make it hard to assemble the clarinet.

I recommend Dr. Slick (`www.doctorsprod.com`) corkgrease. Vandoren and Rico also make quality cork grease.

Tuner

Tuners are helpful as a pitch reference when getting started. They're also helpful in checking pitch on a daily basis and in learning to tune your clarinet properly. Great clarinet players around the world may sound differently, but they all play in tune. Seiko and Korg manufacture inexpensive digital tuners.

Metronome

Metronomes are helpful in finding correct indicated tempos and learning to play steadily. The only way you can tell exactly how fast you played a passage yesterday versus today is to play with a metronome every day. They're absolutely essential as a practice tool, and are one of an ensemble player's best friends.

Inexpensive digital metronomes are manufactured by Seiko and Korg.

Chapter 4

Grasping the Basics of Musical Notation

*L*ike poetry, music began with an oral/audio tradition. Except for some cave wall drawings, nothing was written down. Poets memorized their verse, and all musicians played by ear. They composed songs in their heads and learned songs by listening to someone else play them.

As cultures evolved, they began to record their music on paper, which made it much easier to preserve the music for posterity's sake and distribute the music so other musicians could learn how to play it. While some musicians still play exclusively by ear, those who know how to read and write music have a distinct advantage — they don't have to listen to a tune over and over to play it.

This chapter gives you that edge. For the rank beginner, it functions as a primer for reading music. If you already know how to read music, consider it a refresher course. Throughout the chapter, I explain how to read music by mastering the following essentials:

✔ **Staff:** The grid on which the musical notation is written

✔ **Notes:** Symbols that indicate the relative pitch and duration of sounds

✔ **Symbols:** Signs that represent the rhythmic and temporal aspects of sounds

✔ **Markings over notes:** Indicate the style the composer wants the listener to hear

✔ **Markings under the staffs:** Indicate the expressive qualities of the music

✔ **Markings at the ends of sections:** Indicate the position in the piece — where the player is and where she goes next

Reciting the Musical Alphabet

Written music, like written language, begins with an alphabet, but in music, each letter is a note that represents a sound. Another difference is that the musical alphabet contains only the letters A to G and repeats after every eighth letter to form what we fondly refer to as an *octave*.

Think of the musical alphabet as a vertical alphabet, because the notes represent sounds from low to high and back down, as shown in Figure 4-1.

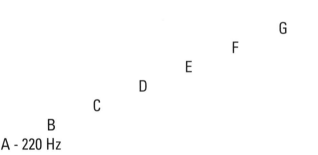

Figure 4-1:
The musical alphabet starts with A (at the bottom), climbs to G, and repeats.

Octave: A miracle of music

The octave is considered a miracle of music, because the same note played higher or lower has an identical quality, varying only in pitch. The A above the middle C, for example, vibrates at 440 hertz. A an octave above vibrates at 880 hertz, while A an octave below vibrates at 220 hertz.

This is a natural phenomenon. Humans can take no credit for creating it, but they can take some credit for discovering it and taking advantage of it through music.

Staffs and clefs: Nothing but treble and bass

When you write the English alphabet, you do it in a straight line — from left to right. Because the music alphabet is vertical, you write it from bottom to top on a *staff*, which sort of functions like a sheet of graph paper containing five horizontal lines. And you don't actually write the letters; the positions of the notes on the staff represent the letters.

Because the musical alphabet has so many notes and the letters repeat themselves, five lines can't possibly accommodate all the notes. To make room for all the notes, musical notation uses two staffs and distinguishes between the two through the use of clefs — the *treble clef* for higher notes (see Figure 4-2), and the *bass clef* for lower notes (see Figure 4-3). In piano music, the staffs are placed one above the other with the treble clef staff on top.

Figure 4-2: The treble clef contains higher notes.

Figure 4-3: The bass clef is for lower notes.

On the treble clef, F claims the first *space* (the space between the lines), followed by A, C, and E, as shown in Figure 4-4. That's right, the notes in the spaces on the treble clef spell FACE: F - A - C - E.

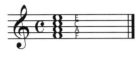

The notes that fall on the *lines* of the treble clef staff are E - G - B - D - F (from low to high), as shown in Figure 4-5. An easy way to remember these notes is by using the mnemonic **E**very **G**ood **B**oy **D**oes **F**ine.

On the bass clef, A claims the first *space* (the space between the lines), followed by C, E, and G, as shown in Figure 4-6. The mnemonic for these notes is **A**ll **C**ows **E**at **G**rass.

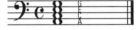

Notes on the *lines* of the bass clef are (from low to high) G - B - D - F - A, as shown in Figure 4-7. To keep this on the tip of your tongue, just remember that **G**ood **B**oys **D**o **F**ine **A**lways.

Figure 4-7:
The notes
on the lines
of the bass
clef spell
Good **B**oys
Do **F**ine
Always.

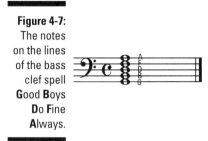

Put all the notes together on the treble and bass clef staffs, and you get the entire picture, as shown in Figure 4-8.

Figure 4-8:
All the notes
on the treble
and bass
clef staffs.

E F G A B C D E F G A B C D E F G A B C D E F G A

Simplifying staffs with ledger lines

Clarinet players toss out the bass clef staff and use ledger lines to modify the treble clef staff to meet their needs. Ledger lines are horizontal lines above and below the staff that extend its range. Clarinetists don't play very far down below middle C, for example, so instead of using the bass clef, they add lines below the staff. They also add lines above the staff to accommodate notes at the top of the clarinet's range, as shown in Figure 4-9.

Figure 4-9:
Ledger lines
extend the
range of a
standard
staff.

The ledger lines below the staff are C (middle C on the piano), A, and F. Ledger lines above the staff are for A, C, E, G, and B. The staff in Figure 4-10 shows all of the notes for the entire clarinet range.

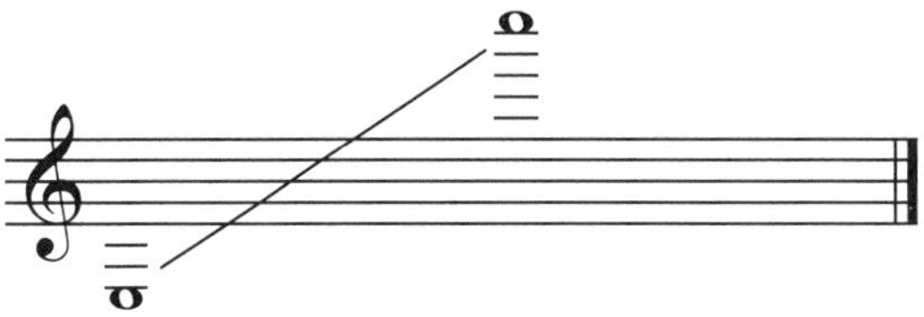

Figure 4-10:
Staff show-
ing all the
notes that
comprise
the entire
clarinet
range.

Locating Notes on a Piano Keyboard

One of the best ways to visualize how written notes correspond to the actual notes you play is to sit down in front of a piano keyboard and look down at the keys. Don't have a piano keyboard available? No worries. That's what the illustrations I provide in the following sections are for.

Pointing out the written notes

Seeing the notes on a piano keyboard is easy — the keyboard is all black and white. Actually, the white keys are the written notes. The black keys are the sharps and flats, which I explain in the following section. As you can see in Figure 4-11, the white keys, like the notes on a staff, follow the alphabet — A, B, C, D, E, F, G — and then repeat themselves.

Middle C is sort of like one of the home keys (A-S-D-F for the left hand and J-K-L-; for the right) on a typewriter or computer keyboard. It provides a point of orientation for the piano keyboard. Throughout this book, I refer to middle C, so having a visual of where it's located on a piano keyboard can serve as a valuable point of reference moving forward.

Identifying sharps and flats

One step up from a written note is a sharp (designated by the ♯ symbol). One step down is a flat (indicated by the ♭ symbol). One of the best ways to visualize sharps and flats is to look at a piano keyboard. On a piano, each octave contains 12 notes. Eight of these notes have letter names assigned to white keys. Black keys account for the remaining four notes — the flats and sharps, as shown in Figure 4-12.

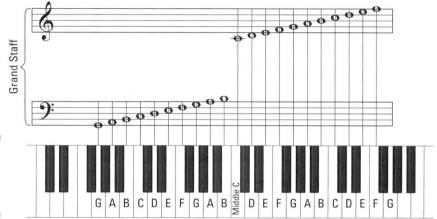

Figure 4-11:
The musical alphabet on piano keys.

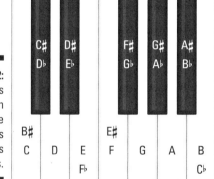

Figure 4-12:
White keys play written notes, while black keys play flats and sharps.

Sharps

A sharp is a half step above its corresponding written note or the black key to the right of the nearest white key (see Figure 4-13). In other words, the black key to the right of the F key plays F♯.

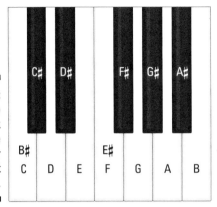

Flats

A flat is a half step below its corresponding written note or the black key to the left of the nearest white key. In other words, the black key to the left of the G key plays G♭ (see Figure 4-14).

Now, you may have noticed that the black key between F and G is to the right of F and the left of G, so does it play F♯ or G♭? The answer is yes — it plays F♯ *and* G♭, which happen to be the same sound.

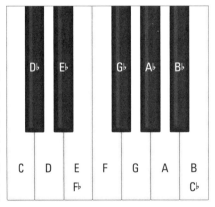

Figure 4-14:
Flats are the
black keys
to the left
of their
nearest
white keys.

Because the black keys play both sharps and flats, these notes are referred to as *enharmonic* — they sound the same but are written differently. A good example of an enharmonic note is E♯. Because E and F have no black key between them, E♯ sounds the same as F♮ (♮ stands for "natural") but is written differently. See Figure 4-15, which shows a staff with one octave of a *chromatic scale* — a scale composed of all 12 half steps in the octave.

Figure 4-15:
Staff with
one octave
of a chro-
matic scale.

Getting Keyed Up with Key Signatures

In a tune with numerous sharps or flats, the staff can become extremely cluttered with special notations. To cut down on the clutter and keep musicians from losing their minds, composers use *key signatures* — a shorthand notation that places the symbols for sharps and flats just to the right of the clef sign on the staff. Key signatures can contain up to seven sharps or seven flats (corresponding to the seven letters in the musical alphabet) plus a key without flats or sharps.

For example, a sharp on the F in the key signature indicates that every time you see an F anywhere in the staff, or above or below it, you play an F♯. Notes without sharps or flats are called either by their letter name alone or the letter name followed by "natural," as in "C natural."

Making exceptions with accidentals

When you first hear the term "accidental" applied to the clarinet, you might assume it has something to do with a note you didn't intend to play. That would be wrong. An *accidental* is a note that is not in the key signature of the music being played. Thus, while the key signature specifies the defaults for flats, sharps, or naturals, *accidentals* mark any exceptions to the rule. For example, if the key signature tells you to play every F as a sharp, but the tune includes one or more Fs played as F♮, then those F naturals are marked accordingly as accidentals (see Figure 4-16).

Figure 4-16:
Symbols for sharp, flat, and natural.

♯ Sharp

♮ Natural

♭ Flat

Accidentals hold until the next bar comes along. (For more about bars, see "Humming a few bars with bar lines," later in this chapter.)

Tuning in to keys and scales

You've probably heard about tunes being composed in the key of C major or D minor. If you're not exactly Mozart (yet), these terms are likely to mean absolutely nothing to you. In fact, most people would never be able to tell the key in which a particular tune is being played or even what a "key" is, regardless of whether it's major or minor.

In music, a *key* is a group (or *class*) of related tones or notes (collectively referred to as a *pitch class*), that are based on or named after a certain note, known as the *harmonic center* or *tonic*. For example, a musical composition might be referred to as being in the key of C, where C is the harmonic center or tonic.

The terms *major* and *minor* refer to the *scale* — the relationship among the tones in a unit of music, such as Do Re Mi Fa So La Ti Do. Think of the notes in a scale as the steps on a musical ladder. You form scales by organizing the steps (notes) into patterns of whole steps (white key to white key on the piano) and half steps (white key to black key). The following sections provide additional details about the major and minor scales, as well as the key signatures that represent them.

Major scales

If you remember the song "Do Re Mi" from *The Sound of Music*, you know that its particular arrangement of eight notes is very uplifting or joyous, which is characteristic of the major scales. Something about the particular order of notes in a major scale makes it sound upbeat — whole step, whole step, half step, whole step, whole step, whole step, half step.

The world of music has 15 major scales in all. Figure 4-17 shows the C major scale with note names and whole and half steps highlighted.

Figure 4-17:
C major scale with note names and whole and half steps highlighted.

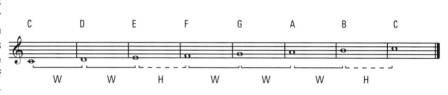

Minor scales

Minor scales follow a different pattern on the musical ladder — whole step, half step, whole step, whole step, whole step, whole step, half step. Actually, minor scales can follow three different patterns, but they all have one thing in common — a lowered third note, which distinguishes minor from major scales.

To hear this different sound, sing or listen to "Brahms Lullaby." (Plenty of Web sites contain audio clips of the music.) The first phrase follows a major scale and the second phrase follows a minor scale.

As with the major scales, the minor scales number 15 — from no flats and sharps to up to seven flats and seven sharps. Figure 14-18 shows a C minor scale with the note names and whole and half steps highlighted.

Figure 4-18:
C minor
scale with
the note
names and
whole and
half steps
highlighted.

Key signatures

Major or minor scales can begin on any one of the 12 notes within an octave. In order to do this, either flats or sharps are used to adjust the patterns of whole steps and half steps that make up each of the scales. The starting note of the scale is called the tonic, and it has a name. For example, when adjusting the pattern for a major scale beginning on E♭ (the tonic for the scale of E♭), we use three flats — B♭, E♭, and A♭. This is where the term *key signature* comes into play — the key signature is the group of sharps or flats placed after the clef on a staff to indicate the key in which the piece is to be played — in the key of E♭, the key signature is comprised of the three aforementioned flats.

The order in which flats are placed on the staff is always B - E - A - D - G - C - F. The order of sharps is F - C - G - D - A - E - B (just the opposite of the order of the flats).

Figures 4-19 and 4-20 show the tonic or starting note for each scale; that is, each key, and the flats and sharps for that key signature.

Figure 4-19:
Twelve
sharp keys.

Figure 4-20:
Twelve flat
keys.

| C major | F major | B♭ major | E♭ major | A♭ major | D♭ major | G♭ major | C♭ major |
| a minor | d minor | g minor | c minor | f minor | b♭ minor | e♭ minor | a♭ minor |

Grooving to the Rhythm

Playing notes in no particular arrangement would be like cracking open a dictionary and reading a bunch of random words out loud. For a tune to be considered musical, its notes must be arranged in a way that produces a melodious rhythm.

Just for fun, try this: Hum a simple, well-known tune to someone and completely distort the rhythm. Chances are pretty good that the listener won't be able to recognize the "tune." Chances are also pretty good that you had a difficult time humming out of rhythm.

Various factors contribute to a tune's rhythm, as named and described in the following sections.

Recognizing a note's value

While the position of a note on a scale represents its pitch, the position says nothing about how long to hold the note. The appearance of the note contains this information, as shown in Table 4-1. A whole note tells you to play the note for a duration determined by the time signature (more on that coming up in the section "Tuning in to the beat with time signatures"). For example, in common 4/4 time, you'd hold a whole note for four beats.

The position of the note's head on the scale tells you the pitch to play. The appearance of the note, including any stems and flags, tells you how long to hold it.

Table 4-1	Note Values
Note	*Value*
o	Whole
♩	Half
♩	Quarter
♪	Eighth
♪	Sixteenth

Because notes have mathematical values, you can add them together. Two sixteenth notes of the same pitch, for example, equal an eighth note. Two quarter notes of the same pitch make a half note. Figure 4-21 shows the math.

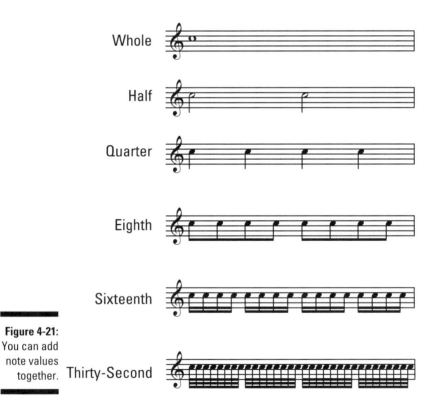

Figure 4-21:
You can add
note values
together.

Advanced players subdivide the longer notes into sixteenth notes most of the time.

Tying notes together

You can add two notes of the same pitch together using a *tie*, which is the musical equivalent of a plus sign. A tie is a curved line segment that connects two notes of the same pitch, as shown in Figure 4-22. For example, if a half note is tied to a quarter note, you play a note that is three beats in duration.

Figure 4-22:
A tie adds
the values
of two notes
of the same
pitch.

Musical notation also uses a type of shorthand to connect smaller note values designated with flags. If several identical note values neighbor one another, instead of drawing a flag for each one, musical notation connects them using a *beam*, as shown back in Figure 4-21. Here, you can see three eighth notes, but you're not adding two notes of identical pitch; you're merely connecting notes of different pitches that have the same value.

Humming a few bars with bar lines

Every staff is divided into measures using vertical lines called *bar lines*, as shown in Figure 4-23. Bar lines divide the notes into groups, making it easier for the conductor to show them to the musicians and making it easier for musicians to read and remember the notes and the rhythm.

Figure 4-23:
Bar lines
divide the
music into
measures.

Tuning in to the beat with time signatures

Just to the right of the key signature on a staff are two numbers, one on top of the other, as in a fraction (see Figure 4-24). Together, they form the *time signature,* but each number represents something different:

✔ The top number determines the number of beats in a bar (or measure). The time signature for a waltz is 3/4, equating to three beats per bar. The time signature for a march is typically 2/4, calling for two beats per measure.

✔ The bottom number indicates the type of note that gets one beat. If the number on the bottom is 2, a half note gets one beat. If the number is 4, a quarter note gets one beat. If the number is 8, an eighth note gets one beat.

Figure 4-24:
The time
signature
controls the
beat.

Accounting for triplets and dotted notes

Triplets and dotted notes provide two ways to further complicate the math involved in establishing rhythm. Fortunately, they represent the last two math problems you have to deal with in this chapter.

Triplets

A *triplet* is a rhythm in which three notes play in the space of two notes of the same value; for example, three eighth notes in the space normally reserved for only two eighth notes. Just remember that triplets are worth two of the notes they're made of. In Figure 4-25, which shows a 2/4 time signature, the eighth-note triplet gets one full beat, while the quarter note triplet gets two beats.

Figure 4-25:
Triplets.

Dotted notes

Some notes have a dot to the right of them. The dot tells you to play the note for its value plus half its value. To play a dotted half note, for example, you play the half note plus a half of a half for a total ¾ note:

$$\tfrac{1}{2} + (\tfrac{1}{2} \times \tfrac{1}{2}) = \tfrac{1}{2} + \tfrac{1}{4} = \tfrac{2}{4} + \tfrac{1}{4} = \tfrac{3}{4}$$

A dotted quarter note would be a ⅜ note:

$$\tfrac{1}{4} + (\tfrac{1}{2} \times \tfrac{1}{4}) = \tfrac{1}{4} + \tfrac{1}{8} = \tfrac{2}{8} + \tfrac{1}{8} = \tfrac{3}{8}$$

Dotted notes are a type of shorthand. Instead of tying together a half note and a quarter note to create a ¾ note, you simply use a dotted half note. See Figure 4-26.

Figure 4-26:
Dotted
notes serve
as short-
hand.

Taking a breather with rests

Watch any band closely for the duration of a tune, and you're likely to see one or more players stop playing for a short period of time. They rest because the sheet music tells them to rest, using one of the rest symbols listed in Table 4-2.

Table 4-2	Rest Values
Rest	*Value*
⬓	Whole
⬓	Half
𝄽	Quarter
𝄾	Eighth
𝄿	Sixteenth

The very shortest rests typically appear within the lines of music and act like commas in a sentence. To get a feel for rests, read the following spooky sentence aloud a couple of times:

> John, who was 12 years old, went down to the dark, dreary, dirty, crime-infested city.

Notice that you kept the flow of the sentence all the way from "John" to "city," pausing slightly on each comma. Slight spaces like these in music are marked as rests.

Unless you're playing an ensemble piece in which you don't play all the time, the longer rests usually appear at the very ends of lines. Here the motion of the music really does stop, and the rest is a true rest.

To determine whether a rest is just a space (a pause) or a real rest, move your arm and hand as you sing along. If you want to keep swinging your arm through a rest, it's just a space. If you actually want to stop swinging, then it's a bona fide rest.

Spicing Up the Music with Staccato, Accents, Slurs, and Tenutos

In an attempt to spice up the music, composers often sprinkle special markings throughout a composition to indicate the style in which they want those notes played. In the following sections, I introduce the various styles and the markings used to indicate those styles.

Barking out notes staccato style

Staccato probably started with the string instruments, so think of it as a plucky style. Instead of strumming your guitar, you pluck the strings. To get a feel for staccato, sing "Twinkle Twinkle Little Star" very fast, replacing all the words with "Ha."

To mark a note as staccato, composers add a dot above or below the note. Figure 4-27 shows "Twinkle Twinkle Little Star" adapted to a more staccato style of play.

Figure 4-27:
Staccato
markings.

Accenting notes for emPHAsis

In written English, writers often stress important words or syllables by italicizing or capitalizing them. If you're reading a passage aloud and come to an italicized or capitalized word, you tend to read it with a little more emphasis.

Although composers don't use italics in their music, they do have a way to emphasize certain notes — by adding *accents,* as shown in Figure 4-28. Here, the composer has accented the notes that accompany the words *star* and *are* in "Twinkle Twinkle Little Star."

Figure 4-28:
Accented
notes.

Slurring your notes

Slurs are the opposite of staccato. Instead of playing each note individually, you tend to blend notes together to create more of a sing-song rhythm. When a composer wants two or more notes slurred, she places a slur mark over all the notes. Figure 4-29 shows "Twinkle Twinkle Little Star" with staccato markings over the quarter notes in bar one and slurs over the quarter notes in bar two. Sing along to get a feel for the difference.

Figure 4-29:
Slurred
notes.

Marking tenutos with a dash

Tenutos tell you to hold a note a little longer than usual. Composers often use these markings to help with slurs and to give the notes in a piece more of a sing-song quality. To hear what tenutos sound like, sing "Twinkle Twinkle Little Star," replacing each word with "Da" instead of "Ha" and following along in Figure 4-30.

Figure 4-30:
"Twinkle
Twinkle
Little Star"
tenuto-fied.

Marking phrases with slurs

Imagine a musical composition as a paragraph comprised of sentences, each of which is comprised of one or more phrases — typically a noun phrase at the beginning and a verb phrase at the end. In music, composers can use slurs to designate a certain group of notes as a phrase — an antecedent phrase, which comes first, followed by a consequent phrase.

Figure 4-31 presents "Twinkle Twinkle Little Star" with the first two phrases (antecedent and consequent) marked by slurs. Sing along to get a feel for the phrases.

Figure 4-31: "Twinkle Twinkle Little Star" divided into phrases.

Twin kle twin kle lit tle star | how I won der what you are

Reaching Beyond the Notes

Music is passionate, or at least it should be, but when you hear some people play, you get the impression that they're just going through the motions. They may be hitting all the right notes, but the music sounds lifeless.

To inject some emotion into the music and create a mood, composers often add *expressive marks* to the notes, as explained in the following sections.

Deciphering dynamic markings

Dynamic markings enable composers to crank the volume up or down along a spectrum from softest to loudest (see Figure 4-32):

- **Pianissimo:** Composers mark the softest measures with p's to create a calm or distant effect — "p" stands for piano, while "pp" stands for pianissimo, which is Italian for "very soft." The more p's, the softer you play.

- **Mezzo:** Mezzo, marked with an "m," is the middle range.

- **Forte:** Forte, marked with an "f," is where the composer begins to crank up the volume. The more f's, the louder: Loud is "f," louder is "ff," and loudest is "fff."

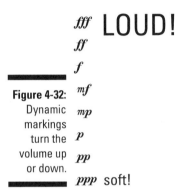

Figure 4-32: Dynamic markings turn the volume up or down.

Spotting crescendos and diminuendos

Compositions often have music that gradually rises in volume (this is called a *crescendo*) or gradually becomes softer (referred to as a *diminuendo*). Either can occur more or less gradually.

Crescendos and diminuendos are both marked with a sideways V, with the open end facing right for a crescendo and left for a diminuendo. Most musical phrases crescendo to the high point or the most important notes of phrases and tend to create tension. Diminuendos, on the other hand, tend to drift off, leaving listeners with a sense of relaxation.

Learning Italian with tempo markings

You can play a tune or portions of a tune fast, slow, or at a comfortable cruising speed. This is what tempo is all about, and if you want to learn about tempo, you need to brush up on your Italian:

- *Adagio* is very slow.
- *Andante* is moderately slow.
- *Moderato* is medium.
- *Allegro* is fast.

Italians also like to add modifiers like *un poco* (a little), and *non troppo* (not too much).

Interior markings are also very important. *Accelerando* means speed up, whereas *ritardando* and *rallantando* both mean slow down.

Following repeat signs and roadmaps

Repeat signs and roadmaps are proof that laziness is the mother of invention. To save time and money and avoid writer's cramp, early composers developed several shorthand techniques, including using repeat signs and roadmaps, which reduce redundancy. The following sections introduce you to these timesaving notations.

Repeat signs

Repeat signs, as shown in Figure 4-33, tell you to play it again, Sam. You repeat the section you just played. If the music contains only one repeat sign, you go back to the beginning and start playing. If it has two repeat signs, the first one (with dots on the right) indicates the beginning of the section you need to repeat, and the second one (with dots on the left) indicates the end, while telling you to go back to the previous repeat symbol. You usually repeat only once unless the notation instructs otherwise.

Figure 4-33:
Repeat
signs.

First and second endings

Tunes often have two or more endings. You play through the first ending, repeat everything leading up to the beginning of the first ending, and then skip to the second ending. The two endings are bracketed and numbered, as shown in Figure 4-34, so you know exactly where to start, stop, and skip.

Figure 4-34:
Repeats are
often used
in songs
with two
endings.

Chapter 5

Assembling, Cleaning, and Caring for Your Clarinet

....

In This Chapter

▶ Putting your clarinet together . . . easy does it

▶ Keeping your clarinet squeaky clean

▶ Giving your clarinet an oil and lube job

▶ Lining up a repair technician if you need one

....

*Y*our clarinet may look about as sturdy and unsophisticated as a Louisville Slugger, but it's actually more akin to a finely tuned Ferrari. You wouldn't think of slamming the doors on your Ferrari, and you'd do everything possible to keep it clean, shiny, and properly tuned up. You need to treat your clarinet with the same sort of tender loving care.

The key system on clarinets is relatively complex and a little delicate — with enough force, metal does bend, so be gentle. To prevent corrosive chemicals from building up inside the instrument, including the mouthpiece, you need to properly clean your clarinet regularly. You also need to keep the pads on the clarinet dry so they don't swell up and leak air when they close on the body of the instrument.

Like a car engine, the metal keys must be lubricated to prevent wear and tear, and some clarinetists feel that the wooden body occasionally must be oiled to keep it from drying out. Finally, just as with that finely tuned Ferrari, you need to know a good mechanic or technician to call on when something breaks or wears out.

In this chapter, you get up to speed on the do's and don'ts of handling, assembling, and maintaining your clarinet for trouble-free use.

Assembling Your Clarinet

Assembling a clarinet isn't exactly rocket science. After all, a typical clarinet comes in about seven pieces (as described in Chapter 2), give or take a few — how difficult could putting together seven pieces possibly be? Well, the challenge isn't in slapping together the pieces, the challenge is in doing it properly without bending or breaking anything.

In the following sections, I offer a few assembly tips and tricks, reveal some places on the clarinet to avoid touching, and then step you through the assembly process. By the end of this section, you'll have a fully (and properly) assembled clarinet.

Assembly tips and tricks

Over the course of their careers, auto mechanics pick up numerous tips, tricks, and techniques that make basic tasks much easier. That's how they can perform a repair that would take you an entire weekend in less than an hour — and do it without breaking anything or skinning any knuckles. To simplify the task of assembling your clarinet, I offer the following tips and tricks I've gathered over my career:

✔ **Set the case on a chair or the floor before you even think about opening it.** The last thing you want to do is dump all those delicate parts out of the case — something that's pretty common when a clarinet player opens the case on his lap.

✔ **Before you begin the assembly, place the reed in your mouth with the bark side down and get it good and moist.** That way, it's ready for you when you're ready for it. Reeds are pieces of wood and need to be moist to vibrate properly.

Hold the reed in your mouth during the entire assembly process. It takes at least 60 seconds for a reed to absorb moisture.

✔ **Before assembling your clarinet for the first time and during the break-in period, apply a dab of cork grease on each cork to help the pieces slide together more easily and seal properly.** This is especially necessary for new clarinets that haven't yet been "worked in." Apply cork grease every fifth time for a new instrument and every tenth time after the first six weeks.

✔ **Twist the pieces together like you screw the lid on a jar**.

Never jam corks together, and never force a fit.

✓ **To avoid bending keys, start with the bell and work up.**

✓ **When you're done, make sure the brand insignia faces up and is centered.** As noted in Chapter 3, the insignias for professional clarinets are stamped on last, after the bell and barrel are moved around to the location for them that produces the best tone quality. Even intermediate-quality clarinets often play best with the insignias on the barrel and bell centered with the keys on the upper and lower joints.

Hands off! Places you should never touch

To avoid bending keys when assembling the clarinet, touch as few keys as possible. To accomplish this, hold the upper and lower joint with the keys facing up. Use the same grip as you'd use when holding a tennis racket, as shown in Figure 5-1. Hold the parts of the clarinet firmly, but not with a death grip, and never touch the following parts:

✓ The cups of the keys on the lower joint

✓ The side keys on the upper joint

Figure 5-1:
Hold the parts of the clarinet the same way you'd hold a tennis racket.

Attaching the bell to the lower joint

Without further ado, begin the assembly by connecting the bell to the lower joint:

1. **Take the bell out of the case with your left hand. See Figure 5-2.**

2. **Grasp the lower joint with your right hand, keeping your fingers away from the keys on the lower part of the bottom joint.**

3. **Twist the bell onto the lower joint so the brand insignia on the bell faces up.**

Figure 5-2:
Attach the bell to the lower joint with the insignia facing up.

Attaching the lower joint to the upper joint

With the bell and the lower joint safely in place, you can now attach the lower joint to the upper joint. Here's how:

1. **While continuing to hold the lower joint with the right hand, grasp the upper joint with your left hand.**

2. **Press down on the keys of the upper joint so the upper part of the bridge mechanism rises, and continue to hold the keys down as you perform Step 3.**

The bridge key connects the keys of the upper and lower joints. You depress the ring keys on the upper joint, which raises the upper part of the bridge mechanism, to keep the keys of the upper and lower joints from jamming together. Make sure the lower part of the bridge key fits under the upper part and doesn't bend into it when you turn the two sections together in Step 3.

3. **Twist the upper and lower joints together so that the lower half of the bridge key is under the raised upper part, and then line up the two keys. See Figure 5-3.**

4. **Release the upper joint keys.**

Avoid bending the bridge keys. The bridge keys are the part of the clarinet that gets bent most frequently and causes the greatest number of repair bills.

Figure 5-3:
Attach the lower and upper joints.

Attaching the barrel to the upper joint

You're halfway there. Now attach the barrel to the upper joint:

1. **Move your left hand to the top of the upper joint.**

2. **Grasp the barrel with your right hand.**

3. **Twist the barrel onto the upper joint, taking care to keep the brand insignia on top, as shown in Figure 5-4.**

Figure 5-4:
Twist the
barrel onto
the upper
joint.

Attaching the mouthpiece to the barrel

Almost there. Now attach the mouthpiece to the barrel:

1. **While holding the upper joint with your left hand, grasp the mouth-piece with your right hand.**

2. **Twist the mouthpiece onto the barrel, lining up the very center of the table (the flat part) of the mouthpiece with the center of the vent key, as shown in Figure 5-5.**

Figure 5-5:
Attach the
mouthpiece
to the
barrel.

Attaching the reed to the mouthpiece

One final piece, and your puzzle is complete. Attach the reed to the mouthpiece:

1. **Place the clarinet on your lap with the flat part of the mouthpiece facing up.**

2. **Loosen the screws on the ligature and slide it onto the mouthpiece down to the top line.**

3. **Slide the butt of the reed under the ligature, and position the reed so that it's even with the tip of the mouthpiece and centered on the table of the mouthpiece.**

4. **When the reed is in position, slightly tighten the ligature screws.**

Cleaning and Storing Your Clarinet

Your clarinet may not cost quite as much as a brand spankin' new Ferrari, but a new clarinet can cost anywhere from a few hundred to a few thousand dollars. Money aside, properly cleaning and storing your clarinet keeps it sounding great and feeling great to play. In the following sections, we show you how to swab, scrub, and shine your instrument and then store it for safekeeping.

Because clarinets aren't cheap and repairmen are usually expensive, proper cleaning and storage of the instrument can save you some serious cash.

Swabbing condensation

As you play your clarinet, condensation accumulates inside it. Warm, moist air flowing through a slightly cooler, dark tunnel tends to do that. Saliva also tends to do that, but that's too icky to mention. Regardless of where all that moisture comes from, it can damage your instrument over time, so every time you finish playing and about every 20 minutes when you're practicing or performing, swab out the moisture. Here's how:

1. **Remove the mouthpiece.**

2. **Drop the swab string into the instrument through the bell, taking care to spread out the swab so that it goes through the clarinet easily, as shown in Figure 5-6.**

3. **Pull the swab string slowly but firmly to pull the swab through the instrument.**

If the swab gets stuck, don't keep pulling. Starting with the outside edges of the swab, work it out of the top of the instrument. Be patient!

Cleaning the keys

Hate to break it to you, but the perspiration on your fingers and in the palms of your hands may be slightly acidic. That's bad news for your clarinet keys, because the acid tends to take the shine off them. Using a silver cloth, gently buff the keys, as shown in Figure 5-7, to liven them up and restore their sparkle. Do this every two or three weeks, or more often if you like.

Figure 5-6:
Swab your
clarinet.

Figure 5-7:
Shine the
keys.

You can pick up a silver cloth at most music and jewelry stores. Some players like to use a high-quality silver polish to make the keys really sparkle. If you do, take great care to use only small amounts on just a few keys at a time, and don't let any of the polish touch the pads — it has the same bad effect as oil.

Giving the mouthpiece a bath

At least once a week, give your mouthpiece a bath in lukewarm, soapy water. Otherwise, various gunk accumulates, which may look and taste terrible and negatively affect your playing. If the mouthpiece goes without a bath long enough, it may even become a health hazard. To avoid getting gunk in your clarinet, don't eat foods containing sugar before you play. If you play after eating, brush your teeth or swish water in your mouth.

If you're washing your mouthpiece in the sink, place a washcloth in the bottom of the sink, just in case you drop the mouthpiece. This can prevent breakage if the mouthpiece slips out of your hands.

When you're ready to wash the mouthpiece, take the following steps:

1. **Fill the sink or a small container large enough to submerge the mouthpiece, up to where the ligature usually sits, with lukewarm water (never hot) and a little hand soap.**

2. **Remove the mouthpiece cap, ligature, and any pad saver you may have for your mouthpiece.**

3. **Being careful not to get the cork wet, dip the end you blow into down into the soapy water, and hold it there for a few seconds.**

4. **Pull out the mouthpiece and use a paper towel or soft cloth to rub any gunk off the mouthpiece, as shown in Figure 5-8.**

   Repeat Steps 3 and 4 until all the gunk is gone.

5. **Turn the mouthpiece over, shake out any water that got inside, and then wipe out any excess water with a tissue.**

6. **Set the mouthpiece upside down on a paper towel, and let it dry for a few minutes.**

7. **Using a cotton swab, rub off any cork grease or dirt from around the cork, and then grease the cork.**

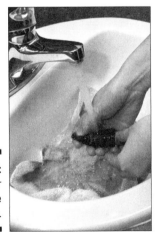

Figure 5-8:
Give your
mouthpiece
a bath.

How 'bout using a humidor for reeds?

If you smoke cigars, you may be wondering whether a humidor would work for reed storage. And the answer is: Yes, it would, but I wouldn't use the same box you use for your cigars — it'll make your reed smell like a cigar, too.

You could also make your own reed humidifier with a Tupperware storage container and orange peelings. Place just a few peelings in the box and change them out every four or five days.

Clarinet storage do's and don'ts

Perhaps even more important than keeping your clarinet clean is storing it properly. Baking it a few hours in a hot car or under direct sunlight can melt the glue that holds the clarinet's pads in place or even warp the instrument. Following are some do's and don'ts for properly storing your clarinet:

✔ Store the instrument in a moderately cool room. Place it on a shelf or on the floor.

✔ Position the case so that the keys of the clarinet face up. If stored with the keys down, the added weight of the case can bend the keys over time.

✔ Never leave your instrument in a hot car, due to the aforementioned reasons.

✔ If traveling by air, always carry the clarinet aboard the aircraft — don't check it as luggage.

Storing reeds

The reed is one of the most delicate parts of a clarinet, so treat it with special tenderness. Always remove your reed after you finish playing, and store it in a humidified reed case. Good reeds are hard to come by, and they last much longer if they're stored in a good reed case.

Several inexpensive cases are available. I recommend the plastic reed cases made by Rico or Vandoren, or, if you want to go all out, check out the reed storage boxes sold by Muncy Winds.

Leaving the reed on the mouthpiece over long periods of time can cause the table of the mouthpiece to warp.

Protecting that reed and mouthpiece!

Clarinets come with mouthpiece caps to protect the mouthpiece in the case and the mouthpiece and reed when the clarinet is outside the case but not in use. Always put the mouthpiece cap on when you lay the instrument down or aren't playing during a rehearsal or performance.

Maintaining and Repairing Your Clarinet

Like a car, a clarinet is easier and cheaper to maintain than it is to repair. Break it in properly when it's new, oil the keys now and again, clean the pads, and keep up on the minor repairs, and your clarinet will last longer and play stronger, and you'll avoid costly repairs.

In the following sections, I show you how to properly maintain your clarinet and track down a good repair technician just in case your clarinet happens to suffer some damage.

Maintaining a brand new clarinet

When you get home with your brand new clarinet, the first thing you may want to do is play it night and day. And that would be wrong. First, you need to break it in properly. Here's how:

- ✔ **Apply a little cork grease to the corks the first three or four times you assemble the clarinet.** See the section "Assembly tips and tricks," earlier in this chapter, for details.

- ✔ **If the instrument is made of wood, play it no longer than 45 minutes a day for the first two weeks.** This is called the break-in period, and most new clarinets do require it.

The advantage of composite, greenline clarinets is that they don't need to be broken in and the bore retains its original dimensions throughout the life of the instrument. See Chapter 3 for details on shopping for a clarinet.

To oil wood . . . or not?

Although many manufacturers discourage oiling the bore of wooden clarinets, some players believe that it helps maintain the moisture level in the wood. These players commonly oil both the outside surfaces and the bore of the instrument with special bore oil.

If you do this, avoid letting any oil touch the pads of the instrument. Always put small pieces of waxed paper under the closed pads so that oil doesn't touch them. If you apply oil to the inside of the instrument, rub a small amount on a swab and gently push the swab through the bore of the instrument. After oiling, set the clarinet parts on a table with the keys facing up.

Nowadays, wooden clarinets are made of woods that aren't soaked in oil. The wood is cut and allowed to cure for several years before being made into clarinets. In its natural state, the wood is a beautiful brownish color. Because many people expect clarinets to be black, they're painted black at the factory. A clarinet can be made from the wood of the customer's choice or provided by the customer. In such a case, the wood is left in its natural state.

Taking care of any ol' clarinet

After the break-in period, you can relax a little and play your clarinet as much as you want. However, you still need to attend to some occasional maintenance duties, as explained in the following sections.

Oiling the keys

A clarinet's keywork is made of metal, and as we all know, metal rusts and wears down. To keep the rust at bay and reduce the wear and tear around the hinges, apply a small drop of instrument key oil on the joint near every screw in the key mechanism once a week (see Figure 5-9).

Keep key oil away from pads. Oil on a pad ruins it. Also, it's possible to put too much oil on the keys — a little dab'll do ya.

Cleaning the key pads

Pads can become sticky, and you may find yourself having to press down on a key harder and harder to pull up the pad. If a pad becomes sticky, place a slightly moistened cigarette paper under it. Gently close the pad on the paper, and then gently pull the paper out from under the pad.

Figure 5-9:
Apply a
small drop
of oil on
the joint
near every
screw.

Finding a good repair technician

If you follow all the advice in this chapter to properly clean, store, and maintain your clarinet, you may be able to avoid having to call on the services of a repair technician. Eventually, however, you're likely to encounter some maintenance or repairs you're not qualified to attend to. When this happens, start looking for a repair technician.

You can track one down by flipping through your town's Yellow Pages, but it's often better to get a recommendation from another musician you know. Ask your clarinet instructor, if you have one, or call around to music stores in your area. You may also want to consider contacting a band director or a professor at one of the local high schools or colleges.

To select a qualified repair technician who meets your needs, ask the following questions:

- **Do you repair only what you sell?** To encourage sales, some music stores repair only what they sell. If you purchased your instrument elsewhere, ask for names of any qualified repair technicians in the area. Many of the best technicians work independently or on contract with music stores, so if the store refuses to subcontract the job to a technician, deal directly with the technician.

- **What is your average turnaround?** Unless you're a preferred customer, the turnaround for most repairs is typically several days. Avoid technicians who keep you waiting for weeks.

- **Are you a woodwind player?** If the technician is a woodwind player, this question is likely to elicit a response including the names of some known teachers or professionals in the area. The technician with the most connections is usually the best.

Part II
And a One, and a Two, and a Three: Getting Started

The 5th Wave   By Rich Tennant

In this part . . .

Coaxing the right notes out of a clarinet requires a full-body commitment. You need to assume the proper stance, hold your head just right, form your lips just so, breathe deeply, and blow fast enough to make the reed vibrate, all while holding the clarinet and moving your fingers to the proper positions. And you thought golf was tough!

In this part, you get your head in the game — along with your back, lungs, lips, tongue, teeth, and fingers so you can start playing notes. You discover how to make your clarinet produce a sound, form that sound into notes, and play a whole lot more notes higher, lower, in between, and even above high C. I also show you how to slur notes to move smoothly from one to the next and tongue to separate notes to give each note more definition.

Chapter 6

Getting Your Body, Lungs, and Lips in the Game

Most people think of the musician and her instrument as two separate entities. Technically speaking, they're right. A musical instrument isn't exactly an appendage of the human body. When you're playing the clarinet, however, you sort of become part of the instrument. You're the bag for the bagpipe — in this case, your clarinet. Without you, the clarinet is just a pretty stick with a lot of holes in it and some bling wrapped around it.

To play your role well, you need to get your body in the game by assuming proper posture, preparing your lungs to breathe for two (you and your clarinet), and forming your lips just so around the mouthpiece. This chapter builds the foundation for initial success and long-term future improvement.

Taking a Stance: Great Posture for Great Breathing

You're the fuel system for your clarinet. As such, you need to fill up your tank by breathing deeply and deliver the fuel as efficiently as possible and as forcefully as necessary. Breathe too shallowly, and you'll run out of gas after the first few notes. Assume a poor posture, and you'll get a kink in the fuel line that prevents you from filling your tank or delivering the fuel forcefully and reliably.

Great clarinet playing starts with a great posture. If you're all twisted and scrunched up, you can't take in the amount of air required to play well or exhale fast enough to make the reed vibrate. You need to stand or sit up straight, relax your shoulders, and hold up your chin.

Work on maintaining good posture throughout the day, regardless of whether you're holding a clarinet. When you're standing, sitting, or walking, keep your back straight, shoulders square but relaxed, and chin parallel to the ground. This helps prevent you from falling into bad habits while playing.

Good posture makes good breathing and blowing possible, because it allows you to breathe deeply and keeps the kinks out of your windpipe. Let the following sections be your guide.

Straightening your back

Slump over in your chair, take a deep breath, and exhale. Now, sit up straight, shoulders straight but relaxed, take another deep breath, and exhale. Unless you're a very unique human specimen, you breathed much more deeply with a straight back than slumped over.

When playing the clarinet, remain conscious of your posture and how it affects your breathing, at least until assuming the right posture becomes second nature to you.

When asked about the key to good clarinet playing, Stanley Hasty, preeminent American clarinet teacher, said, "Keep a straight back."

Raise your music stand so the top of the rack is level with your eyes when you're sitting or standing erect. This forces you to maintain good posture, because if you start slouching, the music becomes more difficult to read.

Keeping your chin up

As you sing "La," let your head droop forward. Notice how the sound gets more pinched and softer. Keeping your chin up, parallel to the ground, takes the kink out of your windpipe and facilitates free movement of air. Keep your head up.

Drooping your head while playing is just like bending a garden hose as you're watering the lawn. It constricts the flow of air.

Breathing for Your Clarinet

When playing the clarinet, you may tend to get winded. After all, you're breathing for two — you and your clarinet. You have to breathe to keep yourself from passing out, take in enough breath to produce notes, and do it all as efficiently as possible.

The fullness of the clarinet sound comes from the volume of air in your lungs. Resonance comes from the speed with which you expel the air. Because of this, your ability to control your breathing has a direct correlation to the beauty of the sound and the length of the musical phrases you can play.

In the following sections, I reveal techniques that help you breathe more deeply and in a more controlled fashion.

Breathing in . . . deeply

Although the human body is designed to breathe from bottom to top, most adults breathe from top to bottom. You can tell, because when you instruct them to take a deep breath, their shoulders rise — a sure sign of top-down breathing. As a result, they're filling their lungs only about half to two-thirds full.

With bottom-up breathing or breathing with your diaphragm, you fill your lungs from the very bottom to the very top, giving yourself a full tank of gas. One of the best ways to practice diaphragm breathing is to lie on your back with your hands on your stomach. As you breath in, notice your hands rising as your stomach expands. As you exhale, notice your stomach flatten. If your chest tends to move more than your stomach, you're doing it wrong.

When playing the clarinet, inhale through the corners of your mouth while keeping the mouthpiece firmly anchored between your top teeth and bottom lip. In other words, don't open your mouth to take a breath. Try to make the air go clear down to your stomach, even though this is physically impossible.

Breathing out . . . completely

When you're playing a woodwind instrument like the clarinet, breathing out is as important as breathing in. I would say it's even more important, but if you don't breathe in enough, you have nothing to blow out.

When exhaling, hiss like a snake, as Tom Martin, clarinetist of the Boston Symphony, tells players. This causes the back and tip of your tongue to rise up and form a wind tunnel inside your mouth that forces the air out at a higher pressure, as though it's hissing out of a punctured tire.

To further improve your breathing, practice the exercise shown in Figures 6-1 and 6-2, developed by Arnold Jacobs, former tuba player of the Chicago Symphony. Jacobs had one lung removed due to lung cancer, yet he could still keep up with the loudest brass section in the country. Here's what you do:

1. **Pretend your hand and arm are part of a sideways gas gauge.**

2. **Place your hand on your abdomen and breathe in for a count of eight.**

3. **Exhale for a count of eight seconds, swinging your arm and hand out as you release pressure.**

   Remember to exhale with a hiss.

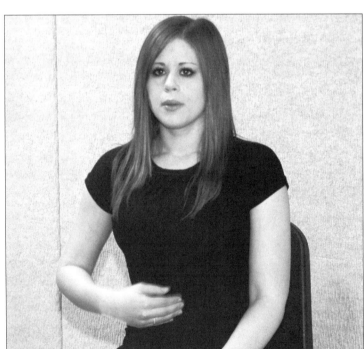

Figure 6-1:
Inhale.

Figure 6-2:
Exhale.

Sounding Off with a Mini-Clarinet

When you ride a bike for the first time, you start out slowly — tricycle first, then a bike with training wheels, and finally a two-wheeler. Taking a similar approach to the clarinet can greatly improve your chances of early success. Start with a mini-clarinet, consisting only of the mouthpiece (with reed) and barrel. As soon as you can consistently produce a full, controlled sound on your mini-clarinet, you're ready to step up to the full clarinet, complete with upper-joint, lower-joint, and bell.

Getting small

When eager musicians first encounter the clarinet, they're intimidated into silence. They're so overwhelmed with the holes and keywork that they can't get the clarinet to utter a sound. The solution is to take the keys and tone holes out of the equation temporarily.

Assemble your clarinet, as explained in Chapter 5, skipping the upper- and lower-joints and the bell. This gives you a mini-clarinet with only the mouth-piece assembly (mouthpiece, ligature, and reed) and the barrel.

After attaching the reed to the mouthpiece, slip a business card under the reed until you feel a slight bit of resistance on the card. The card should be about ⅜ inch from the tip of the reed, as shown in Figure 6-3. The amount of reed above the line is the approximate amount of reed that can and should vibrate inside your mouth.

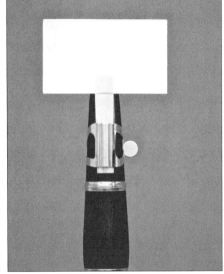

Figure 6-3:
Slide a business card under the reed.

Giving your clarinet some lip: Proper embouchure

Watching someone playing the clarinet, you may assume all the person is doing with her mouth is blowing into the mouthpiece. While that's certainly part of what the mouth does, it's not nearly all of what it does. Several parts of the mouth work together to accomplish the following:

✔ Lower teeth and lip support the reed and control its vibration.

✔ Upper teeth press down to anchor the mouthpiece and create a lever that assists in controlling the reed's vibration.

✔ Lips seal around the mouthpiece to prevent air from escaping as the player exhales.

✔ Tongue directs the air directly into the mouthpiece opening.

How all the parts of your mouth team up to blow just right is called *embouchure,* and it's a key ingredient to coaxing full tones out of your clarinet.

Taking a big drink: The straw analogy

Embouchure is fairly complex, but you can start with a simple comparison to a drinking straw. Hold a drinking straw in your mouth, suck in, and take note of your natural lip position:

✔ You're not biting the straw with your teeth.

✔ Your lips are wrapped around the straw with the top, bottom, and sides of your lips all in on the action.

✔ Your lower lip curves over your bottom teeth just slightly, keeping your teeth from contacting the straw. (Your lower lip isn't all the way inside your mouth.)

You don't talk with your lower lip inside your mouth, so don't play the clarinet that way, either.

Holding your mouth just so

Before placing the mouthpiece in your mouth, get your jaw and lips into position. Imagine yourself applying lip balm, curling your lips just over the surface of your teeth to support your lips and stretching them out so they're not all wrinkly when you apply the lip balm. (See Figure 6-4.)

Roll all of your lower lip into your mouth and then roll it back out while saying the "mu" part of the word "music." Notice that your lower lip curves against your bottom teeth just enough to cover the biting surface as it does when you're drinking from a straw.

Now smile with your lower lip, and frown with your upper lip. Notice that your top lip forms against your eye teeth like when you say "vuum." Figure 6-5 illustrates the muscle flow required to achieve proper embouchure.

Figure 6-4:
Hold your lips as if you're applying lip balm.

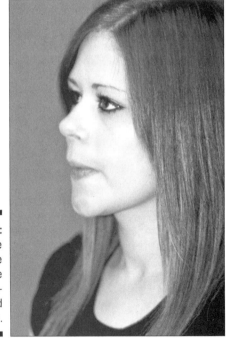

Figure 6-5:
Apply gentle pressure using the facial muscles around your mouth.

The reed rests against the lower lip, which is curved against (not over) the bottom teeth.

Holding your tongue just so

To maximize the force of your breath coming into the mouthpiece, use your tongue to form a wind tunnel and then hiss like a snake.

Taking another drink with the clarinet

When you've mastered the nuances of how to hold your mouth and tongue, you're ready for the mouthpiece:

1. **Slide the mouthpiece into your mouth until your lower lip is near the mark that you made on the reed.**

2. **Let your top teeth touch the mouthpiece about ¼ inch from the tip.**

   The only difference between the straw analogy and the mini-clarinet is that your top teeth touch the mouthpiece. When you're drinking from a straw, your teeth typically never touch the straw.

3. **Form your lips into the "mu" and "vuum" positions (smiling with the bottom lip while frowning with the top lip).**

4. **With your right hand, raise the mini-clarinet until it's almost straight out.**

   Keep your lower lip in the smile position and avoid raising it up as you raise the mini-clarinet.

5. **Close the corners of your mouth around the mouthpiece, and take a long, slow drink.**

6. **Blow back out as you hold your jaw and lips exactly like they were when you drank in, making a hissing sound with the mouthpiece for eight beats.**

   You're not playing any notes here, just making the hissing sound, which lets you know that you haven't changed the shape or tension of your bottom lip.

7. **Repeat steps 5 and 6 several times until you feel comfortable blowing out.**

Maximum reed vibration occurs when the reed rests on a firm, narrow ledge. By stretching your lower lip just over the biting surface of your bottom teeth, you create such a ledge.

Breathing in and blowing out

As you're playing the clarinet, the natural impulse is to open your mouth to take a deep breath, which is very inefficient. Every time you open your mouth, you then have to reposition the mouthpiece and reestablish the proper embouchure.

A more efficient method is to keep the clarinet clamped between your upper and lower jaws while breathing in through the corners of your mouth, as shown in Figure 6-6. This keeps the mouthpiece in place while opening a passage for incoming air.

Playing that big band sound: Adjusting the leverage and air

When you're blowing air into your clarinet with it sticking straight out from your mouth, you won't hear anything but hissing air. As explained in Chapter 2, in order to vibrate, the reed must close half the distance between itself and the mouthpiece before it can vibrate. Unless you partly close the reed with leverage, it doesn't vibrate.

Closing the reed by biting on it is possible, but I don't recommend it. Biting down to close the gap between the reed and the mouthpiece makes it very difficult to articulate and to produce the high notes. It also limits the amount of control you have on the reed. The correct way to close the gap is to maintain your embouchure while lowering the clarinet. Essentially, the clarinet acts as a lever that puts upward pressure on the reed, as shown in Figure 6-7.

Figure 6-6:
Breathe in through the corners of your mouth.

Using your clarinet as a lever, make your first sound with your mini-clarinet:

1. **Take a deep drink with your clarinet pointing straight out, as shown in Figure 6-8.**

   See the previous sections for more about the drinking analogy.

2. **Blow out while gradually bringing the end of the mini-clarinet down so that you feel the leverage of the reed against your lower lip. Do this while maintaining the shape of your embouchure.**

   You should feel some pressure on your lower lip, which is a good thing.

3. **Keep lowering the mini-clarinet until you get a sound.**

   Expect the sound to go from hissy to airy at first.

4. **Keep lowering the mini-clarinet until you hear a G above the staff.**

   If possible, play the note on a piano or tuner first, so you know what it's supposed to sound like.

   If you're able to play G3, the leverage and embouchure tension is perfect. Figure 6-9 demonstrates the proper clarinet position with excellent embouchure.

5. **Play the sound for at least eight seconds — count "one-one-thousand, two-one-thousand, three-one-thousand. . . ."**

   The sound should be pleasant and not harsh.

Figure 6-7:
Use the clarinet as a lever to close the gap between the reed and mouthpiece.

Figure 6-8:
Take a drink with your mini clarinet held high (Track 1).

Figure 6-9:
Proper mouthpiece position with excellent embouchure (Track 2).

Chapter 7

Playing Your First Notes

· ·

· ·

Anyone who's ever swung a golf club knows that fundamentals are everything. Start with the wrong stance and grip, and you're likely to be slicing, hooking, and topping the ball all day long, perhaps even throwing your back out in the process. Start with the right grip, stance, and backswing, and your odds of success soar — hopefully along with the ball.

I'm not suggesting that you swing your clarinet, but to play a tune correctly, you must start with the proper fundamentals — especially the correct hand and finger positions and embouchure. Starting out right greatly improves your chances of success and saves you loads of time later trying to unlearn bad habits. In this chapter, I show and tell you how to properly handle your clarinet and play your first few notes.

Talk about starting with the basics! This chapter assumes you're standing (or sitting) there holding a fully and properly assembled clarinet. If you're not, head to Chapter 5 first, and double-check to make sure the center of the reed is aligned with the vent key. I'll be here when you get back.

Letting Your Fingers Do the Talking

Unlike golf, playing the clarinet is a team sport, with ten players per team — your ten fingers, that is. And before they can start playing the game, you have to make sure every player is in the correct position. In other words, hold the instrument properly with your fingers in all the right places.

The following sections introduce you to the proper hand, finger, and thumb positions, from your mitts to your digits. I won't ask you to do anything complicated like actually moving your fingers. For now, your hands and fingers simply need to know where to stand, so they're ready to jump into action.

Your hands pull double duty — they hold the instrument while getting all the fingers and thumbs in position so they can do their jobs.

Double-checking your right thumb position

Your right thumb does all the heavy lifting. It supports the clarinet as you play it. To determine the correct thumb position, here's what you do:

1. **Wave as if to say goodbye with your right hand.**

   Note that the nails of your fingers face upwards, your thumb doesn't move, and your thumbnail points back at you, as shown in Figure 7-1.

2. **Place the clarinet on your knee with the thumb rest facing you.**

3. **While keeping your hand in the goodbye position, slide your thumb up to the thumb rest, so your thumb touches it between the knuckle and thumbnail.**

   This is the strongest part of your thumb. (See Figure 7-2.)

4. **Close your index finger on the first tone hole, as shown in Figure 7-2.**

When your thumb is in the proper position, you should be able to lift the clarinet up off your knee and move it up and down, as shown in Figure 7-3, without squeezing it.

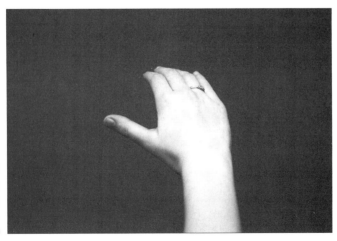

Figure 7-1:
Wave
goodbye.

Figure 7-2:
Slide your right thumb up to the thumb rest and place your index finger on the first tone hole.

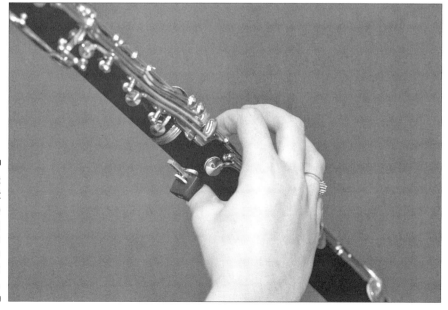

Figure 7-3:
Correct thumb positioning enables you to lift the clarinet with one hand.

WARNING!

Don't apply a death grip. The thumb rest lets your thumb rest while still allowing it to support the clarinet. Your thumbprint doesn't touch the clarinet. Because the top of the thumb touches the thumb rest between the knuckle and the nail, only the side of the thumb touches the clarinet. Allowing the thumbprint to touch the clarinet and squeezing the clarinet repetitively with improper thumb positioning over long periods of time may actually lead to carpal tunnel syndrome.

Getting your left hand in the act

Your left hand is just hanging there like a limp noodle. Wake it up, because it has some work to do:

1. **Hold up your left hand with your palm facing away from you and your thumb in the two o'clock position.**

   If you grew up with digital clocks, check out Figure 7-4 to figure out what the two o'clock position looks like.

2. **Press your thumbprint against the tone hole on the back of the instrument.**

3. **Press your index finger against the first tone hole on the upper joint to seal it shut (see Figure 7-5).**

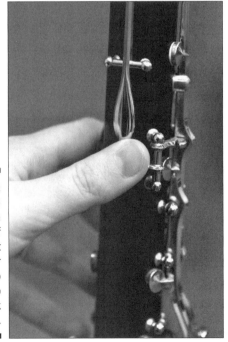

Figure 7-4: Seal the tone hole on the back of the clarinet with your left thumb in the two o'clock position.

Figure 7-5:
Your left
index finger
closes the
first tone
hole on the
upper joint.

Holding your fingers in the right positions

If you've ever played "Whack a Mole" or watched someone play it, picture in your mind how the player stands holding the hammer above the holes just waiting for that unfortunate mole to pop up. If you were octopus man with eight hammers, you'd probably hold a hammer just above each hole for maximum mole-whacking efficiency.

In the same way, you want your fingers in the optimum positions to close the tone holes and press the keys. In the following sections, I show you how to hold your fingers just right.

Trill keys are not thumb rests. Don't support the clarinet with the trill keys. Players who fail to support the clarinet with their right thumb often rest the first (bottom) trill key of the upper joint on their right index finger (see Figure 7-6). This is a big no-no. It ruins the right-hand finger positions and doesn't do a whole lot of good for that trill key, either.

Figure 7-6: Don't rest the trill key on your index finger, as shown here.

Making O's and C's

Let your arms dangle at your sides and note the natural curvature of your fingers. Your fingers are not straight unless you consciously make an effort to straighten them. This natural curvature is just what you're shooting for to establish the correct finger position for playing the clarinet.

Lift your right hand, retaining that natural finger curvature. Using your right index finger and thumb, form the letter O, as shown in Figure 7-7.

Now lift your right index finger slightly to form the letter C, as shown in Figure 7-8. Notice that the finger opens a gap between itself and your thumb without changing its natural curvature.

Playing the clarinet is all about forming O's and C's. Pressure on a finger closes the O. Relaxation opens the finger to form a C. The curvature of the fingers never changes.

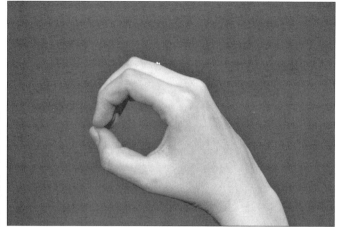

Figure 7-7:
Forming an
O with your
right index
finger and
thumb.

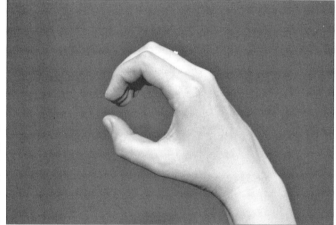

Figure 7-8:
Lifting your
right index
finger to
form a C.

When you curve the index finger correctly, the rest of the fingers will follow suit. The index finger is the sergeant.

Don't wiggle your fingers. Your fingers should be curved and move at the knuckles. Fingers that wiggle tend to be flat and farther from the tone holes. This prevents you from playing as fast as you can with fingers curved and close to the tone holes. Finger coordination is also much more difficult with flat fingers.

Don't let your pinkies droop

Pinky fingers tend to get lazy and droop, as shown in Figure 7-9. Don't let them nod off. Just like the other fingers, your pinkies should curve above the keys they're in charge of playing. They need to be in position to make the play when it comes their way.

Figure 7-9:
Don't let
your pinkies
droop like
this.

Playing Your First Note on the Whole Clarinet

In Chapter 6, you play a scaled-down version of the clarinet consisting of the mouthpiece (reed attached) and barrel. With the remaining three parts of the clarinet in place, you're now ready to play your very first note — E♮ on the staff:

1. **Place the clarinet in your mouth.**

2. **Close the thumb hole with your left thumb.**

3. **Close the top tone hole of the upper joint with your index finger.**

4. **Take a deep breath, as explained in Chapter 6.**

5. Form the proper embouchure, as explained in Chapter 6.

6. Blow out for eight seconds, maintaining your embouchure.

Figure 7-10 shows the fingering chart for E2, which is the first line E on the staff. A *fingering chart* is a picture of the clarinet's tone holes and keys used to illustrate which tone holes are closed and which keys are pressed to produce each note. The filled-in circles represent tone holes that remain closed and keys that must be pressed. Clear circles represent open tone holes and keys you don't press.

Figure 7-10:
Fingering
chart for E2.

Play E2 on the staff for eight beats — two tied whole notes. Remember, a whole note is equal in duration to eight eighth-notes that are tied together, as shown in Figure 7-11.

Figure 7-11:
Play E2 on
the staff for
eight beats
(Track 3).

While playing your first note, maintain good embouchure (refer to Chapter 6 for more details):

- ✔ Take a drink on the big clarinet.
- ✔ Keep your lower lip in the "mu" position and your top lip in the "vuum" position.
- ✔ Point your chin and smile to make a narrow ledge with the lower lip.
- ✔ Slide your lower lip down the reed near the mark defined for playing mini-clarinet (see Chapter 6).
- ✔ Hiss inside your mouth to make the air move fast.

Launching Notes with Your Tongue

Playing the clarinet is like speaking, except for the fact that your mouth plays an entirely different role. When you speak, you create the base sound in your voice box, and then form the sound with your mouth, tongue, and lips. When you play the clarinet, you don't use your voice box. Instead, your mouth and the mouthpiece function as the clarinet's voice box. Your tongue starts the sound and directs airflow over the reed to produce the main base sound. The clarinet then forms the sound into distinctive notes.

To make a note even more distinctive, you can *tongue* to begin the note. To tongue a note, touch the tip of your tongue to the tip of the reed and release it with a T sound before hissing. Try it without the clarinet by saying "T-heeee."

Imagine you're holding a faucet handle with your right hand and you want to get a drink of water. As soon as you turn that handle, the water starts pouring out, because it's ready and waiting, pushing against the valve until that valve opens and lets it go. Use the same technique to tongue. Press your tongue against the roof of your mouth and let air build up behind it like the water pressure builds inside the pipe. Release your tongue and blow —"T-heeee."

Always tongue the first note of a piece by starting with "T-heeee." For more about tonguing, check out Chapter 9. Head back to the preceding section, "Playing Your First Note on the Whole Clarinet," and play E♮ on the staff again, this time launching it with your tongue.

Adding More Notes to Your Repertoire

Getting over that first note on the whole clarinet is like taking your very first step. Now that you have a feel for playing notes, learning new notes becomes easier and easier.

Take a deep breath and play the notes shown in Figure 7-12. Notice that E2 is played by closing the thumb and top tone hole on the upper joint. After playing E2, add one finger at a time to play each successive lower note. Use the fingering chart in Appendix A to help you remember which tone holes to open and close for low D2, C2, B1♭, A1, and G1. For coverage of F1 and F♯1, see Chapter 8. For coverage of B♮, see Chapter 13.

Slur your notes to produce a smooth transition from one note to the next, as explained in Chapter 9. To slur the notes, keep moving the air with the hiss sound as you play from one note to the next.

Figure 7-12:
Play E - D -
C - B♭ - A - G
(Track 3).

Take a deep breath and play the notes shown in Figure 7-13 all in one breath.

Figure 7-13:
Play E - D
- C - B♭ - A
- G - A - B♭
- C - D - E
(Track 3).

If you're having trouble closing that bottom tone hole, you're not alone. People with small hands or short fingers often have trouble reaching that hole. Try aiming your finger down toward the bottom keys.

Gimme an F! Gimme a G!

To add F and G to your repertoire, follow the notes provided in Figures 7-14 through 7-16. Keeping your left thumb in the two o'clock position, use it to close the tone hole to play F and open the tone hole to play G, and then play the repeated exercise.

Figure 7-14:
Play F and G
and then the
repeated
exercise
(Track 4).

Take a deep breath and play the exercise shown in Figure 7-15 all in one breath to add F and G to the notes you already know. Use the fingering chart in Appendix A to visualize which tone holes to open and close and which keys to press, and to learn to relate the notes you play to the notes you see on the staff.

Figure 7-15:
Add F and G to the notes you already know (Track 4).

Play Bᵇ in Figure 7-16 and then play it along with other notes, as shown in the figure. When playing Bᵇ with the other notes, take a full breath and play the notes all in one breath.

Figure 7-16:
Bᵇ exercise (Track 5).

Digging an F♯ and low B♭ out of the final two tone holes

Literally and figuratively, you've covered all the tone holes except for the final two, which enable you to play F♯ (same as G♭) and B1♭. (For B1♭, cover the top hole on the lower joint instead of the middle hole.)

Play F♯ (same as G♭), as shown in Figure 7-17, and then play the exercise, also shown in the figure.

F♯ and G♭ are *enharmonic* notes, which sound the same but are written differently, as explained in Chapter 4.

String these new notes along with a few others you've picked up by slurring the notes shown in Figure 7-18. Remember to take a deep breath and play the notes all in one breath.

Figure 7-17:
Play F♯ by itself and then with other notes (Track 5).

Figure 7-18:
Slur the G scale (Track 5).

Getting all choked up with throat tones

REMEMBER

When most people first hear the term "throat tones," they assume it refers to the sounds patients make when doctors instruct them to "Say 'Ahhhh.'" Actually, throat tones have nothing to do with *your* throat. They have everything to do with the keys near the "throat" (top) of the instrument.

The fingers that play these notes also cover the tone holes, so they have to be in two places at the same time, which can be quite a trick.

To find the correct position for your left index finger, hold the clarinet like a flute and let your left index finger arch over the A and A♭ keys, as shown in Figure 7-19. Touch the A key with the inside of the first knuckle and the G♭ key with the inside corner of the second knuckle. This is why I call A and A♭ *knuckle notes.*

Now hold the clarinet in normal position while keeping your first finger arched over the A and A♭ keys, as shown in Figure 7-20. Let the first finger slightly overlap the top tone hole. When the left hand is in proper position, the index finger closes on the clarinet at a 45-degree angle to the instrument. The left thumb covers the thumb hole in a two o'clock position in relation to the vent key above it.

Figure 7-19:
Hold the clarinet like a flute to find the correct finger positions for A and A♭ — the knuckle notes.

Figure 7-20:
Fingering position for A and A♭ with the clarinet in normal position.

To check your left-hand fingering positions, finger first line E on the staff. If your thumb and index finger make an X when you pull them off the clarinet, you have the correct left hand position (see Figure 7-21).

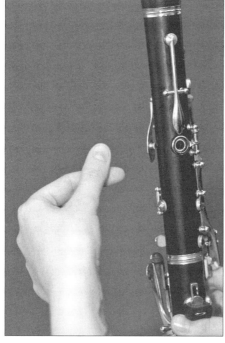

Figure 7-21:
Thumb and index finger crossed when removed from clarinet.

Play A in Figure 7-22, and then play the exercise that follows it with repeats. Be sure to touch the A key with the index finger just as you touched it when holding the clarinet in flute position. Slur the notes, making sure you roll your finger from the F♯ tone hole as you touch the A with the inside corner of the first knuckle of your top finger.

Figure 7-22:
Play A followed by the F♯, A, F♯, A exercise (Track 6).

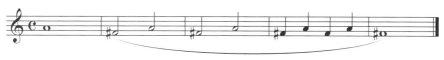

Play A♭ with the fingering indicated in Figure 7-23, and then play the exercise that follows it three times. Slur the notes, touching the A♭ key with the inside corner of the second knuckle.

Figure 7-23:
Play A♭
followed by
the A, A♭, A,
A♭ exercise
(Track 6).

To play throat tone B♭, raise your left thumb off the thumb tone hole and touch the vent key with the upper right corner of your thumb, as shown in Figure 7-24.

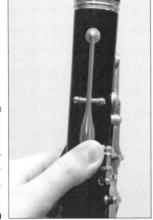

Figure 7-24:
Touch the
vent key
with your
thumb to
play B♭.

Play B♭ in Figure 7-25, and then play the exercise that follows it, slurring the notes as shown in the figure. Repeat this measure several times.

Figure 7-25:
Play B♭
followed by
the B♭, A,
A♯ exercise
(Track 6).

Stringing all those notes together

After playing all the notes individually and in small groups, pull it all together by practicing the exercises shown in Figures 7-26 through 7-29. Use one deep breath to play all the notes in each exercise.

Figure 7-26:
Practice
(Track 6).

Figure 7-27:
More
practice
(Track 6).

Figure 7-28:
More
practice
(Track 6).

Figure 7-29:
More
practice
(Track 6).

Chapter 8

Heading Lower, Higher, and In Between

*I*f you've worked through Chapter 7, you've mastered, to use an airplane analogy, the take-off and the landing, but you haven't explored all that air between the runway and the stratosphere. With respect to playing the clarinet, you have several notes in your repertoire but still have room for many more.

In this chapter, I show you how to play the lowest notes and the notes from B in the staff to C above the staff (see Chapter 4 for the ins and outs of staffs and notes), including the pinky notes. I also provide numerous exercises to help you hone your technique, smoothly connect the lower notes to the higher notes, and then fill in all the gaps with the chromatic notes. By the end of this chapter, you'll be able to play all the notes in the clarinet's normal range.

The clarinet's normal range is from low E to high C above the staff. In Chapter 10, you reach even higher to play notes above high C.

Playing the Pinky Notes

How low can you go? Only your little fingers know for sure. Using your little fingers to press the keys farther down the lower joint of the clarinet, you can cover more tone holes to produce lower and lower notes. Because you use your little fingers (on both hands) to press these keys, the notes they make are often referred to as the *pinky notes*. All of them are below low G, and you cover all the tone holes to play each of them.

REMEMBER

Whether you cover tone holes with your fingers or by pressing keys to close pads over tone holes, you get the same effect — lower notes.

Exploring the low pinky notes

You play pinky notes with your little fingers on *both* hands, but you don't have to start out that way. To get started, try playing the low pinky notes one hand at a time.

Low right-hand pinky notes

ON THE CD

Start with the right-hand pinky notes — low E, F, F♯ (G♭), G, and A♭ (G♯). Play the pinky note exercises shown in Figures 8-1 to 8-4 with the little finger on your right hand. Remember to start the first note of each exercise with "T-heeee." For more about launching notes with your tongue (saying "T-heeee"), see Chapter 6.

Figure 8-1:
Play G to F
(Track 7).

Figure 8-2:
Play G to E
(Track 7).

Figure 8-3:
Play G to
F♯ (G♭)
(Track 7).

Figure 8-4:
Play G to
A♭ (G♯)
(Track 7).

Now let your little finger do the walking with the right-hand pinky walk game, as shown in Figure 8-5. Repeat it over and over playing it faster and faster.

Figure 8-5:
Play the
right-hand
pinky walk
game
(Track 7).

Low left-hand pinky notes

Your left hand gets to take its turn by playing the left-hand pinky notes — E, F, and F♯ (G♭), and G. Play the pinky-note exercises shown in Figures 8-6 to 8-8 with the little finger on your left hand. Remember, these three notes can also be played with the right-hand pinky as well. Knowing how to play them with either pinky enables you to alternate pinkies when possible so your fingers won't get all tangled up when playing between the pinky notes, as discussed in Chapter 13.

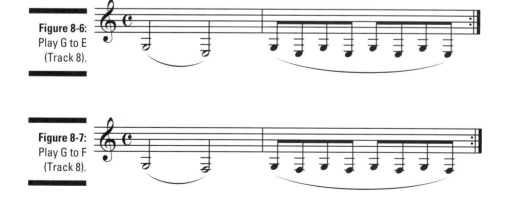

Figure 8-6:
Play G to E
(Track 8).

Figure 8-7:
Play G to F
(Track 8).

Figure 8-8:
Play G to
F♯ (G♭)
(Track 8).

Your little left finger gets to take a walk, too. Play the left-hand pinky walk game, shown in Figure 8-9, over and over, increasing your speed each time you play it.

Figure 8-9:
Play the left-
hand pinky
walk game
(Track 8).

ON THE CD

When low E follows low F, play low E with both pinkies as shown in Figure 8-10. Play the exercise shown in Figure 8-10 over and over, playing faster each time you repeat it.

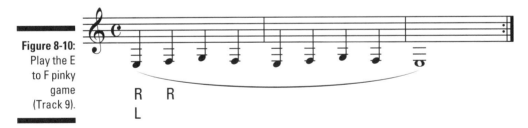

Figure 8-10:
Play the E
to F pinky
game
(Track 9).

Aiming high: Playing the fifth line F and continuing upward to G, A, B, and C

The higher notes — F, G, A, B, and C — hang out on the top line of the staff and above it. To play each of these notes, add the vent key as you finger a lower note with the same tone holes covered. Because all five of them are actually related to the lower notes, think of them as cousins.

To produce any of these notes, keep the fingers in position to play the note's lower "cousin" while pressing the register key on the back of the upper joint.

The higher notes (clarion register and above) require a good embouchure and fast-moving air:

- ✔ Rest the reed on a flat, narrow ledge, as explained in Chapter 6.

- ✔ Make sure you have enough reed inside your mouth. Remember the business card tip from Chapter 6.

- ✔ Use your tongue to form a wind tunnel for producing fast air, as explained in Chapter 6. Hiss like a snake as you blow.

To make fast air, hold your finger at the bridge of your nose and arch your tongue inside your mouth to aim the air at your finger as you blow (see Figure 8-11). While you're playing, imagine blowing at this imaginary mark on the bridge of your nose.

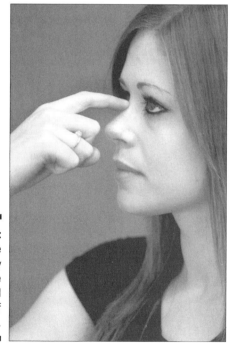

Figure 8-11: Produce fast air by directing the air toward the bridge of your nose.

You form the inside of your mouth to form a wind tunnel for the same reason plumbers use an elbow, as shown in Figure 8-12, to connect two lengths of pipe: to maintain pressure along the entire length of the connection. If the elbow was larger and bowl-shaped (like your mouth), the pressure would decrease inside the elbow before reaching the next length of pipe. In the same way, if your oral cavity remains bowl-shaped, air pressure decreases when air flows from your windpipe into your mouth. The air slows down before reaching the clarinet. To produce fast air, try to shape the inside of your mouth into an elbow rather than a bowl.

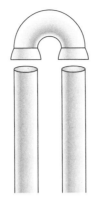

Figure 8-12:
Your mouth connects your windpipe to the clarinet like an elbow connects two lengths of pipe.

While playing low B♭ with fast air, press the register (vent) key with the tip of your finger and keep on blowing, as shown in Figure 8-13. Hold this note for at least six beats. Do it right, and you should get a fifth-line F. This exercise is known as the "Wild Leaps" game, because you jump from a low B♭ to the fifth-line F.

Figure 8-13:
Play the "Wild Leaps" game to jump from B♭ to the fifth-line F (Track 10).

After producing a good fifth-line F, add more fingers one at a time to produce the E and D, as shown in Figure 8-14. By playing them in one breath, you play with a more controlled and pleasant sound.

Figure 8-14:
Try to play the quarter note part of this exercise in one breath (Track 10).

Playing pinky notes in the staff

Play both the right- and left-hand pinky notes in the staff using the same technique you use to play the other higher notes: Finger the low note first and then add the register key to play the note's higher cousin. The following sections show you how to play the right- and left-hand pinky notes in the staff.

Right-hand pinky notes in the staff

Start with the right-hand pinky notes in the staff — B, C, C♯ (D♭), D, and E♭ (D♯). Play the right-hand low note pinky walk, and then add the register key to play the notes' "cousins," as shown in Figure 8-15. As you play the first note of each exercise, focus on the "mu" and "euww" parts of your embouchure, launch each note with "T-heeee," and keep your wind tunnel going. Start slowly, and gradually increase your speed with each repetition.

The music in Figures 8-15 through 8-18 is on the CD.

Figure 8-15: Play the right-hand pinky note walk, adding the register key (Track 10).

Play the lower and upper pinky note walk again with flats instead of sharps, as shown in Figure 8-16.

Figure 8-16: Play the lower and upper pinky note walk with flats instead of sharps (Track 10).

Left-hand pinky notes in the staff

Your left hand gets to take its turn by playing the left-hand pinky notes in the staff — B, C, C♯ (D♭), and D. Play the pinky note walk shown in Figure 8-17 with the left-hand little finger, using the register key to play the "cousin" notes.

Figure 8-17:
Play the left-hand pinky note walk, adding the register key (Track 10).

Play the left-hand pinky note walk again with D♭ instead of C♯, as shown in Figure 8-18.

Figure 8-18:
Play the lower and upper left-hand pinky note walk with D♭ instead of C♯ (Track 10).

Using both pinkies for B2

Now that you've limbered up each pinky separately, use them together to play from C2 to B2 or when ascending and C2 follows B2. By using both pinkies in tandem, you avoid a clumsy flip-flop of little fingers.

Perform the exercise shown in Figure 8-19, changing from B2 to C2, and repeat it several times, increasing your speed with each repetition.

Figure 8-19:
Play this
exercise
several
times
(Track 11).

Putting all of the higher notes together

Switching from using each pinky solo to using them together in a duet (and vice versa) can be a challenge. To develop the manual dexterity required to change notes smoothly, play "Your First Scale," as shown in Figure 8-20, all in one breath.

Figure 8-20:
Play "Your
First Scale"
all in one
breath
(Track 12).

For some additional practice, play "Worm Song with Higher Notes" all in one breath, as shown in Figure 8-21.

Figure 8-21:
Play "Worm
Song with
Higher
Notes" all in
one breath
(Track 12).

To challenge yourself further, play a longer piece that requires you to take a few breaths and change registers. Play the clarinet solo from the second movement of Schubert's "Unfinished Symphony," as shown in Figure 8-22. Follow the breath marks as you play this famous clarinet solo. (For more about registers, see the following section "Changing Registers: A Tricky Transition.")

Figure 8-22: Play the clarinet solo from the second movement of Schubert's "Unfinished Symphony" (Track 12).

If you're having trouble playing some of these higher notes, try troubleshooting the problem by playing this game: Close your eyes and play a low B♭. While you're playing, have someone else touch the vent key. The sound should jump up to F3, which is its higher cousin note. If it doesn't, check for the following problems:

✔ Reed not resting on a narrow ledge

✔ Too little reed inside your mouth

✔ Missing fast air

Changing Registers: A Tricky Transition

The entire range of notes you can play on your clarinet is divided into three registers:

✔ **Chalumeau:** The lowest register, consisting of notes low E (E1) to B2♭, in the staff

✔ **Clarion:** The middle register, consisting of notes B2 in the staff to C3 above the staff

✔ **Altissimo:** The high register, consisting of notes C3 above the staff to C4

Changing registers can be quite a challenge, because you're often going from using very few fingers to using many fingers. In the following sections, I show you how to change registers and provide suggestions on how to smooth the transition. (In this section, I explain how to change from the chalumeau to the clarion register. In Chapter 10, you discover how to change from clarion to altissimo.)

The register change from the chalumeau to the clarion register presents one of the most challenging fingering issues clarinet players encounter. Many of the notoriously difficult passages in the clarinet literature involve this register change.

Playing from two places at once: The F♯ to A connection

Negotiating register changes requires strong hand and finger coordination. The main challenge is with the tone holes, especially going from the F♯ tone hole to the A key, so this is a logical place to start.

In Chapter 7, I show you how to play the knuckle note, A, with good left-hand position. When going from F♯ to A, use the same flute hand position I recommend in Chapter 7 for the throat tones. Without good hand positioning, you'll be unable to move smoothly between the A key and the top tone hole of the upper joint. Remember, your index fingers are the sergeants — the rest of your fingers follow them.

Here's a great game for learning how to properly position your fingers for changing back and forth between F♯ and A: Play A while continuing to close the F♯ tone hole with your index finger. Do it again, but this time let your index finger roll off the tone hole as it touches the A key (see Figure 8-23).

Figure 8-23:
Play A, keeping the F♯ tone hole closed, and repeat while letting your index finger roll off the tone hole (Track 13).

Keeping the right hand down for register changes

Keeping the right hand down during a register change eliminates many of the coordination problems when going from lots of fingers on the clarinet to just one or two. Keeping the right hand down isn't cheating. In fact, the throat tones actually sound better with right-hand fingers down, as I explain in Chapter 11.

Keep the right hand down as you perform the register change exercises shown in Figures 8-24 to 8-28. As you play the throat tone note, close all of the right-hand tone holes and press any of the pinky keys.

A comma at the end of a slur indicates a place to breathe. Follow the breath marks in all the music you see in this book. *Never* breathe between two register-change notes when performing exercises.

Figure 8-24:
Slur D to A, C to A, and B to G (Track 13).

Figure 8-25: Slur the phrases as shown in this exercise (Track 13).

Figure 8-26: Slur D to B♭, C to B♭, and B to B♭ (Track 13).

Figure 8-27: Slur the phrases as shown in these exercises (Track 13).

Figure 8-28: Slur above staff and then down below staff (Track 13).

Going Chromatic to Plug the Gaps

When learning the alphabet, you recite all the letters from A to Z. If your teacher had decided to let you skip a letter or two, you would have had difficulty reading words that used the missing letters. The same is true for music — you need to know all the notes in all the registers.

Chapter 7 and the first part of this chapter introduce most of the notes in the chalumeau and clarion registers. The missing notes are the sharps and flats in these registers. On a piano, these are the black keys a half step above or below their neighboring white keys. (For notes in the third, altissimo, register, turn to Chapter 10.)

Each octave contains a dozen notes separated by tone half steps. The dozen notes in any octave comprise the octave's *chromatic scale*. By playing a chromatic scale from low E to C above the staff (C3) you learn all the letters of the alphabet you need to know at this point.

Perform the exercise shown in Figure 8-29, playing the second part slowly at first and then increasing speed as you repeat the exercise. The first line on the chromatic scale, E♭, is a half step lower than E2. Note that the half steps in the chromatic scale appear as sharps or flats. Certain notes may be enharmonic and written in two different ways. For example, E♭ is enharmonic to D♯; they're written differently, but they sound the same. (For more about enharmonic notes, check out Chapter 4.)

The remaining exercises in this section (Figures 8-29 through 8-34) appear in Track 14 on the CD.

Figure 8-29:
Slur as
shown and
repeat
playing
faster
(Track 14).

D♭ (also known as C♯) is a half step lower than D. Play D♭, as shown in Figure 8-30. Play slowly at first and then repeat, playing faster. Finger the D♭ or C♯ as shown in bar one of the exercise and then play the exercise over and over.

Figure 8-30:
Play slowly
at first, and
then pick
up speed
(Track 14).

A♭ (also known as G♯) is a half step lower than A. Play A♭, as shown in Figure 8-31. Play the second part slowly at first and then go faster and faster as you repeat.

Figure 8-31:
Slur as shown and increase speed as you practice (Track 14).

Low F♯ (also known as G♭) is a half step lower than G. Play low F♯ as shown in Figure 8-32. Keep in mind that F♯ (G♭) is a pinky note, and you can use either of two fingerings to play it. In Figure 8-34, I show you the fingering to use when playing the chromatic scale. When you play this finger combination, imagine doing the pinky walk in which you alternate pinky fingers.

Figure 8-32:
Try this exercise (Track 14).

One more fingering, and you'll be ready to play the lowest octave of the chromatic scale: E2 to low E (E1). To avoid an awkward flip-flop of the right-hand index finger and the second finger in chromatic passages, play low B with the fingering shown in Figure 8-33. The extra key is called the *fork key*, and you press it with the third finger of the right hand.

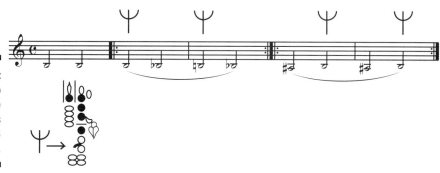

Figure 8-33:
Two possible fingerings for low B (Track 14).

Play a complete chromatic scale from E2 down to low E (E1), as shown in Figure 8-34. Keep practicing until you can play it down and back up in one breath.

Figure 8-34:
Play a chromatic scale from E2 to low E and back up (Track 14).

Higher chromatic notes for the clarion register

Now apply the chalumeau chromatic fingerings to the clarion register. As you did when learning the other notes of the clarion register, all you have to do is finger the chalumeau notes with the addition of the vent key. Remember to use the fork key for F3♯ when ascending and the G3♭ when going back down, as shown in Figure 8-35.

Figure 8-35:
Play E to B2, then continue up to C3 in sharps and back down to B2 in flats (Track 14).

One final fingering

To avoid flipping from F2 to F♯ (F to G♭) in chromatic passages, play F♯ (G♭) as shown in Figure 8-36.

Figure 8-36:
Play F♯ with chromatic fingering (Track 14).

Putting it all together: The whole enchilada

Drum roll . . . and now the full chromatic scale. . . .

Practice the full chromatic scale, as shown in Figure 8-37, from low E to C above staff and back down to low E. Practice until you can play it fast enough to play the entire scale up and down in one breath. Many clarinetists play full chromatic scales as part of their daily warm-up routines.

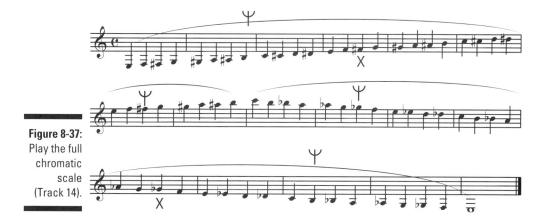

Figure 8-37:
Play the full chromatic scale (Track 14).

Chapter 9

Playing Between the Notes: Slurring and Tonguing

In This Chapter

▶ Slurring notes to smooth the transitions between notes

▶ Slurring with added accents and crescendos

▶ Tonguing to produce special effects

▶ Mixing articulation with slurring and tonguing

A s you play your clarinet, you move from one note to the next. How you transition between notes is called *articulation*. You articulate in two ways, depending on the desired effect. To move smoothly from one note to the next, you *slur*. To make each note more distinct, you *tongue* the notes, briefly touching the tip of your tongue to the reed to stop its vibration, creating space between the notes. Either way, you keep the air flowing to connect the notes.

This chapter introduces you to clarinet articulation, explains how slurring and tonguing contribute to articulation and relate to one another, offers guidance on how to slur and tongue properly, and provides plenty of exercises for developing your clarinet articulation technique.

Getting Connected with Articulation

"Articulation" is a funny word. It describes how things are connected, including bones in a skeleton and syllables in a word, but it's also defined as the "act of giving utterance or expression." Both meanings apply to the clarinet: Articulation refers to the expression of notes and the connections between them. It's sort of like articulation in speech — the formation of the various sounds that comprise words and sentences. In speech, you generally articulate in two ways: by stringing sounds together to form words and by pausing to indicate spaces between words.

When playing the clarinet, you also articulate in two ways:

- ✔ **Slurring:** Controlling the flow of air to transition smoothly between notes.

- ✔ **Tonguing:** Stopping the reed vibration to add definition to notes.

When playing slurred or tongued notes, remain focused on the goal, but aim for closer targets:

- ✔ **Goal:** Keep your air moving towards the end of the phrase. Imagine a bowling ball rolling down the lane and striking the pins. You want to keep that same steady momentum and steady air flow when slurring or tonguing.

- ✔ **Closer targets:** Move your air towards closer targets along the way just as, in speech, you move toward important words in a sentence. In clarinet playing, the closer targets are accented notes and the intensity crescendos that lead up to them. See "Adding accents" and "Producing intensity crescendos," later in this chapter, for details.

As you speak, you don't even think about articulation, because it's second nature. With practice, clarinet articulation can and should become just as natural and effortless.

Slurring to Smooth Transitions

Slurring means keeping the air flowing or blowing *through* notes rather than blowing *each* note. The purpose of slurring is to transition smoothly from one note to the next, leaving no spaces between the notes. Consider the way singers connect notes: They continue from one note to the next in one breath until they come to a natural break.

The best way to experience a slur is to sing the first line of the "Star Spangled Banner" using "ah" in place of the words, without stopping to take a breath. That's one "ah" for the entire phrase starting with "Oh José" and ending with "can you see?" Notice how you're moving your air through the melodic line. Now sing the same song beginning a new "ha" at every syllable. Pretty choppy, eh? When you slur the notes of a musical phrase, you want smooth, not choppy.

In the following sections, I explain how to slur on the clarinet and then reveal ways to add nuances to your slurs with accents and intensity crescendos.

Slurring smooth and steady

Slurring on the clarinet is easy. You simply exhale one long continuous breath while playing the notes in the slurred phrase.

Try it yourself. Play the phrase shown in Figure 9-1 all in one breath. Remember: No stopping your breath between notes.

Figure 9-1:
Slur the notes by playing them with one continuous breath (Track 15).

Don't confuse slurs and ties. Although they look kind of similar in musical notation, ties enable composers to add notes together, whereas slurs indicate the transitions from one note to the next. (To identify the difference between slurs and ties, check out Chapter 4.)

Adding accents and intensity crescendos

Constant air flow is essential in slurring, but that constant airflow can and should vary in intensity as you play notes and phrases. By pushing more air in different ways and at different times, you produce accents and intensity crescendos that emphasize notes and help transition to a higher pitch:

- **Accent:** An added quick push of the diaphragm muscles makes a sudden change in volume that adds emphasis to a note.
- **Intensity crescendo:** The diaphragm muscles move the air faster more gradually to ramp up to a higher pitch or lead into an accent.

In other words, you maintain fast air as you play normally, increase air flow intensity to produce a crescendo, and deliver a burst of air to add an accent. It's all about moving air.

Although accents are always preceded by intensity crescendos, you're likely to find that accenting notes without leading into them with intensity crescendos is easier at first. In the following sections, you practice accents and intensity crescendos alone and then together.

In musical notation, an accent looks like a "greater than" sign above the note. An intensity crescendo looks either like a "less than" sign over a note that precedes an accent or as a line between two notes. In the case of intensity crescendos that "skip up" from one note to the next, a line is the best notation. See Chapter 4 for more about musical notation.

Adding accents

While the purpose of slurring is to transition smoothly from one note to the next, you often need to accent notes within a slurred phrase the same way you change the inflection of your voice to stress certain words or syllables in a sentence. In music, accents serve two purposes:

- ✔ To emphasize a note's importance.
- ✔ To create pulses on the beats to make the music more rhythmic or dance-like. Musicians have a saying that "Music is either song or dance." Dances are songs with a more predominant pulse.

When playing the clarinet, you add accents with your diaphragm and *intercostals* — your chest muscles. To feel these muscles, place your hands on either side of your body just below the rib cage and pant like a puppy dog.

Try accenting a note simply by changing your air flow. Say "T-heeee" and keep the "eeee" part going as you blow more air to change the stress (represented by capital letters): "T-heeeeEEEEeeee." Notice that you're not raising your voice, but the more air you push, the louder it gets. You do exactly the same thing to accent a note on the clarinet: Just by blowing more air, you increase the note's loudness. When you're doing this on the clarinet, it gets even louder because of the reed vibration.

Play the low C, as shown in Figure 9-2, keeping the sound going as you accent the note with your diaphragm muscles. When playing an accent, remember to keep the air flowing and simply change its intensity from "heeee" (strong air flow) to "EEEE" (stronger air flow).

Figure 9-2:
Play the low C accented notes as you crescendo to the final note (Track 16).

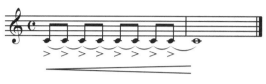

Producing intensity crescendos

An *intensity crescendo* is an increase in air flow for slurring up to an accent or to a higher pitch rather than pumping up the volume or amplitude of a note. Unlike an accent on a note, an intensity crescendo leads up to the next note.

You use both intensity crescendos and accents in speech. If someone constantly introduces you with the incorrect name and home town you may correct them by saying something like "No, *Nick*, my name is *Mary*, and I am from *Denver*, *not* Portland!" Figure 9-3 shows how this sentence might appear in musical notation marking the accents and crescendos.

Figure 9-3:
Accents and intensity crescendos in a sentence.

No, Nick, my name is Mary, and I am from Denver, not Portland!
    >   >   >   >

Producing an intensity crescendo is like accelerating on an entrance ramp from the city limit of 35 miles per hour to the highway limit of 70 to blend in smoothly with any traffic. When transitioning between notes on the clarinet, you need to accelerate your air in order to transition smoothly between different pitches or frequencies. If you're moving from low B to B in the staff, for example, you're changing pitch from 220 to 440 cycles per second. That means the reed vibration frequency changes from 220 to 440 cycles per second, as well. To support the increasing vibration, supply more air. Fail to do so, and the reed stops vibrating — the note stalls.

As you're transitioning to a higher note, ramp up the air speed in sync with the note, so sufficient air is available to play that note.

When moving from higher to lower notes you still ramp up your air to account for the differences in resistance from going from a short air column (the result of having lots of open tone holes on the clarinet) to a long air column (the result of many closed tone holes on the clarinet). I talk about this in Chapter 13.

Preceding accents with intensity crescendos

Although you can certainly produce an accent by itself (just blow real hard), doing so sounds as though you're punching at the notes — something you'd never do when using accents in speech and should never do when accenting notes on the clarinet. To avoid this unpleasant effect, lead into all accents with an intensity crescendo.

To ramp up to an accent with an intensity crescendo, drag out the note (holding it to its fullest value) and speed up the air before accenting the next note. Don't back off the air before the accent. As you're practicing this, take extra time for the intensity crescendo and really lead the sound before accenting the next note. Move your fingers very precisely as you accent the note after the intensity crescendo.

Play the exercise shown in Figure 9-4. The line between two note heads marks each intensity crescendo. Stretch each note prior to the accented note, so you can feel the crescendo before accenting the next note. Take all the time you need to feel the crescendo before accenting the next note. (Although you never accent every note in a musical line during a performance, this is a great way to feel the moving air with every note.

Figure 9-4:
Lead into every accent with a crescendo (Track 16).

Play the exercise shown in Figure 9-5, replacing every other accent (the second, fourth, sixth, and so on) with intensity crescendos, so the air keeps moving forward towards the next accent (closer target) and ultimately to the end of the phrase. (By replacing half the accents with intensity crescendos, you retain the moving air but with a smaller degree of air motion than you use to produce accents.)

The bottom line is that the air should move forward for every new slurred (and tongued) note. This is exactly what singers do.

Figure 9-5:
Replacing accents with intensity crescendos (Track 16).

Play the exercise shown in Figure 9-6, replacing the accents on the second and third beats with intensity crescendos. Officially, this is called *sostenuto* or sustained playing. Unofficially, I call this "taffy music," because you're stretching out the notes.

Figure 9-6:
Replace accents with intensity crescendos using tied eighth notes to show subdivision of the half notes (Track 16).

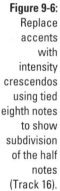

Mastering the Fine Art of Tonguing

Your tongue plays a key role in reciting the alphabet, but it really gets a workout with letters like D and T, and, for most people, it naturally flies into the correct position for each letter you want to pronounce. Try moving it to a different position when pronouncing a particular letter. Chances are pretty good that the letter doesn't sound quite right and that your tongue feels awkward. Your tongue also serves an important function when you're playing the clarinet. Knowing why, when, how, and where to place the tongue significantly improves your sound and can actually make playing much easier.

Clarinetists tongue notes for five different reasons. They do it to

✔ Start notes

✔ Separate repeated notes and successive notes that change pitch

✔ Increase response of notes

✔ Make the music sing more

✔ Add space between notes

In the following sections, I explain how to tongue to produce these effects and provide exercises to improve your tonguing ability and make tonguing feel more natural.

Playing the clarinet is like speaking, except for the fact that your mouth plays an entirely different role. When you speak, you create the base sound in your voice box and then form the sound with your mouth, tongue, and lips. When you play the clarinet, you don't use your voice box. Instead, your mouth and the mouthpiece function as the clarinet's voice box. Your tongue starts the sound and directs air flow over the reed to produce the main base sound. The clarinet then sculpts the sound into distinctive notes.

Brushing up on the basics: Aiming for the tip rail

Tonguing is simply a matter of touching your tongue to the reed to stop its vibration, but the reed is a pretty big target. You want to make sure you touch it in the right place, with the right part of your tongue, and apply just the right amount of pressure. Tonguing technique affects not only the sound, but also your tongue's freedom of movement and physical endurance.

When tonguing, make sure you're touching the correct part of your tongue (the tip) to the correct place on the clarinet (the tip of the reed). Touching your tongue too far below the tip of the reed causes extraneous sounds, slows down your tongue, and leads to tongue fatigue. To tongue properly, aim for the tip rail.

The *tip rail* is a stationary object that acts just like the hard palate (the roof) of your mouth. When you touch the tip of your tongue against the tip of the reed, the reed bends up and touches the tip rail the same way you touch the tip of your tongue against your hard palate to say "T" or "D."

Time for some target practice. Remove the reed from your mouthpiece. Place the mouthpiece in your mouth and say "T" repeatedly while touching your tongue to the tip rail.

The purpose of this exercise is to increase your awareness of the tip rail as the true target you're aiming at. It really helps players understand that they're not really tonguing the reed, but simply touching the reed to move it to the tip rail, which functions like the hard palate. This works like a charm to clean up sloppy articulation.

Now try to hit the target (the tip rail) while playing some notes — still without the reed. Play the repeated eighth notes shown in Figure 9-7. You should hear a high hiss and a high thudding sound as you play each note. If you're tonguing down in the baffle of the mouthpiece, you hear a low thudding sound instead. Try making your T's louder and louder.

Figure 9-7:
Tongue the
repeated
eighth notes
without the
reed
(Track 17).

Starting notes: Going on the attack

Whenever you begin playing a piece or a passage, go on the attack — a tongued attack, that is. An *attack* is the manner in which you begin playing a piece or a passage, and for clarinet music, all pieces begin with a *tongued attack*. This launches the piece or passage with force and makes the initial note more distinctive.

The amount of force on attacks depends on the mood and style of the piece you are playing.

To tongue a note, touch the tip of your tongue to the tip of the reed and release it with a T sound before hissing. Try it without the clarinet by saying "T-heeee."

Imagine you're holding a faucet handle with your right hand and you want a drink of water. As soon as you turn that handle, the water starts pouring out, because it's ready and waiting, pushing against the valve until that valve opens and lets it go. Use the same technique to tongue. Press your tongue against the roof of your mouth and let air build up behind it like the water pressure builds inside the pipe. Release your tongue and blow — "T-heeee."

A tongued attack is typically indicated by the letter "t" or "tu," because the tongue usually behaves the same way it does when pronouncing "T" or "Tuh." You can, however, use a different letter or syllable to tongue notes, such as "D" or "Deh," which is usually preferable when fast tonguing. (See Chapter 14 for more about fast tonguing.)

Separating repeated notes and successive notes that change pitch

You can tongue staccato or non-staccato style to separate notes that change pitch. With staccato, you tongue at the beginning and end of the note, as explained later in the section "Adding space between notes staccato style." Non-staccato, the most common form of tonguing, is more subtle but still adds space between the notes. To tongue non-staccato style, here's what you do:

✔ Touch the tip of your tongue to the tip of the reed, bending the reed to the tip rail.

✔ Resist the urge to move your jaw. You don't move your jaw when pronouncing "D" or "T," so don't do it when you're tonguing on the clarinet. All motion should be *inside* your mouth.

✔ Keep the air flowing. Stop the reed vibration, not the air flow.

With the reed in place, tongue the eighth notes shown in Figure 9-7, touching the tip of the reed instead of the tip rail to separate the repeated notes with "Tee-tee-tee."

Practice tonguing to separate notes by playing "Boogie Woogie" (see Figure 9-8) and "Ode to Joy" (Figure 9-9).

Figure 9-8:
Play
"Boogie
Woogie,"
separating
repeated
notes with
"tee"
(Track 18).

Figure 9-9:
Play "Ode to
Joy," tongu-
ing all the
notes with
"tee"
(Track 19).

To remember to keep the air flowing while tonguing, practice the following exercise:

1. **Hold your clarinet between your knees and only with your left hand, as shown in Figure 9-10.**

2. **Place your right hand on your tummy.**

3. **Play "Twinkle Twinkle Little Star" faster and faster, as shown in Figure 9-11.**

   If you feel your tummy move as you tongue, you're stopping your air between tongued notes. That's a no-no. Keep the air moving and make a bigger crescendo to end the phrase.

Figure 9-10:
Hold the
clarinet
between
your knees
and place
your right
hand on
your tummy.

Figure 9-11:
Play
"Twinkle
Twinkle
Little Star"
with the left
hand while
holding your
tummy with
the right
hand
(Track 20).

To check for excessive jaw motion when you tongue, place your right hand on your mouth, instead of on your tummy, as shown in Figure 9-12, and play "Twinkle Twinkle Little Star" (see Figure 9-11). If you feel your jaw moving, try taking a little more mouthpiece into your mouth.

Figure 9-12: This time hold your chin instead of your tummy when playing "Twinkle Twinkle Little Star."

Tonguing for response

At certain pitches, your clarinet may seem unresponsive. It squeaks, makes no sound at all, or emits some other odd utterance. Tonguing can make the clarinet more responsive, especially when you're skipping up or down to certain notes.

Where's that squeaking coming from?!

Ever wonder why the clarinet squeaks? It's because that vibrating column of air in your clarinet naturally tries to divide itself into smaller segments. Those squeaks are very high harmonics — very high notes you may want to play someday. You can purposely divide the column of air in two by opening the vent key.

Changing the column of air from five segments to three or three to one, however, isn't as easy as pressing the vent key. Because of this, you have to tongue some notes to skip down to them or tongue high notes to skip up to them.

Downward skips

To skip down to a note, add an intensity crescendo before tonguing the notes shown in Figures 9-13 and 9-14. (Remember, the sign for an intensity crescendo is a line connecting the heads of the two notes involved.)

Figure 9-13: Play "The Entertainer" to practice tonguing downward skips (Track 21).

Upward skips

To skip up to a note, add an intensity crescendo before tonguing the notes. Play "Mary's Skippy Lamb," shown in Figure 9-14, leading into each note with an intensity crescendo.

Figure 9-14: Tongue both the upward and downward skips in "Mary's Skippy Lamb" (Track 22).

Tonguing to sing more: Legato tonguing

Slurring produces a sing-song quality, but sometimes it's just not enough for a particular song or phrase. To make the notes sing even more, combine tonguing with small breath accents — a technique called *legato tonguing*. Jazz and pop clarinetists often use legato tonguing, marked with dots or dashes under the slurs.

Practice legato tonguing by playing the notes shown in Figure 9-15. Make the legato notes sing more than the slurred notes in this exercise by moving your air and tonguing the notes with "D-heeee" instead of "T-heeee." This gives the legato notes a softer beginning.

Figure 9-15:
Dots or accents under slurs indicate legato tonguing.

For more practice with legato tonguing, play "Danny Boy," as shown in Figure 9-16. Play the piece with slurs only the first time through, and then add legato tonguing, so you can get a feel for the difference between the two.

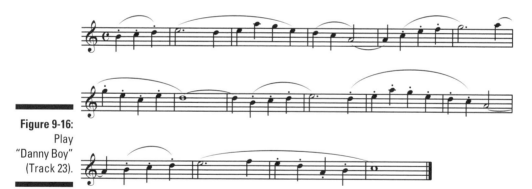

Figure 9-16:
Play "Danny Boy" (Track 23).

Adding space between notes staccato style

Staccato is the opposite of slurring. In slurring, you transition smoothly from note to note. In staccato, individual notes are much more distinct. Because staccato adds spaces between notes, taking away some of the sound, it makes the music sound lighter.

To play staccato, tongue to start and stop the note. In other words, start and end the note with a "T" as in "T-heeee-T."

Play an open G starting with T-heeee and ending with T, as shown in Figure 9-17.

Figure 9-17:
Play an open G staccato style followed by a succession of staccato eighths (Track 24).

The amount of time the tongue spends on the reed determines the space between staccato notes, while the middle sound (the "heeee" between the two T's) determines the actual length of the note. You can play staccato notes in three different lengths:

- **Aught:** Commonly referred to as *ball bouncing staccato*, aught as in "daughter" is the longest interim sound, usually with eighth notes or triplets, as shown in Figure 9-18. This long staccato makes the clarinet sound a little like a guitar.

- **O:** Dot is medium-length staccato, a shorter interim sound that's clearer than it is long. See Figure 9-19.

- **U:** Dut staccato is very short (secco) making the music sound very crisp, as shown in Figure 9-20.

Figure 9-18:
Use Aught staccato when you play this "A-La-Guitar" exercise (Track 25).

Figure 9-19: Use Dot staccato when playing this clarinet solo from the first movement of Beethoven's *6th Symphony* (Track 26).

Figure 9-20: Use Dut staccato when you play "In the Hall of the Mountain King" from the *Peer Gynt Suite* by Grieg (Track 27).

Mixing Articulation with Slurring and Tonguing

When you speak, you naturally coordinate **airflow** with tongue movement and other articulatory organs for the desired effect. You can do the same on the clarinet by combining slurring with tonguing to produce different sounds. The most common mixed articulation is

slur slur tongue tongue

Other common mixed articulations include the following:

slur slur tongue

slur slur slur tongue

tongue slur slur slur slur

When playing mixed articulations, make sure all the notes are audible, just as all the syllables of words are audible as you pronounce the word.

Always make an intensity crescendo on the last slurred note before tonguing. Otherwise it loses volume and disappears.

To get more comfortable with mixed articulation, play the exercises shown in Figures 9-21 to 9-24, following the articulation marks.

Figure 9-21:
Slur slur
tongue
tongue:
"Arkansas
Traveler"
(Track 28).

Figure 9-22:
Slur slur
tongue:
"Irish
Washer
Woman"
(Track 29).

Figure 9-23:
Tongue
slur slur
slur tongue:
"Rakes of
Mallow"
(Track 30).

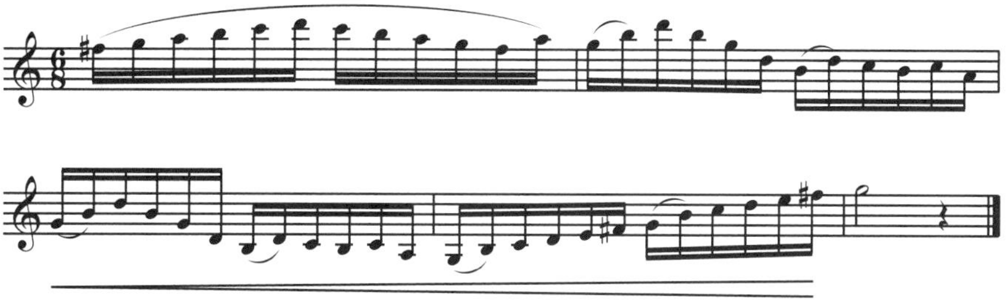

Figure 9-24:
Tongue
slur tongue
tongue
tongue:
Mozart's
"Rondo"
(Track 31).

Chapter 10

Rising Above and Beyond High C

*B*eginning clarinet players often suffer from *acrophobia*, or a fear of heights — high notes, that is. The phobia isn't completely irrational. C above the staff or higher can be tough to play, and because these notes appear less frequently in most music than notes in the clarion or chalumeau registers (see Chapter 8), you have to practice them more to add them to your comfort zone.

By practicing the high notes, however, you increase your comfort level and actually become a better clarinet player overall. Playing the high notes forces you to hone your skills, because they demand that you do everything right. You must maintain proper embouchure and produce the fast air that is so important to good tone.

In this chapter, I reveal the not-so-well-kept secrets of hitting the high notes, introduce you to the fingerings for C3♯ above the staff to high G, and let you in on some alternate fingerings to keep your fingers from getting all tangled up when transitioning between the high notes.

High notes played by inexperienced clarinetists can be somewhat annoying to bystanders, which may make you so concerned about bothering others that you actually avoid playing these high notes. To become less self-conscious about it, consider practicing in a room distant from other members of the household. If you're practicing in a bedroom, open the closet — clothes tend to absorb sound.

Producing the Altissimo Notes

The secret to producing the *altissimo notes* (high notes) on a clarinet is no secret at all. It's more about mastering the basics:

- Choosing a reed with the right amount of resistance
- Maintaining the correct embouchure (see Chapter 6 for embouchure basics)
- Producing fast air

The following sections give you the lowdown on hitting the high notes.

Stepping up to a harder reed

Soft reeds are great for playing notes in the lower registers, because they vibrate more easily. However, they're too floppy to vibrate at the required frequency for playing high notes.

When you're ready to step up to the higher notes, step up to a harder reed, too — a 3½ or 3¾ hardness should do the trick. (For more about shopping for reeds, check out Chapter 3. For even more about reeds, check out Chapter 17.)

If you're doing everything right and still can't hit the high notes, you probably need a slightly harder reed.

Maintaining correct embouchure

A true test of your clarinet embouchure is your ability to play the high notes. To form the proper embouchure, here's what you do (see Chapter 6 for more details on proper embouchure):

- Rotate your lower jaw slightly forward.
- Curve your lower lip against your bottom teeth as when making the "mu" sound in "music."
- Smile with the bottom lip, so it stretches tight against the teeth — just enough lip to cover the biting surface and form a very narrow ledge.

✔ Support the mouthpiece with your upper lip in the frown position as when making the "vuum" sound. Your top teeth should touch the mouthpiece about ¼ inch from the tip.

✔ Make sure you have enough reed in your mouth for it to vibrate properly — about a half inch. Re-mark your reed with a business card under it as explained in Chapter 6. Position your lower lip just below the mark (down towards the ligature).

An inability to hit the high notes can often be traced to the lower lip. To be sure your lower jaw is rotated forward and the correct amount of lower lip curves against your lower teeth, perform the following exercise:

1. **Play low D, as shown in Figure 10-1, making a mental note of the sound.**

2. **Buzz low D again without the clarinet, using only your lips. (See Figure 10-1.)**

   To buzz low D, hold the point of your chin down with your right hand and stretch your lower lip against your bottom teeth as you do when making the "mu" sound. As you do this, blow out and let your bottom lip buzz.

3. **If you're having difficulty buzzing the note, make the necessary adjustments.**

   Try the following:

   • **If you can't buzz the note:** Make sure your lower lip isn't inside your mouth, and try again. You can't buzz a note with your lip inside your mouth.

   • **If the buzz sounds lower than the low D you played:** Stretch your lower lip tighter against your bottom teeth and try again.

4. **Play low D on the clarinet with your lower lip in the buzz position. (See Figure 10-1.)**

5. **As you play, pull the mouthpiece out of your mouth and continue to blow to buzz the D. (See Figure 10-1.)**

6. **Repeat steps 4 and 5, but this time, start by playing D2 and then slide the mouthpiece out of your mouth to buzz low D, as shown in Figure 10-2.**

   Because the tension on the lower lip never changes, you should be able to pull the mouthpiece out of your mouth and go to a buzz while playing D2 or any other note, high or low.

7. **Repeat step 6, but this time, start by playing G above the staff and then slide the mouthpiece out of your mouth to buzz low D, as shown in Figure 10-3.**

Now you should have a much better feel for the correct positioning of your lower lip. Remember, if you can't buzz the note, your lower lip is probably out of position.

Figure 10-1:
Play low D, buzz low D, play low D again, and then go to a buzzed D (Track 32).

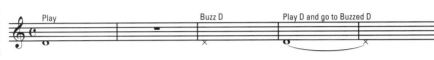

Figure 10-2:
Play D2 and slur to a buzzed low D (Track 32).

Figure 10-3:
As you play G3, pull out the mouth-piece and buzz D1 (low D) (Track 32).

Don't change your embouchure when playing from low notes to high notes.

Letting 'er rip with fast air

Producing fast air is important for playing all notes, but for the high notes, you need to transform your lungs and airway into a turbocharger to make the reed vibrate fast enough to play the higher frequencies. Do everything I recommend for producing fast air in Chapter 6, but do it better and perhaps more pronounced:

- ✔ **Breathe out with your diaphragm.** Doing this increases the force and volume of air.

- ✔ **Curl and arch your tongue to form a wind tunnel for concentrating the air and driving it more directly at the reed. The air must strike the reed in a perpendicular fashion (think of a T).** You may need to arch your tongue higher for the higher notes.

- ✔ **Sculpt your cheeks to an inward position, as shown in Figure 10-4, by hissing like a snake.** This further concentrates the column of air.

Figure 10-4: Hold your cheeks against your teeth for more concentrated airflow.

Meeting More Cousins: The Overtones

In Chapter 8, I introduce you to the high pinky notes that hover above the staff and encourage you to consider them cousins to their lower note counterparts. They're cousins because to change from the lower note to its higher note cousin, all you do is open a vent hole. Heading even higher above the staff, you meet even more cousins — second and third cousins called the *overtones,* which require you to open even more vent holes.

Overtones are tones inside tones, which Pythagoras discovered eons ago. To hear what they sound like on the piano, hold down the keys for the Cs above low C while striking a low C. The overtones make the strings for the notes you're holding down (low C's higher harmonics) ring sympathetically with the other Cs' sounds.

These higher harmonics are actually the squeaks you hear when you unintentionally hit the high notes on your clarinet. In the following sections, I show you how to intentionally play these notes.

Fingering notes C3♯ above the staff to F4♯

The notes from C3♯ above the staff to high F4♯ are "second cousins" of notes below the staff. For "second cousin" notes, you open an additional vent hole (for a total of two), dividing the column of air into five segments, which steps you up to the next register. (For more about opening vent holes to change registers, see Chapter 8.)

To learn the notes from C3 to F4♯, perform the following exercise (see Figure 10-5):

1. **Play the lowest note in each of the overtone series (the *fundamental*).**

2. **While performing Step 1, open the vent key to produce the middle register *(third overtone)*.**

3. **Continue holding the vent key while opening the top tone hole on the upper joint.**

   This steps you up to the next register.

Opening one more vent hole for high G

The high G above C3 is a "third cousin" to low A. To play it, open one more vent hole (three in all), dividing the air column into seven parts.

Try it. Play low A, E, and C3♯, and then lift the third finger of the left hand to open one more vent hole, as shown in Figure 10-6.

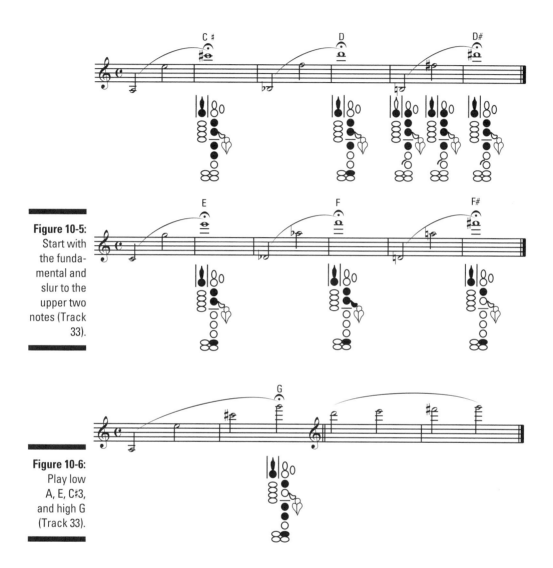

Figure 10-5: Start with the funda-mental and slur to the upper two notes (Track 33).

Figure 10-6: Play low A, E, C#3, and high G (Track 33).

Putting it all together

Practice moving between high notes by performing the exercise shown in Figure 10-7. Start each repeated measure with quarter notes and increase your speed as you repeat it several times.

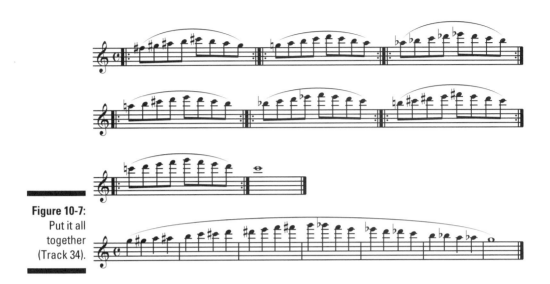

Figure 10-7:
Put it all
together
(Track 34).

Improving Finger Coordination with Alternate Fingerings

Playing the high notes is quite a challenge, requiring impeccable embouchure, fast air, and manual dexterity. However, even the nimblest of fingers can get all tangled up when transitioning to and from these highest of notes, as you move from very few fingers on the clarinet to more fingers. In addition, some of the higher notes simply don't respond very well with the standard fingerings.

To avoid awkward finger changes between notes and improve the response of the high notes, alternative fingerings for the high notes can come in very handy. Fingerings for altissimo notes fall into the following categories:

- ✔ Diatonic
- ✔ Chromatic and trill
- ✔ Short skip
- ✔ Wide skip

Diatonic fingerings are the most basic and common for notes above C3♯. These fingerings are taught first because they work best in playing scales. You already learned these standard fingerings in the previous sections — "Fingering notes C3♯ above the staff to F4♯" and "Opening one more vent hole for high G." In the following sections, I reveal alternate fingerings for these same notes.

Chromatic and trill fingerings

Chromatic notes are the half steps between notes — on a piano, you tap the black keys. On a clarinet, you play chromatic notes by opening and closing keys and tone holes.

Transitioning between adjacent chromatic notes on the clarinet using diatonic (standard) fingerings can be very awkward because so many fingers are involved. To avoid awkward finger changes, use chromatic fingerings when possible. Chromatic fingerings (to play, for example, C above the staff to C♯) usually involve moving just one or two fingers as opposed to several.

Chromatic fingerings also come in handy for trilling — quickly alternating from one note to the note a whole step above it (for example C to D). Moving quickly between notes a whole step apart can be as tricky as moving between chromatic notes. To avoid these awkward transitions, you may use chromatic fingerings as trill fingerings. (For more about trilling, see Chapter 14.)

Play C3 - C3♯ and then trill C - D, F4 - F♯, and F3♯ - G4, as shown in Figure 10-8.

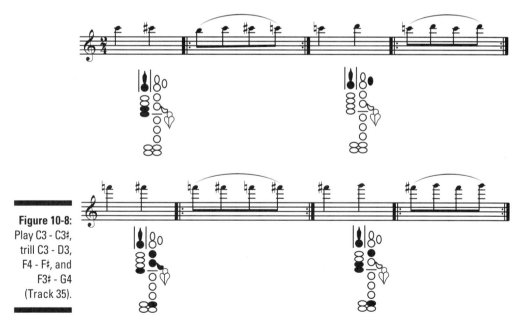

Figure 10-8:
Play C3 - C3♯,
trill C3 - D3,
F4 - F♯, and
F3♯ - G4
(Track 35).

Short-skip fingerings

A *short skip* is an interval between notes that's less than a fifth; for example, A to D, which is a fourth. Short-skip fingerings require the use of more fingers than trill or chromatic fingerings, but fewer fingers than diatonic (scale) fingerings. You use short-skip fingerings in the following three cases:

- ✔ When the high note is the top note of an *arpeggio* — a chord with notes played in quick succession instead of simultaneously.

- ✔ When playing intervallic skips or leaps of thirds and fourths to a high note; for example A to D, which is a fourth.

- ✔ To improve the intonation of a high note played by itself.

Play the skips to the high notes using short-skip fingerings, as shown in Figure 10-9. Play each repeated group faster as you become more comfortable with the fingerings.

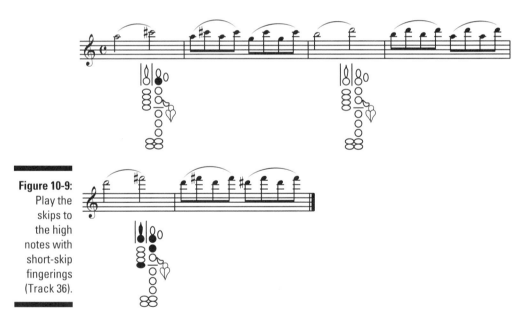

Figure 10-9: Play the skips to the high notes with short-skip fingerings (Track 36).

Wide-skip fingerings

A *wide skip* is an interval between notes that's a fifth or greater; for example B3 to G4 or F to F4. Wide-skip fingerings for high notes use as many fingers and keys as possible. This makes the clarinet "longer." The longer the clarinet, the greater the resistance, which results in better response for high notes.

Use wide-skip fingerings to play E4♭, F4, F4♯, and G4, as shown in Figure 10-10. Perform the exercise slowly using all indicated fingerings.

Figure 10-10: Skip to the high notes with wide-skip fingerings (Track 37).

Part III

Above and Beyond: Essential Intermediate Techniques

The 5th Wave   By Rich Tennant

"Going up, the scale."

In this part . . .

You can play "Hot Cross Buns" like a pro, but that's not going to get you an invitation to jam with the Boston Pops. Before you can even hope to make it to "the show," you need to hone your skills and develop some more advanced clarinet-playing techniques.

In this part, you develop skills for refining your clarinet playing to add fullness, color, and focus to your sound. I show you how to reach high and hit the top notes (without blowing out your eyeballs or eardrums), tune up for the proper pitch, develop faster tonguing and fingering techniques, make your practice sessions more productive, produce some very cool special effects, and tweak your reed for optimum performance and sound.

By the end of this part, you still may not be ready for the Boston Pops, but you will be ready to jam with teachers and friends and have the confidence to step on stage for your first or next performance — maybe even a solo!

Chapter 11

Achieving a Great Clarinet Tone

*T*one is the sound a clarinet makes when a particular individual plays it. It's unique to every clarinet and every individual player. As soon as you hear a great clarinet player, or even a pretty good one, you'll want to sound like that when you play, too. You'll want to be able to hit the lowest low notes and the highest high notes with color and focus. You'll want that full clarinet sound no matter how loudly or softly you play. You've come to the right spot. Here you discover how to give your sound quality and character by mastering the four components of great tone: responsiveness, pitch, color, and focus.

As an added bonus, I explain how to make the normally wheezy-sounding throat tones resonate and how to play quietly while maintaining magnificent tone.

A competent clarinetist plays almost all the notes in tune, but great clarinetists have both great tone and great intonation.

The Four Essential Qualities of Great Tone

Although tone varies among clarinets and clarinetists, all great tones exhibit the following four qualities:

- ✔ **Responsive in all registers:** The clarinet and the clarinetist playing it must be just as *responsive* as any pianist playing her piano. In other words, your reaction time in playing any note in a particular piece should be the same as the time it takes to press a key on a piano.

- ✔ **In tune and on pitch:** Whether the music is classical or jazz, Hungarian or American, good clarinet sounds are in tune. Playing *in tune* means your instrument plays each note at its proper frequency. Sometimes people say "playing *on pitch*," which means you actually play the note at its proper frequency. When notes are out of tune, some people say you're *off-key*.

- ✔ **Consistent in tone color:** Tone color is the timbre or character in a voice or musical instrument. For example, a piano, saxophone, and clarinet all playing the same note sound distinctly different by nature of their tone color. Likewise, two people playing the same note on the same clarinet produce a different tone color by the way they play. The most important point about tone color is that it must remain consistent.

- ✔ **Consistent in tone focus:** Focus is the width or breadth of the sound, and it generally affects how well the sound projects. Good tone flows in a stream instead of a spray.

Successive tones in songs are like colored ribbons. As the ribbon follows the shape of the melodic line, from high to low, it maintains the same color and focus unless you change it intentionally to produce a special effect.

Tone: A matter of taste and culture

Tone is a matter of personal taste. It used to be more of a cultural thing, too. Every country, and sometimes each area in the same country, had its own unique clarinet sound. Thanks to the Internet, TV, and digital music, now you can hear players from anywhere in the world with the turn of a dial or the press of a button. Consequently, clarinetists from around the world are beginning to sound more alike.

Fortunately, even with this growing uniformity in tone, you can find as many terrific sounds on the clarinet as there are fabulous clarinet players.

Producing Great Tone: Step by Step

When you're sitting in a concert hall listening to a clarinet solo, you're probably not thinking about auto racing, but the process for producing great tone is similar to that of driving a racecar:

1. **Start your engine: Increase amplitude to facilitate reed vibration, for maximum responsiveness.**

   You must supply a sufficient volume of air to make the reed move up and down, and have enough reed inside your mouth for it to vibrate freely. Without sufficient amplitude (a function of air volume and reed vibration), the clarinet remains silent.

2. **Shift into drive: Apply leverage to the reed to produce proper pitch.**

   By applying leverage to the reed, you move it closer to the mouthpiece facing and put it in gear, allowing the reed to vibrate. The amount of leverage you apply largely controls the pitch. (Of course, to achieve proper pitch, your clarinet must also be in tune, as discussed in Chapter 15.)

3. **Hit the gas: Deliver fast air to add color.**

   Producing fast air is like stepping on the accelerator. In the case of your clarinet, fast air adds color to your tone.

4. **Steer: Adjust pressure on the reed, as needed, to keep the tone focused.**

   When you're moving forward, steering becomes a whole lot easier. On the clarinet, you steer the sound to keep it focused by adjusting the position of your top teeth on the mouthpiece along with pressure from the corners of your top lip, which changes the leverage on the reed.

Although all four components need to be present at all times, most players find it useful to approach tone as a step-by-step process. In the following sections, I explain each "step" in greater detail, telling you how to add each component of great tone to the mix.

Cranking up amplitude for increased response and fullness

Picture a guitar lying on a chair. Pluck a string, and it makes a sound. Pull the string out farther when you pluck it, and it plays a louder, fuller sound. That's what amplitude is all about. The farther up and down an object vibrates, the greater the amplitude. The reed on a clarinet follows the same principle: The farther up and down it vibrates, the greater the amplitude and the fuller the sound.

The response of all the notes on the clarinet, from low to high, depends on the amplitude of the reed. Making the reed vibrate with sufficient amplitude to produce the high notes is most difficult, so when you're working on amplitude, do everything you do to produce high notes, as explained in Chapter 10:

✔ Have enough reed vibrating in your mouth — about a half-inch. The business card trick I present in Chapter 6 can help you correctly place your lower lip on the reed to ensure that you have enough — but not too much — reed in your mouth. Eventually, you'll develop a "mind's eye" to make proper placement more instinctive.

✔ Rest the clarinet reed on as narrow a ledge as you can form with your lower lip, as explained in Chapter 6.

Play the excerpt from Modest Mussorgsky's "Night on Bald Mountain" shown in Figure 11-1. This is a great exercise for checking the amplitude of your sound. If the high notes don't come out, make some embouchure adjustments, as discussed in Chapter 6, until they do.

Figure 11-1: Excerpt from Modest Mussorgsky's "Night on Bald Mountain" (Track 38).

Gaining leverage over pitch

Good tone at any pitch is in tune. Whether it's Willie Nelson crooning a lonesome love song or Pavarotti belting out a few verses of "Nessun Dorma," the notes are "on the money" in tune. The same is true of clarinet tone — it must remain in tune with itself and any other instruments playing with it.

Two factors contribute to pitch: the length of the clarinet and the leverage of the embouchure. In Chapter 15, I show you how to change the length of your clarinet to tune it. Here I explain how to adjust the leverage of the embouchure to produce notes at their proper pitch.

To apply upward pressure to the reed, use your mouth and the clarinet to create a teeter-totter, as shown in Figure 11-2. Sitting on one side of the teeter-totter are your top teeth. Sitting on the opposite side is the entire weight of the clarinet. In between is the fulcrum on which the teeter-totter teeters and totters, the narrow ledge formed by your bottom lip.

Notice that the lower lip is a greater distance down the reed than the top teeth. This is called a *non-opposed embouchure,* because your teeth are not opposite or in line with one another. In non-opposed embouchure, the upper and lower teeth are positioned in a 1:3 ratio from the tip of the mouthpiece:

- ✔ **Upper teeth:** About a quarter-inch down from the tip of the mouthpiece

- ✔ **Lower teeth:** About three-quarters of an inch down from the tip of the mouthpiece and slightly covered by the lower lip

As you move your lower teeth (and lip) down the reed, you begin to feel more pressure on your lower lip as you lower the clarinet, because your top teeth gain more leverage, increasing the downward pressure on the mouthpiece. This gives you greater control over how much leverage is applied than you'd get from biting down on the mouthpiece with an *opposed embouchure.*

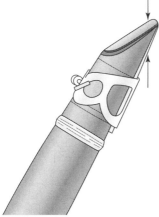

Figure 11-2:
The lower lip is a greater distance down the reed than the top teeth.

With your upper and lower teeth at their proper positions on the mouth-piece, use the clarinet to apply more or less leverage on the reed:

✔ Holding the clarinet high, applying no leverage, produces no sound.

✔ When you lower the clarinet, increasing leverage, the clarinet begins to produce a sound, although it's very flat at first. Remember, you did this when you made your first sounds on the mini-clarinet in Chapter 6.

✔ Bring the clarinet closer to your body, near a 30-degree angle with your body, and you start to get good pitch that's well focused. If you bring the clarinet too far down, you apply too much leverage, which makes the sound sharp and thin.

Play F3, as shown in Figure 11-3, raising and lowering the clarinet to produce the different pitch levels, from flat to sharp. Remember to keep your chin down and embouchure in position. Don't bite down, and don't let your bottom lip follow the reed up as you raise the clarinet. Think of raising the clarinet off the reed and then bringing the reed back down on the lip when you see the arrow pointing down — but your lower lip must maintain contact with the reed.

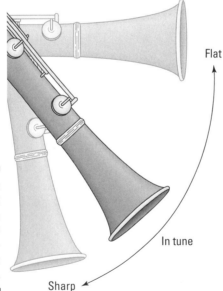

Figure 11-3: Raise and lower the clarinet to produce different pitch levels.

Flat

In tune

Sharp

ON THE CD

Play the F until it's in tune, and then play the scale down and back up, as shown in Figure 11-4.

Figure 11-4:
Play F3
whole note
and then
scale down
and back up
(Track 39).

Adding a dash of color

Color adds intensity or brightness to the tone. Imagine a large orchestra play-ing a dark, heavy piece. Then a piccolo enters on a very high note. The con-trast in color is immediately noticeable, rising from the orchestra's darkness to the bright, cheery sound of the piccolo.

With a clarinet, the more high overtones a sound has, the more intense or brighter it is. As explained in Chapter 10, overtones are higher harmonics that resonate with the fundamental frequency. By delivering fast air, you pro-duce more overtones.

Color is primarily a function of air speed, so adding color is a matter of pro-ducing fast air:

✔ Breathe deeply using your diaphragm.

✔ Hold a high tongue position to transform the inside of your mouth into a wind tunnel. Narrow your wind tunnel vertically by raising your tongue and hissing like a snake. Narrow the tunnel horizontally by sculpting your cheeks inward, toward your facial bones.

Never let your cheeks puff out like Louis Armstrong. Your cheeks should be cheek to cheek with your teeth. In other words, your cheeks should *feel* your teeth. Otherwise, you transform your oral cavity into a big bowl that reduces the air pressure.

Play the music shown in Figure 11-5, keeping your tongue high to produce fast air. While you play, keep the ribbon analogy in mind. Produce fast air to make the tone brighter. Lower your tongue to darken the sound.

Figure 11-5: Use fast air to add color to your tone (Track 40).

Avoid letting your tongue follow the notes down as you play lower on the clarinet. Otherwise, the color runs out of the lower notes.

When you're comfortable making fast air to brighten your tone, take the ultimate test, shown in Figure 11-6. This exercise challenges your ability to maintain fast air over wide skips.

Figure 11-6: The ultimate test (Track 41).

When playing passages that skip to high notes, practice them with the high note first, to establish the correct air speed required to produce the high note. By playing the high note first, you know how much you have to ramp up your air speed when transitioning from a lower note to produce an instant response on the high note. I realize this may seem a little backward, but it really works to reinforce the necessity of delivering fast air for the high notes.

Focusing your sound

Focus in a clarinet sound determines its projection in the same way narrowing a beam of light makes it more intense and enables it to travel farther. Like a public speaker, you need to play to the back of the room without screaming. On the clarinet, you accomplish this through *focus*. Another way to look at focus is this: As you narrow the focus, you narrow the ribbon of your sound.

When you have the amplitude and pitch just right and you're playing on pitch, you're almost there in terms of focus. Your sound just needs a little fine-tuning, and I do mean "little" and "fine." Major adjustments could result in major setbacks. As you play your full, colorful, in-tune notes, focus your sound by making the following adjustments:

✔ While you're playing, shift your top teeth slightly back toward the tip of the mouthpiece. This changes the leverage on the mouthpiece, placing more upward force against the reed. Be sure to shift your top teeth *while playing,* just as a driver moves the steering wheel slightly when driving down a relatively straight road.

✔ Increase top lip support. To do this, add more "euww" by pressing your top lip inward and down against your eye teeth. Remember, the top lip frowns as the bottom lip smiles.

To practice focusing your sound, play the music shown in Figure 11-7, as follows:

1. **Start the sound on F3 with the clarinet slightly off your lower lip.**

2. **Gradually increase the leverage to bring the sound to pitch.**

3. **As you continue playing down the scale, hiss "T-heeee" to blow the air toward the bridge of your nose.**

4. **As you play, gradually move your top teeth back on the mouthpiece to focus the sound to the width you desire.**

5. **Play the exercise a second time, doing all the same things but tonguing the scale instead of slurring.**

   The purpose of playing the exercise a second time, tonguing the scale instead of slurring it, is to gain experience maintaining focus both when tonguing and when slurring. Everything is slightly different when you tongue notes.

Figure 11-7: Make minor adjustments as you play, to improve focus (Track 43).

Play the Russell Dagon focus exercises shown in Figures 11-8 to 11-10 by adjusting the focus of the pitches as you ascend from the beginning E1. (Russell Dagon is retired Principal Clarinetist of the Milwaukee Symphony and Professor of Clarinet at Northwestern University.)

Figure 11-8:
Follow the Dagon pattern to F3 (Track 43).

Figure 11-9:
Follow the Dagon pattern to C3 (Track 43).

Figure 11-10:
Follow the Dagon pattern to E4 (Track 43).

Clarinet playing has its *ups* and *downs:* Keep your head and air up. Keep your chin, upper lip, and clarinet down.

Playing Softly with Good Tone

The clarinet plays softly better than any other wind instrument. It can play softly, to very softly (the Italians call it *sotto voce,* or "soft voice"), to diminuendo, to no sound at all, just as a bell rings and fades to silence. Composers know it. That's why they write so many passages for the clarinet at the quiet dynamic levels.

Now, you might think that playing softly means delivering *less* wind. Au contraire. Playing very softly with tone color actually requires *more* air. You essentially do what stage actors do to whisper to the audience at the back of an auditorium — you use more breath support, not less.

To play softly on the clarinet, you reduce the amplitude to cut down the volume, while increasing the breath support to maintain reed vibration and the color of the tone. To play *pp* (*pianissimo,* or "very soft") or make diminuendos to no sound, do the following:

✔ Lower the clarinet slightly to increase lip pressure on the reed, reducing the amplitude. Amplitude is a function of air volume and reed vibration, so you can reduce amplitude by restricting reed vibration while at the same time delivering more air to project the sound.

✔ As you make a diminuendo, or play at a very quiet dynamic, increase the breath support from your diaphragm. Otherwise, the reed stops vibrating entirely and the sound abruptly stops.

✔ As you apply more lip pressure, you decrease the amplitude of the "diving board mode" of reed vibration. (See Chapter 17 for more about the modes of reed vibration.) To allow the ears of the reed (the corners of the tip) to continue vibrating, also increase the downward pressure of the top lip at the corners of your mouth. To do this, frown more with the "eeuw" word. (For a whole lot more about reed parts, vibration, and fixing problems with a reed, visit Chapter 17.)

Practice playing from loud to soft by performing the exercise shown in Figure 11-11. Begin playing B fortissimo and then diminuendo to infinite, just as a bell rings and then fades to silence.

Figure 11-11:
Play from loud, to very soft, to silent (Track 44).

To develop a better feel for playing ultra-softly, play the Mozart Adagio *ppp* or sotto voce, as shown in Figure 11-12.

Figure 11-12:
Play the Mozart Adagio very softly. First play it loud to establish the breadth of focus in your tone, then repeat it, playing it softer each time (Track 45).

Chapter 12

Shaking It Up with Vibrato, Glissandos, Bends, and Scoops

*N*ot all singers and musicians are equally skilled and gifted. On one tier are competent players who can hit all the notes. On the next are intermediate players, who play all the notes smoothly and have developed their own unique sound. And on the top tier are the standouts, who can do something special with their voice or their instrument. Through various techniques they've picked up or invented, they add a third dimension to their ribbon of sound.

Over the years, musicians have developed all sorts of techniques for plucking, squeezing, and puffing unique sounds out of their instruments. In this chapter, I reveal about a half-dozen special effects for the clarinet and explain how to produce them. With these skills and enough practice, you begin to step up your playing to the next tier and add some tools to your repertoire that can make you a much more creative clarinetist.

Exploring Vibrato's Roots

Vibrato is the pulsating effect in the sound of an instrument or a vocal tone. The pulsation is mostly heard as recurring cycles of pitch variation from just above the pitch to just below it and back. It can also involve very slight repeated cycles of deviation in the volume or amplitude of a note. It occurs most frequently and is most noticeable on the longer note values. Undoubtedly, it began with vocalists.

In the 1600s, long before the clarinet was even invented, string players began using vibrato. Over time, members of the woodwind family adopted it in concert music, including contemporary music, and in popular *idioms* (styles of music), including jazz and folk, as explained in the following sections.

Vibrato in jazz: A match made in heaven

Jazz clarinet without vibrato is like chili without chili powder. All A-list jazz clarinetists use vibrato. Buddy DeFranco, famed jazz clarinetist, says predecessors Artie Shaw and Benny Goodman influenced his own approach with their use of jaw vibrato.

In DeFranco's view, Shaw used a style that imitated string vibrato and Benny Goodman preferred a fast vibrato, probably influenced by the Chicago Dixieland Style players he'd heard in his youth.

Folksy vibrato

Folk music comes from a vocal tradition and often needs a dash of vibrato to express the right spirit and personality. This is especially true of Klezmer music, part of Jewish tradition around the world. Clarinet also plays an important role in the folk music of Eastern Europe, Russia, Greece, Turkey, and Italy, where clarinet players infuse their music with a lot o' vibrato.

Classical vibrato

In some circles, using vibrato in classical music is the equivalent of having your cellphone play the "Crank Dat Soulja Boy" ringtone in the middle of a performance of Beethoven's Ninth. On the other hand, until recently, classical clarinetists in England commonly used vibrato. Jack Brymer, a famous English performer, purports that Richard Mühlfeld, the clarinetist for whom Brahms wrote his sonatas and quintet, used a very pronounced vibrato. Noted American symphonic clarinetists who use (or used) vibrato include Harold Wright (Boston Symphony), Anthony Gigliotti (Philadelphia Orchestra), Stanley Drucker (New York Philharmonic), and famed soloist Richard Stoltzman.

A contemporary take

Contemporary composers often have an "anything goes" mentality . . . as long as "anything goes" works. This equips them with all the tools they need to fully express their creativity. So it's no surprise that many contemporary composers call for vibrato as a special effect. Alban Berg was one of the first and asked for it in his "Four Pieces." More recently, Shulamit Ran notated it in her piece entitled "For an Actor," and Libby Larsen required vibrato in her work "Dancing Solo."

Vibrato and you

How you choose to season your clarinet playing with vibrato is primarily a matter of personal taste, cultural tradition, and the type of music you're play-ing. When playing music born of a vocal tradition, such as folk and jazz, clari-net vibrato is always acceptable and sometimes essential. Vibrato also works well when playing along with string instruments, because string musicians use it almost all the time.

Vibrato is just another color in your tone palate. A computer can produce a good clarinet sound, but only a human being can react to a melodic line and bring out its emotional content. Making subtle color changes by using vibrato is one way to do this. No one would tell a painter to not use purple when painting a scenic picture of a sunset, nor should anyone limit the tonal spectrum in any type of music. Striking the right mood depends on the artis-tic sensitivity of the musician. Good clarinetists maintain consistency in the color and breadth of the music ribbon as they move from note to note in the melodic line (see Chapter 11), but fantastic players make subtle changes in the intensity and color when playing the longer note values.

Giving Your Clarinet a Pulse

Good vibrato begins with solid fundamentals, so don't even think about shak-ing things up until you have a firm footing on a solid foundation. Producing and controlling straight clarinet tone, as explained in Chapter 11, is key to learning vibrato and doing it right.

When playing vibrato, you adjust two of the parameters of good tone explained in Chapter 11:

✔ **Amount of pitch variation within the pulses or cycles:** Pitch variation is determined by how much above and below the pitch each cycle goes. The sharper, then flatter each cycle goes, the greater the pitch variation and the greater the amplitude of the vibrato. See Figure 12-1. (Many saxophone players refer to these pitch variations as *undulations.*)

✔ **Speed of the pulses or cycles:** The speed of pulses is determined by the number of pulses or cycles per beat.

Figure 12-1:
The sharper, then flatter each cycle goes, the greater the vibrato pitch variation and amplitude.

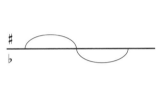

In the following sections, I introduce you to the two types of vibrato, show you how to play each type, and offer guidance on controlling your vibrato through pitch and speed variation.

Use vibrato mostly on longer note values.

Recognizing the two flavors of vibrato

Vibrato comes in two flavors:

✔ *Jaw vibrato (lip vibrato)* makes pitch variations within each of the pulsations. This is the vibrato of choice among saxophone players and most clarinetists, especially jazz players.

✔ *Glottal vibrato (diaphragm vibrato)* affects the amplitude (volume) within the repeated pulsations to produce a controlled quiver in the sound. Many singers opt for glottal vibrato, and flute players use it extensively. Glottal vibrato used to be the vibrato of choice for classical clarinetists of an older generation.

Jaw vibrato versus glottal vibrato is not an either/or choice. You can use either type when playing different tunes or within the same tune. You can also combine the two techniques when playing funkier music.

Getting warmed up with jaw vibrato

Good vibrato may not make your teeth chatter, but chattering your teeth (sort of) is just what you need to produce jaw vibrato. Think Gospel jaw, as explained earlier in the sidebar "Beware of faux vibrato," and you have a pretty good idea of how to implement this technique.

In jaw vibrato, you move your lower jaw repeatedly up and down to subtly change pressure on the reed, resulting in recurring differences in pitch. Another way of looking at it is this: As your jaw moves up and down, your lower lip is on and off the reed. That description is just a way of *looking* at it — the lip never actually breaks contact with the reed. As the jaw moves, it increases and decreases lip pressure on the reed.

Legendary jazz clarinetist Buddy DeFranco uses jaw vibrato, as does wizard jazz clarinetist Eddie Daniels.

To get a clearer idea of the correct jaw motion for jaw vibrato, pay attention to how your jaw moves when saying "Yo-Ee" and "Ya-Ee."

Controlling changes in pitch

To learn how to make subtle changes in vibrato width, practice the following exercise, exaggerating the sharp and flat part of each cycle:

1. **Push up on the barrel of the clarinet with your right thumb so the mouthpiece presses against your top teeth, as shown in Figure 12-2.**

   Pushing the mouthpiece against your top teeth helps you feel the stability of pressure on the mouthpiece, which helps you relax and release lower lip pressure on the reed for the flat portion of each cycle.

2. **Play a sustained G2 (open G), starting with "T-heeee."**

3. **As you play the note, move your lower lip away from the mouthpiece, reducing lower lip pressure on the reed, by saying "Yo-Ee." Keep repeating "Yo-Ee" to make the pitch go flat and then back in tune with the eighth-note rhythms shown in Figure 12-3. The Yo part of the cycle makes the pitch go flat, and the Ee part makes it go sharp.**

4. **Play a sustained open G with eighth-note, triple, and sixteenth-note pulses using "Yo-Ee."**

   The pulses or cycles should follow this sequence: in tune - flat - sharp - in tune - flat - sharp, over and over again, as shown in Figure 12-4.

Add lip pressure for the sharp part of each cycle, and reduce lip pressure for the flat part of each cycle.

Figure 12-2:
Push the clarinet up to press the mouthpiece against your top teeth.

Figure 12-3:
Play a sustained G2 alternating pitch flat and then back in tune (Track 46).

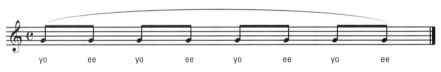

Figure 12-4:
Play a sustained open G with eighth-note, triple, and sixteenth-note pulses (Track 46).

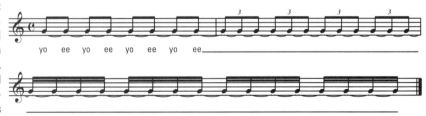

Controlling the speed

Listening closely to vocalists who use vibrato, you're likely to notice that the speed of the pitch changes can vary from crazy-fast, Snow White vibrato that sounds like the bleating of a lamb (tremolo), to super-slow vibrato (wobble). Somewhere in between are various speeds that listeners find pleasing and are appropriate for different styles of music, individual tunes, or even different passages in the same tune.

To develop speed control over your vibrato, practice the following exercise:

1. **Start with eighth notes, saying "Yo" for the first eighth note and "Ee" for the second eighth note.**

   By this time, "Yo-Ee" often turns into just "Yo" or "Ya," as in the exercise used for pitch change in Figure 12-4. Try "Yo" and "Ya" to determine which works best for you.

2. **Play the exercise in Figure 12-4 at different tempos, which naturally changes the speed of your vibrato.**

3. **Play Buddy DeFranco's vibrato exercise, shown in Figure 12-5.**

Figure 12-5:
Buddy
DeFranco's
vibrato
exercise
(Track 47).

Opting for glottal vibrato

Although most players prefer jaw (lip) vibrato, some still favor glottal style. To make glottal vibrato, substitute "Tee-hee" for the "Yo-yo" or "Ya-ya" I introduce in the previous section. Play the music in Figures 12-3 to 12-5 using "Tee-hee-hee-hee." The sound actually changes volume slightly within each of the pulses.

In glottal vibrato (which flute players use), you produce fast recurring pulses inside each longer-value note (usually four or five for most tempos). The "he" makes an accent, which becomes a recurring pulse inside each note. Alternate in blowing harder and softer — harder to produce the pulse and then softer so that the volume falls off before the next pulse.

Jazzing it up

To make your vibrato jazzier, break the rules and allow the pulsations to change color, focus, or both (for more about color and focus, see Chapter 11):

- ✔ **Color:** To change color, position your tongue to blow air toward the end of your nose instead of upward toward the top of the bridge.

- ✔ **Focus:** To broaden the focus, raise the bell of the clarinet slightly, as most modern jazz and Dixieland players do. (Modern jazz players use a slower vibrato than Benny Goodman used. Dixieland players use a fast vibrato.)

Play the popular Hungarian folk song shown in Figure 12-6, with different speeds of vibrato on each of the slower notes.

Figure 12-6:
Popular
Hungarian
folk song
(Track 48).

Honoring tradition: Vibrato in classical clarinet

Many classical players, including Harold Wright and Anthony Gigliotti, used vibrato. Theirs was subtle, and you had to really listen for it, because they kept the color and focus constant. Think of the ribbon of the sound subtly changing color shadings. Classical vibrato on the clarinet uses the same jaw or glottal vibrato, but the focus of the sound (the width of the musical ribbon) never changes.

When adding vibrato to a classical piece, keep the basic color and retain the focus, for a more subtle touch. Regardless of style, always remember that the most successful vibratos are added to sound — sound with vibrato, not vibrato with sound.

Going Gershwin with Glissandos

Listen to the beginning of George Gershwin's "Rhapsody in Blue." Because it's cited so often in discussions and used as the standard demonstration of a glissando (or *gliss,* for short), it's almost synonymous with the word and borders on becoming cliché. Yet this piece truly exemplifies what a gliss is all about. To describe it in words, it sounds like when the fire engine just turns on its siren, quickly rising from a low tone to an ear-piercing shriek. Clarinets are the only woodwind that can pull off a gliss, and it can really add pizzazz to a tune.

In the following sections, I introduce the two types of glissandos — scalar glisses and smears (slides) — and show you how to execute each of them. Regardless of how much use you make of glisses, practicing them is a great tongue-positioning exercise.

Glissandos are commonly used only in jazz, folk, and contemporary music.

Scalar glisses

Most glisses are simply parts of scales with some chromatic notes added to the mix:

- ✔ Execute the gliss solely with your fingers. Fill in skips between notes with parts of the scale from the key the music is written in.

- ✔ Fill in skips between notes with a chromatic note or two from the C scale. Again, fill in skips between notes with a scale and one or two added chromatic notes.

Play "Just a Closer Walk with Thee" as shown in Figure 12-7, with glisses where you see lines connecting the notes.

Figure 12-7:
"Just a
Closer Walk
with Thee"
(Track 49).

Change focus during a scalar gliss to jazz it up even more. (For more about changing focus, see Chapter 11.)

Smears (also known as slides)

Another type of glissando, like the one in Gershwin's "Rhapsody in Blue," is a *smear* (or *slide*). It's the dirtiest and jazziest of them all. In smears, the fingers slide off tone holes as the pressure point on the reed moves. This also makes the color and focus of the sound change as you slide between the notes.

To execute a smear, do the following pretty much at the same time as you slide between the notes:

- ✔ Slide your fingers off the tone holes (instead of lifting them, as you normally do). The color changes as your fingers slide off the tone holes.

- ✔ Change your tongue position as when you say "Doe-weeee."

- ✔ Ease up on your jaw pressure and slide the reed down your lower lip to change its pressure point ("sweet spot") closer to the tip of the reed; then slide the reed up your lower lip to slightly above its normal position. "Sweet spot" is clarinet player slang for the point where your lower lip touches the reed with best results in sound and response.

This works a little differently for every player, so experiment and practice until it sounds just right.

Practice your smears by playing the music shown in Figure 12-8. The music starts with small intervals and gradually increases the size of the interval until you can play a full octave smear.

Figure 12-8:
Start with the B3 to C3 smear and add smears from A3 to C3, G3 to C3, F3 to C3, E2 to C3, D3 to C3, and C2 to C3 (Track 50).

Bending and Scooping Notes

In soccer, you can bend the ball by adding spin when you kick it. Although your foot connects with the ball at a single point, the ball curves in the direction of the spin. On certain instruments, including the harmonica and clarinet, you can bend or scoop notes to make them "curve" up or down slightly as you play them, adding emotion and personality to jazz and folk music.

In the following sections, I define bending and scooping, and explain how to produce these special effects.

When practicing bends and scoops, first sing what you want to hear, and then try playing it on the clarinet. You may also benefit from listening to some good blues singers or jazz sax players, to get the sounds in your head.

Bending a note

Bends occur inside notes, lowering the pitch and then raising it back to pitch. In musical notation, bends appear as an upside-down half-moon and are essentially the flat-to-sharp side of a wide vibrato cycle.

To make a bend, use a technique similar to jaw vibrato:

1. **Start a note on pitch.**

2. **Drop your jaw to loosen lip pressure, lowering the pitch.**

3. **Increase jaw pressure to bring the note back to pitch.**

Play the exercise in Figure 12-9 with bends on the descending notes of a C major scale.

Figure 12-9:
Bend
descending
notes of a C
major scale
(Track 51).

Scooping a note

A scoop occurs at the beginning of a note, lowering the pitch at the beginning of the note and then raising it back to pitch. In musical notation, scoops appear as a short line preceding the note. They're essentially the same flat-to-sharp side of a very wide jaw vibrato cycle.

To scoop a note, here's what you do:

1. **Drop your jaw to loosen lip pressure on the reed just before you start a note.**

2. **Add lip pressure as you play the note, raising it to pitch.**

Play the exercise shown in Figure 12-10 with scoops in front of the notes.

Figure 12-10:
Scoop
descending
notes of a C
major scale
(Track 52).

Chapter 13

Taking Your Fingers to the Next Level: Additional Fingerings

In This Chapter

▶ Exploring alternate fingerings for the pinky notes

▶ Enriching the normally wheezy throat tones

▶ Climbing above G in the extended altissimo range

S ome fingerings are essential — without them, you can't even play "Hot Cross Buns" or "Mary Had a Little Lamb." Others are more or less optional. Alternate fingerings can make the pinky notes easier to play and can reduce the likelihood of getting your pinkies all tied up in knots. Some fingerings can improve your tone by adding fullness and resonance to the throat tones. Additional fingerings extend the altissimo register of the clarinet so you can hit those really high notes.

In this chapter, I introduce you to fingerings that can simplify and enhance your clarinet playing. When you're first starting out, you may not need to know this stuff, but as you progress, you'll find these additional fingering options quite handy.

Preventing Pinky Entanglement

Your pinkies are demure little things, the smallest and weakest of the entire finger tribe. In normal day-to-day activities, they follow the other fingers, pretending to help, but the other fingers all know they're the ones doing the heavy lifting.

On the clarinet, however, your pinkies get quite a workout. They're called into action to help play all the notes below low G (as well as G♯ or A♭) and to add resonance and fullness to some of the notes in the altissimo register (more about that later in this chapter in the section "Adding Fullness and Resonance to the Throat Tones").

Unfortunately, your pinkies aren't the nimblest or most muscular of the bunch. Just try dialing a phone with your pinky or using it instead of your index finger to flip the pages of this book. Because your pinkies are weaker fingers, using the standard pinky fingerings to play notes below low G may get your pinkies all tangled up. To avoid this, try some alternate pinky fingerings, courtesy of inventor Iwan Mueller.

Except for low A♭ and its higher cousin E♭, and A♭ above the staff and its lower cousin D♭, all pinky notes have alternate fingerings. Use these alternate fingerings as necessary, to avoid having to slide the same pinky to move between successive pinky notes.

Play the pinky note combinations shown in Figures 13-1 to 13-3, alternating the use of your pinky fingers. When you're playing these combinations, think of letting your pinkies take a walk.

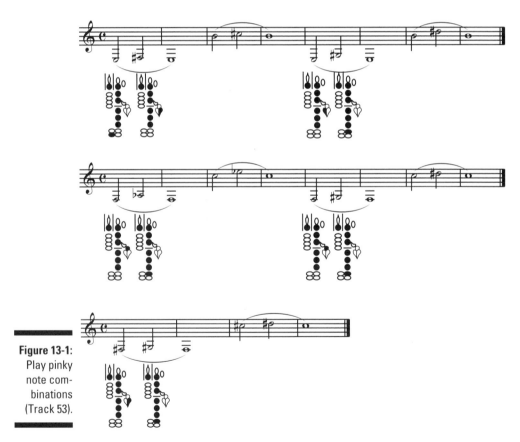

Figure 13-1:
Play pinky note combinations (Track 53).

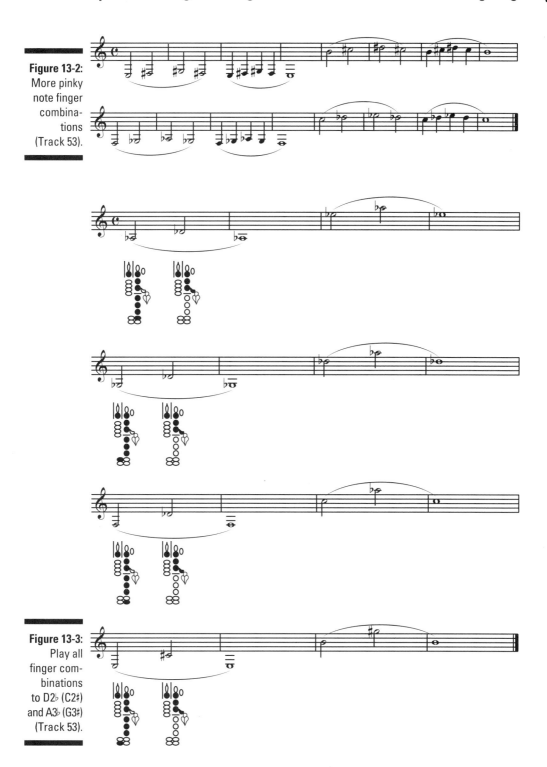

Figure 13-2: More pinky note finger combinations (Track 53).

Figure 13-3: Play all finger combinations to D2♭ (C2♯) and A3♭ (G3♯) (Track 53).

Thanks, Iwan Mueller!

Iwan Mueller was the first to add duplicate fingerings for the pinky notes on the clarinet. He did this in the early 1800s, to enable clarinetists to play between two pinky notes without having to slide from key to key with the same finger.

Thanks to Mueller, you can now play an E-major scale without getting all tangled up going between B, C♯, and D♯, or play an A♭ scale without getting all tangled up going between C, D♭, and E♭.

The easiest way to figure out the alternation of pinky notes is to start with E♭ or low A♭ and work backward. This also works with A♭ or D♭ below the staff.

Adding Fullness and Resonance to the Throat Tones

If the thought of playing notes with your throat makes you gag, relax. Throat tones have more to do with your fingers than your throat. They're called throat tones because you play them in the "throat" of the clarinet, up near the barrel joint.

To play the throat tones, you open almost all the tone holes on the clarinet. When you're playing B2♭, your clarinet is essentially about 9 inches long. (Clarinet length is measured from the mouthpiece to the first open tone hole, as I explain in Chapter 2.) Compare that to playing B2 natural right next to it, which plays on a clarinet that's 26 inches long!

The longer the clarinet, the greater the resistance and the fuller the sound. When you shorten the clarinet by opening so many tone holes, the notes sound kind of wheezy and tiny compared to the notes around them. In addition, having the least resistant note right next to its most resistant counterpart makes maintaining the width and color of the tone ribbon difficult when playing passages with throat tones mixed in.

Fortunately, an acoustical phenomenon called *end correction* can help. End correction is a property of vibrating sound waves in wind instruments. The vibrating column of air (the sound wave) extends farther down the instrument, way past the first open tone hole.

To experience end correction, grab a friend and try this:

1. **Play a low E1 on your clarinet while your friend moves his hand up and down in a slicing motion at the bell, as shown in Figure 13-4.**

2. **Note the distortion in the sound.**

3. **Play E1 again while your friend makes the slicing motion farther and farther away from the bell.**

4. **Note that the sound is still distorted at some distance from the bell, meaning that the sound wave extends the entire length of the clarinet and then some.**

For a low E, all the tone holes are closed, making the first open "tone hole" the bell itself. The vibrating column of air producing the sound extends from well below the open tone hole (the bell, in this case) and reaches all the way up the instrument.

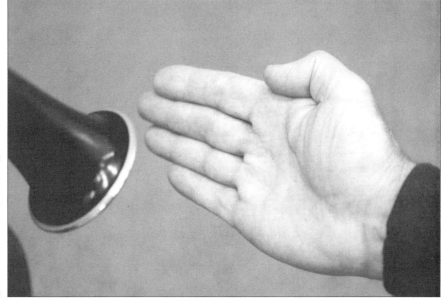

Figure 13-4:
Play low E1, while your friend cuts the sound wave away from the bell.

To improve the sound of the throat tones using end correction, close additional tone holes farther down the clarinet while playing the throat tones. This extends the length of the vibrating sound wave for added fullness and color, producing *resonated throat tones.*

Play each of the throat tones in Figure 13-5 first with the normal fingering and then with resonated throat tone fingerings for each respective note. Notice how much fuller and more colorful the resonated throat tones sound.

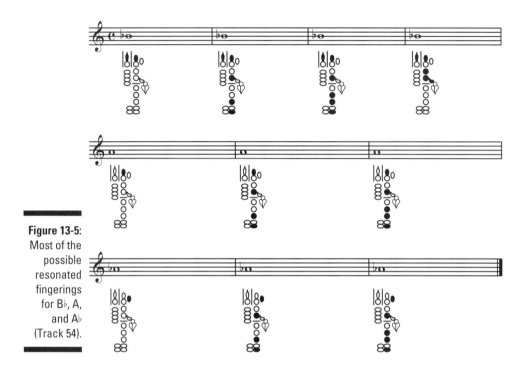

Figure 13-5: Most of the possible resonated fingerings for B♭, A, and A♭ (Track 54).

Getting a feel for throat tones

To develop a better feel for throat tones, perform the exercises shown in Figures 13-6 to 13-9 with the fingerings indicated below the throat tone notes. Notice how much fuller the resonated notes sound when compared to the nonresonated throat tones.

Figure 13-6: Matching the fullness of the C's with resonated fingerings for B♭ and A (Track 55).

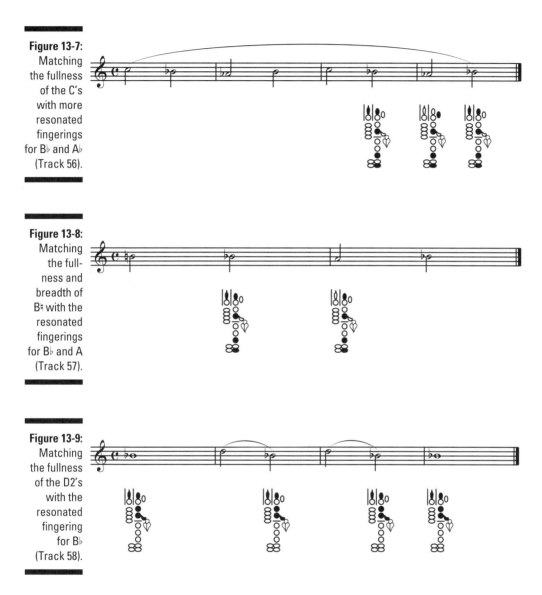

Figure 13-7:
Matching the fullness of the C's with more resonated fingerings for B♭ and A♭ (Track 56).

Figure 13-8:
Matching the fullness and breadth of B♮ with the resonated fingerings for B♭ and A (Track 57).

Figure 13-9:
Matching the fullness of the D2's with the resonated fingering for B♭ (Track 58).

In case you're wondering why I didn't introduce these fingerings earlier in the book, it's because they're kind of awkward for playing fast passages. However, these fingerings are common, so be sure to add them to your repertoire. Use them whenever possible to add fullness and color to your sound. As you gain familiarity with these fingerings, they become much less awkward.

Improving your throat tones

Hone your skills at playing resonated throat tones by playing a nice, even-sounding scale with the resonated fingerings for B♭ and A, shown in Figure 13-10.

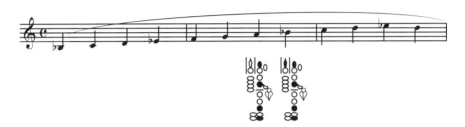

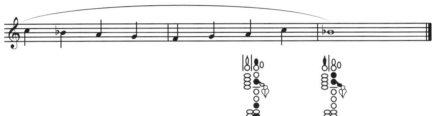

Figure 13-10:
Scale using resonated fingerings for B♭ and A (Track 59).

Play the passage from the *New World Symphony* shown in Figure 13-11, noting that the B2♭ throat tone sounds like a real note instead of a poor excuse for a note.

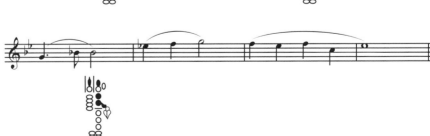

Figure 13-11:
Dvorak's *New World Symphony* second spiritual opening (Track 60).

Letting Your Fingers Do the Climbing: Rising Above High G

The normal range of the altissimo register tops out at G4, but the clarinet is capable of playing the notes all the way up to high C4. This gives the instrument a range of more than four octaves. Hanging out on the peaks of this extended altissimo range are five notes: G4♯, A4, A4♯, B4, and C4.

Playing above high G may seem excessive. These notes aren't exactly the staple of most clarinet repertoires, so you may be wondering why I'm recommending that you practice these notes. Two good reasons:

✔ Playing the absolute highest notes makes producing high notes in the normal range seem like no big deal. High G, the highest note in the normal range, is no longer the highest note, so you feel more confident playing it.

✔ Composers such as Aaron Copland include the upper altissimo notes in their clarinet solos. Gioachino Rossini wrote high A's in his music in the early 1800s, and Camille Saint-Saëns included one in his "Sonata for Clarinet" later in the same century.

To play the upper altissimo notes, just change registers two more times. (For more about navigating register changes, see Chapter 8.)

A clarinet is like a set of 14 bugles, all of different lengths. Instead of having to swap out 14 separate instruments, however, you simply change the "length" of the clarinet by opening tone holes. Keeping the clarinet long plays the low notes. To skip up to higher "cousins" of the note you're playing, while fingering the low note, you simply open one or more of the top tone holes, effectively shortening your clarinet.

When playing the highest notes, in addition to opening more tone holes, pay attention to the following essentials:

✔ **Optimum embouchure:** Form a narrow ledge with your lower lip. Say "mu" with the bottom lip and "vu" with the top lip. (See Chapter 6 for more about forming a proper embouchure.)

✔ **Enough reed vibrating over the mouthpiece facing:** Double-check the amount of reed vibrating freely by inserting a business card under the reed. (See Figure 6-3.) This indicates the approximate amount of mouthpiece you should have in your mouth. If the reed is proper strength and the air is moving fast enough, this is often the problem. The solution is to move your lower lip approximately ½₂ inch farther down the reed while keeping your top teeth where they were.

✔ **Very fast air:** At high B4, the reed vibrates 1,760 times per second. To accomplish this, you need to deliver a very fast air stream. Breathe deeply and make a small wind tunnel by sculpting your cheeks against your teeth and hissing like a snake, "T-heeee."

Play each group of cousins in the fourth register (some players call these *seventh partial notes*), as shown in Figure 13-12, using the fingerings shown beneath the notes.

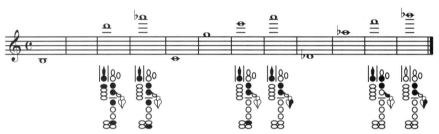

Figure 13-12:
Play each group of cousins in the fourth register (Track 61).

Play each group of cousins in the fifth register of the clarinet (some players call these *ninth partial notes*), as shown in Figure 13-13.

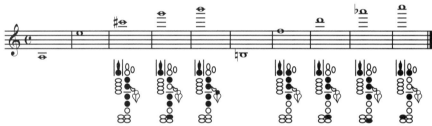

Figure 13-13:
Play each group of cousins in the fifth register (Track 62).

Put it all together and play the A, B♭, and C scales, as shown in Figure 13-14.

Figure 13-14:
Play the A, B♭, and C scales (Track 63).

Chapter 14

Turbo Tonguing and Faster Fingering

*B*ase competency on the clarinet is commendable, but being able to play well and fast is essential for playing all types of music and keeping up with a band or orchestra. You must play well — fast, slow, and in between.

Musicians and composers play a never-ending game of raising the bar. Composers write increasingly challenging pieces, and musicians take up the challenge. Likewise, musicians often improvise, doing something on the clarinet that the composer may never have heard or even thought possible. As a result, many composers who write music for the clarinet have grown to expect clarinetists to be able to pull off some pretty fancy gymnastics. To meet these expectations and be able to play pieces like Igor Stravinsky's *The Firebird* or John Corigliano's "Clarinet Concerto," you have to train hard, just like an Olympic athlete, to raise your game to the next level.

This chapter cranks up the speed, challenging you to articulate and slur faster and faster, showing you how to do it, and providing exercises to hone your skills.

Gearing Up Your Tongue

Fast tonguing isn't all that special. It's the same as tonguing, explained in Chapter 9, only faster. To tongue quickly on the clarinet, here's what you do:

> ✔ Keep a constant flow of air between the tongued notes.
>
> ✔ Use a syllable that keeps the tongue muscle relaxed and doesn't create too much space between the notes. "De" works better than "Te," because your tongue spends less time on the reed.
>
> ✔ Organize the tongued notes into manageable groups of "syllables."

In the following sections, I show you how to recognize fast tonguing in musical notation and explain the essential ingredients for fast tonguing in greater detail.

Tonguing is still tonguing, whether you do it fast or slow. As you work on fast tonguing skills, pay attention to the tonguing fundamentals explained in Chapter 9.

Recognizing fast tonguing in musical notation

Composers, especially piano players who know little about clarinets, often place dots over notes in fast passages to indicate articulated notes. They want the music to sound light. That's all fine and dandy on the piano, but it often confuses clarinetists, who interpret the dots as calling for *secco* (very short) staccato. They try to play the passage that way and get all tied up. The moral of the story is to take these marks with a grain of salt and tongue the notes lightly, but not with short staccato style.

If you overreact to the dots by using a staccato syllable, your tongue either gets tired in a hurry and starts tripping on notes or just can't move fast enough.

Maintaining constant air flow

Tonguing on the clarinet, especially fast tonguing, requires constant airflow with little tongue. In other words, keep blowing. Use the tip of your tongue to briefly stop the reed vibration instead of stopping the air.

You're talking with the clarinet. When you speak a sentence, you keep the air flowing and use your lips and tongue to form the syllables and words. When you're speaking with the clarinet, keep the air flowing, too, using your tongue to articulate the notes. For additional details on maintaining air flow, see Chapter 9.

Keeping your tongue relaxed

When you're fast tonguing, don't let your tongue get all stressed out. Relax. Say "Tee," noting how hard your tongue presses against the roof of your mouth. Now say "Dee," and notice how much less pressure you use. When you're fast-tonguing, don't articulate with a staccato "Tee." Use a softer syllable. One of the following will do:

✔ Da

✔ Dee

✔ Du

Try each one to see which works best for you. Everyone has different preferences, so none of these choices is right or wrong.

The amount of time the tongue presses the reed against the tip rail determines the actual space (no sound) between notes. At fast tempos, you don't need much space between tongued notes. A clear and quick "D" is plenty.

To see just how much more relaxed your tongue and throat are with softer syllables, perform the following exercise:

1. **Place your hands lightly on your throat.**

2. **Say or sing "Tee" repeatedly very fast for at least six beats.**

3. **Say or sing "Dee" repeatedly very fast for at least six beats.**

Notice how much more relaxed your tongue and throat become when you eliminate T's from the tonguing syllable.

For staccato eighth and sixteenth notes at slow tempos, tongue with syllables that include T, such as "Tut." For staccato or nonstaccato eighth and sixteenth notes at fast tempos, tongue with syllables that start with D, such as "Dee."

Grouping tongued notes, syllable style

No matter how slowly you speak, you utter each word as a tight collection of syllables. You don't say "com-mu-ni-cate"; you say "communicate," slurring the syllables. In the same way, group each succession of tongued notes so that the notes play like syllables that make up a word. Try it without the clarinet first:

1. **Say several four-syllable words, repeating them faster and faster — for example, "Miss-i-ssip-pi," "Tall-a-hass-ee," "Col-o-ra-do."**

2. **Repeat the three words, this time adding "Da-Da-Da-Da" or the syllable of your choice after each word — for example, "Miss-i-ssip-pi," "Da-Da-Da-Da," "Tall-a-hass-ee," "Da-Da-Da-Da," "Col-o-ra-do," "Da-Da-Da-Da." Which was easier to say?**

   The take-home lesson here is that "Da-Da-Da-Da" is easier to say and comes out more quickly than genuine four-syllable words, because the "Da" syllables are not part of a complex word.

3. **With the metronome set to quarter note = 120, try vocalizing by alternating four-syllable words with "Da-Da-Da-Da" — for example "Ok-la-ho-ma," "Da-Da-Da-Da."**

   This step should really drive home the point that fast tonguing groups of notes is no different than slurring syllables when pronouncing a word.

When learning to play articulated passages, sing the tongued notes "Da-Da-Da" style before you try to play them.

Playing tongued sixteenth notes with accents on every downbeat raises your comfort level in grouping tongued notes. Perform the exercises shown in Figures 14-1 to 14-3. (The scale pattern shown in Figure 14-1 was first introduced by Kreutzer, who was a violinist, but clarinetists, including Baermann, and pianists, including Hannon, borrowed it for their books.)

Start slowly and then increase the tempo as you repeat each exercise four or five times. Try to accent all the downbeats and upbeats in each measure. When the fast tempo makes accenting all the notes impossible, accent only the downbeats and add crescendos in place of the eliminated upbeats. (For more about how to accent notes, check out Chapter 9.)

Figure 14-1:
Play the Kreutzer-Hanon returning scale on F in sixteenths (Track 64).

Figure 14-2:
Play the
Hanon
C-scale
pattern in
sixteenths
(Track 65).

Figure 14-3:
Play
"Boogie
Woogie"
(Track 66).

Play "Mazel Tov Simen Tov," as shown in Figure 14-4, playing all tongued notes with necessary accents and crescendos to the ends of phrases. Start slowly and then play faster and faster, using clear "Da's" for the tongued notes. Gradually increase the tempo to quarter note = 120 and then up to quarter note = 132.

Figure 14-4:
Play
"Mazel Tov
Simen Tov"
(Track 67).

Limbering Up for Faster Fingering

Playing fast slurred passages requires nimble and strong fingers, but more than just the fingers is involved. Familiarity with the notes and your own confidence contribute significantly to finger speed. Any hesitation slows you down.

Pairing notes and fingerings instinctively

To play fast, you must play instinctively. Your fingers must know what to do so they don't have to wait for orders from your brain. Professional athletes describe it as playing "in the zone."

Before you can play in the zone, however, you need to prepare in the practice studio. Learn the notes and their corresponding fingerings. Highlight the most unusual and difficult fingerings, and practice them even more until they're second nature.

One of the most efficient ways to build familiarity with notes is to learn patterns through a thorough knowledge of scales and arpeggios. See Chapter 16 for details and additional practice tips.

Gaining confidence at fast tempos

Speed is relative. Normally, you probably aren't comfortable driving 70 miles per hour in a 30-mile-an-hour zone, but if you just exited the highway, driving 30 miles an hour feels like a crawl.

The same is true for playing fast passages on the clarinet. To build your comfort and confidence levels, devote some practice time every day to playing fast. Use a metronome, and increase the speed of passages just one notch a day.

Undertaking strength training

Pressing down on tone holes and keys requires a certain amount of finger strength and endurance. I'm not about to recommend that your fingers pump iron or do pinky pushups, but your fingers do need to complete a practice session at least five days a week to perform some finger calisthenics on the clarinet.

When performing finger calisthenics, alternate finger groups just as you might alternate the use of different muscle groups in your weekly workout routine.

Developing smooth finger coordination

As your fingers scurry about on their various paths to tone holes and register keys, they're apt to crash into one another along the way. To prevent this from happening, work on your *raw technique,* or your coordination between the fingerings of two notes.

After you've learned all the notes and fingerings and are familiar with a passage, playing it smoothly usually comes down to ironing out the wrinkles in one or two places where you find the fingering most difficult. This removes the areas where your fingers get tripped up and enables you to maintain fluid, rhythmic finger movement throughout the piece.

To sharpen your raw technique and train your fingers to move rhythmically, practice daily trill and tremolo studies, as explained later in this chapter in the section "Practicing your fast fingers technique."

Pulling it all together

You're comfortable playing fast, you know the fingerings for all the notes, and your fingers are strong and well coordinated. Now you need to bring it all together and toss in some additional fundamentals so you can play those fast slurred passages on the clarinet and make them sound good, too. Here's what you need to do:

- ✔ Maintain constant air flow between the tongued notes. (Yeah, I know I've said that about 50 times already, but it's *that* important.)

- ✔ Always crescendo to the final notes of runs, because note response improves with proper breath support. (See Chapter 9 for more about crescendoing to notes.)

- ✔ Keep your fingers close to the tone holes and keys, as explained in Chapter 7. Famed performer and teacher Elsa Verdehr recommends having "sneaky fingers." Good hand and finger position makes raw technique much easier.

- ✔ Group slurred notes into manageable groups, making it more natural to play fast runs and rhythmic pulses. Adding accents can help.

✔ Move the fingers in a rhythmic fashion. Fast fingers are not wildly wiggling fingers. Some clarinet players find it helpful to snap the fingers down in a very precise fashion when playing fast.

Add accents to fast passages to gain some traction. Practice the accents until they become second nature. You may choose to play a fast passage with less predominant accents, but if you get into trouble, use the accents.

Practicing your fast fingers technique

The best way to hone your raw technique is by doing trill and tremolo studies. These studies include both narrow and wider skips, as well as isolate the finger changes between notes.

Perform the trill studies shown in Figure 14-5, which include note combinations that often give players the greatest difficulties. Always begin with C - D and G - A, because these give your weakest fingers a workout.

When you're first performing the exercises, identify the note combinations that give you the greatest difficulties, and then practice these combinations daily until they no longer seem difficult.

Figure 14-5:
Trill studies to challenge your fast fingers technique (Track 68).

Play the elongated scales in thirds, as shown in Figure 14-6. These are attributed to David Weber, famed former clarinet instructor at the Julliard School of Music. Practice the exercises in Figures 14-7 to 14-9 with crescendos, keeping your fingers curved and close to the clarinet, and adding accents on both downbeats and upbeats. When faster tempos make accenting both downbeats and upbeats impossible, replace the upbeat accents with crescendos.

These exercises are great for integrating the coordination required for playing between two note units such as you did in the trill studies or the elongated thirds. Note that they progress into longer passages in which scales and wider skips are often juxtaposed. If possible, play these exercises in other keys as well.

Figure 14-6: Play the elongated scales in thirds (Track 69).

Figure 14-7: A mix of trill studies and scales (Track 70).

Play the Hanon exercise in A major, as shown in Figure 14-8. This particular exercise combines skips and scales and is excellent for honing technique. Now play the same Hanon exercise in the key of A♭, as shown in Figure 14-9, accenting the first sixteenth note of each beat.

Figure 14-8: Hanon exercise in A major, changing the key signature to three sharps (Track 71).

Figure 14-9: Hanon exercise in the key of A♭, with accents on the first sixteenth note of each beat (Track 71).

Chapter 15

Tuning Up for Proper Pitch

*G*reat clarinet players are masters of the Double T: tone and tune.

  ✔ *Tone* is the character of the sound, which varies according to the instrument and the person playing it. Every clarinet player has a unique tone.

  ✔ *Tune* is the frequency of each note, which doesn't (or, at least, shouldn't) vary according to the instrument or the person playing it.

In a choir, for example, each singer has a unique voice (tone), but all singers must sing notes in tune (at the same pitch) for the group to sing with one voice. An out-of-tune singer or musician is a real standout, and not in a good way. However, a singer or musician with a unique, high-quality tone who sings or plays in tune stands out in a good way, particularly during solos.

Chapter 11 discusses tone in greater detail, providing several techniques for developing good tone on the clarinet. When you're playing in a band, you also want to make sure your instrument is in tune. Frequency variations of only a few cycles per second for any note really stand out and may ruin an otherwise stellar performance. In this chapter, you discover what tuning to the proper pitch is all about, how to tune your clarinet, and how to identify and correct common pitch problems.

Grasping the Concept of Tuning to the Proper Pitch

If you're not already well schooled in the concepts of tuning and pitch, put down that tuning fork and brush up on the basics. Pitch relates to two aspects of the notes you play, the notes themselves and the intervals between them:

- **Notes:** Each note has a distinct pitch. (Pitch is the same as frequency.) A2 plays at a frequency of 440 Hz. A half step up is A2♯ (or B2♭), which plays at a frequency of 466.16 Hz. Another half step up, or a full step up from A2, is B2, at a frequency of 493.88. When members of a band are playing the same note, they must all play it at the same pitch to be "in tune."

- **Intervals:** An interval is the distance, measured in frequency, between notes, or how much higher or lower one note is compared to another. For example, the interval between A2 and B2 is 53.88 Hz. As a convenience, musicians refer to the distance between notes in terms of half steps (the shortest distance between two notes), steps, seconds, thirds, fourths, and so on. For example, B2 is a step up, or a second, from A2. The distance between B2 and D2 is two steps up, or a third.

To determine the distance between notes, count the lines and spaces the notes are on, along with the lines and spaces between them, as shown in Figure 15-1. There are different kinds of thirds (major and minor), but this estimation gets you close enough.

Figure 15-1:
The interval between B1 and D1 is a third.

To play in tune, both the notes and the distance between them must be in tune.

High-quality clarinets (beginners as well as advanced) come close to being in tune, but no clarinet comes from the factory perfectly in tune. In addition, a number of variables can affect a clarinet's pitch, including room temperature, humidity, and the volume at which the notes are played.

Tuning to European musicians

When describing pitch as frequency, it's tempting to think of pitch as a purely scientific phenomenon. However, culture also plays a role. Proper pitch for a particular note in the United States is not always the same as proper pitch for the same note played in other countries.

For example, European musicians play at a higher pitch than Americans. They play A at a frequency of 444, whereas musicians in the U.S. play A between 440 and 442. This discrepancy explains why an American clarinetist may have difficulty playing along with a CD recorded by a European clarinetist.

Variations also are more pronounced on the clarinet because you don't just press one key for each note, as you do on a piano. With the exception of A and A♭ in the staff, you use multiple keys and tone holes to produce each note. As a result, almost all notes on the clarinet are a compromise between the pitch tendencies of the lower and higher notes that each finger combination produces. In other words, tuning often becomes more art than science.

Warming Up in the Bullpen

Tuning a chilly clarinet is nearly impossible. When the instrument is cold, the air inside it is cold, too. That cold air vibrates at a lower frequency because cold air molecules tend to be sluggish. This results in a lower pitch for every note you play. Before you tune your clarinet, warm it up. Either of the following methods, preferably both and in the order presented here, can do the trick.

Warming the outside first: The ol' armpit trick

A safe way to warm up your clarinet is to hold the upper and lower joints in your armpits, where your body temperature is the highest. Well, other places may be warmer, but. . . . Place the upper joint under one armpit and the lower joint under the other, and try to remember not to shake hands with anyone! Hold the upper and lower joints in place for a few minutes until they heat up to about room temperature. (The amount of time varies, depending on how cold the instrument is.)

This not only warms the instrument, but it prevents any cracking that may result when the interior of the clarinet heats up faster than the exterior. Players who live in very cold climates should always warm their clarinets in their armpits if the clarinet is very cold from being outside.

Warming the inside with a low E

When the outside of your clarinet is at least room temperature, you're safe to start warming your clarinet from the inside out. Play a low E, the note that results in the longest column of air. After playing low E, continue to warm up by playing other low tones and scales until the notes sound just about right. When they do, you know the clarinet is warm enough to start tuning it.

Professional players who play under bright lights have the opposite problem. Because bright lights create heat, the pitch in woodwind instruments can become sharp during performances, requiring frequent tune-ups throughout the performance.

Tuning Your Clarinet: Two Methods

You tune your clarinet using either of two methods, depending on whether you're practicing or playing alone, or performing with others:

- ✔ **Tuning by ear:** When playing with others, making instruments in tune with one another is more important than making them in tune with some ideal frequency, so you must tune by ear.

- ✔ **Using a tuner:** When you're practicing or playing alone, use a tuner. A tuner is a mechanical device that plays notes in tune and may also indicate whether a particular note is out of tune, either sharp or flat.

In the following sections, I explain how to tune your clarinet using each method.

Regardless of which method you follow to tune your clarinet, when your instrument is in tune, make a mental note of the barrel's position so you get used to that pitch. Pitch perception is in your head, so playing the same length clarinet all the time can increase your sensitivity to variations from the norm. Pulling out the barrel to play in tune also affects reed response, which is another reason to try to play with a consistent barrel position.

Tuning by ear

To tune by ear, one musician plays the tuning note while all the other musicians listen. Then all the musicians tune their instruments to the tuning note.

Figuring out which tuning note to play

The clarinet plays a note that's different from the tuning note, as explained in the following list:

- ✔ In orchestras, the oboe gives the pitch — an A concert, which is B2 for the clarinet.

- ✔ In bands, the first-chair clarinet gives the pitch — a B♭ concert, which is C for the clarinet.

- ✔ Most bands also have the first clarinet player give an F concert, which is open G for the clarinet. The open G (G2) is given so that those who play mostly in this range (clarinets who play the second clarinet part) can be more in tune.

- ✔ When playing with a piano, the piano always gives the tuning notes. For clarinets, it should be an A concert (B2 for the clarinet) and F concert (G2 for the clarinet). You need to tune to both B2 and G2 to establish a balance. G2 tends to be flat if you pull out the barrel joint far enough to make B2 play in tune. The band also tunes to two notes, B2♭ (clarinet C) and F (clarinet G2) for the same reason.

Whoa! You're probably wondering what this is all about and why the clarinet must play notes that differ from the tuning note. The difference comes from the fact that the tuning note is sounded by a concert-pitch instrument, whereas most clarinets are transposing instruments:

- ✔ **Concert-pitch instruments:** These instruments play notes that match the corresponding pitch on the piano. Playing C on a concert-pitch instrument matches C on the piano. Concert-pitch instruments include all the strings, along with the flute, oboe, trombone, bells, and xylophone. One type of clarinet, the C clarinet, is a concert-pitch instrument, as explained in Chapter 2.

- ✔ **Transposing instruments:** These instruments are built in different keys. For example, the most popular clarinet is the B♭ clarinet, written in the key of B♭. Because B♭ is a whole step below C, a B♭ clarinet must play C a whole step higher, as D. To play concert A, the clarinet must play B. The clarinet (except for the C clarinet), saxophone, trumpet (except for the C trumpet), and tuba are all transposing instruments.

Fortunately, music is usually written in different keys for transposing instruments, so you don't really have to think about it during a performance. You do need to think about it when tuning your instrument. If you're playing a B♭ clarinet and the oboe sounds concert A, you play a B. With an A clarinet, because A is three half steps below C, you need to play three steps higher to compensate; when the oboe plays concert A, you must play C, three half steps above A.

Making the right adjustments

For greatest success in tuning by ear, listen closely to the note and let it register in your inner ears (inside your brain) before you play your note. Here's the method I recommend, which I refer to as the "Half-Note Rest Follows Half-Note" method:

1. **Listen to the tuning note, which should be at least two slow beats in length.**

2. **Leave a half-note rest space so your brain has time to register the note.**

3. **Play your note and listen to determine whether it is the same pitch level as the tuning note. See Figure 15-2.**

Figure 15-2:
Take a half-
note rest
and then
play your
note (Track
72).

4. **Make adjustments until your note matches the tuning note.**

   If you're playing with a piano, have the pianist repeat the tuning note. Be patient — it's worth the extra time to repeat the procedure until you're in tune.

5. **If you're out of tune, make some minor adjustments to correct your pitch:**

   • **Sharp:** If the note sounds sharp, pull out the barrel, twisting it back and forth like the lid of a jar as you pull, a distance equivalent to about the thickness of a dime and then gradually a bit more. It doesn't hurt to pull the barrel out a distance equivalent to about the thickness of a nickel. When you're done pulling, twist to realign the barrel so the brand signature is in front and centered with the A key. If you're consistently sharp, you may need to get a longer barrel. Try a 67-mm barrel instead of the standard 66-mm barrel. (See Chapter 3 for more about choosing a barrel.)

- **Flat:** If the note sounds flat, push in the barrel. If you're consistently flat, you may need to get a shorter barrel. Instead of using a 66-mm barrel, try a 65-mm barrel.

Making minor adjustments during a performance

During a performance, your clarinet is likely to heat up. Your hands, the lights, the stage heat, your breath, and increased lip pressure can all make you play sharper. To make minor adjustments to account for these changes, try adjusting the length of the clarinet at other joints:

✔ If you're in tune with the tuning note but go sharp in the middle of a piece, pull out the mouthpiece slightly to make a minor adjustment. It's easier to give the mouthpiece a quick bump or tug during a rest than it is to twist out a barrel joint.

✔ If open G is flat but the upper notes are in tune, pull the upper and lower joints slightly apart, no more than the thickness of a dime. This affects the notes where tone holes of the lower joint are covered.

✔ Pull out the bell (where it attaches to the lower joint) slightly for B2 and to achieve a richer sound. Many professionals like to pull out the bell because it makes the clarinet longer. Remember, the longer the clarinet, the greater the resistance and the fuller the sound.

Using your tuner

For $50 or less, you can pick up an electronic "chromatic" clarinet tuner at your local music store or purchase one online. I found one online for $26.95 that runs on a 9-volt battery (not included). It includes an LCD meter and LED lamps that indicate pitch (sharp, flat, or in tune) for the LEDs and a sliding scale for the LCD meter. It also has automatic note selection so the tuner can tell which note you're playing. You can use a tuner in three ways, as I explain in the following sections.

Tuning with your tuner by ear

Listen to the pitch the tuner plays and tune by ear, as explained earlier in the section "Tuning by ear."

Letting the meter do its job

Play the notes in the chromatic scale as you watch the meter to see whether you're in tune, flat, or sharp. (See Figure 15-3.)

Figure 15-3:
A chromatic tuner indicates whether you're in tune, flat, or sharp.

Tuning by intervals: The basics

Train your ear to tune by intervals. (For more about intervals, see "Grasping the Concept of Tuning to the Proper Pitch," earlier in this chapter.)

Most clarinet players discover that tuning by intervals is easier than tuning by specific notes, because intervals, especially fourths and fifths, tend to be easier for most folks to recognize. Before getting into specifics about fourths and fifths, practice the following exercise to train your ear to recognize correct intervals:

1. **While looking at the tuner, tune to the first of the two notes in the desired interval.**

   For example, if you're tuning to a fourth and you choose C and F as the two notes, use the tuner to tune the clarinet to C.

2. **While looking at the tuner, play the second note of the interval as you hear it in your inner ear and as you watch the needle on the tuner, and make minor embouchure and leverage adjustments until it is in tune.**

   To follow along with the example, play F as the second note.

3. **Play the first note again with the tuner to make sure it's in tune.**

4. **While looking away, play the second note of the interval with the same pitch you heard when you played it with the tuner.**

   As you're playing the second note, glance back at the tuner to see whether the second note is in tune.

5. **If the second note is in tune, you should now have a better idea of how the interval between the two notes sounds.**

   If the second note is not in tune, correct the pitch of the note as you continue playing it, and then skip back to Step 3 and try again.

The easiest intervals for most people to recognize in their inner ear are fourths and fifths, because they've heard plenty of songs with fourths and fifths in them and can readily identify the interval. It all boils down to having the right interval stored in the memory of your inner ear and then comparing the sound of the interval you play to the sound of the stored interval. The tuner doesn't do it for you; the tuner only helps confirm what your inner ear is telling you.

In the following sections, I show you how to tune to intervals already stored in your inner ear through popular tunes, including "Here Comes the Bride" and the music from the movie *2001: A Space Odyssey*.

Checking intonation on fourths

To hear what a fourth sounds like, sing Mendelssohn's "Wedding March" ("Here Comes the Bride"), or "Christmas Carol," "O Tannenbaum," or "I've Been Working on the Railroad."

To hear fourths in tune on the clarinet, perform the exercise shown in Figure 15-4 with a tuner, following the procedure explained in the previous section.

Checking intonation on fifths

To hear what a fifth sounds like, hum the beginning notes of the theme from the movie *2001: A Space Odyssey,* which is the opening of Richard Strauss's "Zus Spach Zarathrustra."

To hear fifths in tune on the clarinet, perform the exercise shown in Figure 15-5 with a tuner, following the procedure explained in the previous section, "Tuning by intervals: The basics."

Figure 15-4: Check the intonation on fourths. Repeat the play-tune pattern with each interval (Track 73).

Figure 15-5: Check the intonation on fifths. Repeat the play-tune pattern with each interval (Track 74).

Recognizing Your Clarinet's Pitch Tendencies

Even when your clarinet is officially "in tune," not all the notes fall perfectly in step. Every clarinet has certain *pitch tendencies,* notes that are slightly out of tune. Several factors can contribute to a clarinet's pitch tendencies, including the following:

- ✔ Even if it's fresh from the factory, your clarinet itself isn't automatically in tune.

- ✔ The tone holes and keys do double duty, so they're involved in playing both low and high notes, and their location on the instrument has to be a compromise.

- ✔ Slight variations in the mouthpiece mean that differences in chambers and bores can greatly affect intonation.

Half the challenge of playing in tune is your ability to recognize the pitch tendencies of your clarinet and make the necessary adjustments — usually by choosing fingerings to play the problem notes in tune.

You can "lip" notes higher or lower by increasing or decreasing tension on the lower lip, but reserve this technique for extremely minor adjustments. Lipping notes causes instability in the tone and changes the focus of notes and, hence, the width of the ribbon of whatever line of notes you're playing. (See Chapter 11 for more about maintaining a stable ribbon of sound.)

Correcting general pitch tendencies

Two pitch tendencies are fairly predictable, regardless of idiosyncrasies related to the clarinet. Fortunately, they're pretty easy to correct:

- ✔ **Low and loud:** When they get all warmed up, clarinets tend to play slightly on the flat side on very low notes played at a very high volume. If you're playing very low and loud, push the barrel in as much as possible, to keep the pitch up.

- ✔ **Soft and slow:** Most notes on the clarinet play slightly sharp at very soft dynamic levels. Because the slow movements of many pieces are marked at the quieter dynamic levels, try pulling the mouthpiece out a slight bit before you play them.

When you need to make very minor tuning adjustments, jiggling the mouthpiece out of the barrel a bit is easier than twisting the barrel out from the upper joint.

Letting your fingers do the work: Alternate fingerings for problem notes

Adding a tone hole here or opening a key there can help you correct out-of-tune notes with fingerings. The following sections highlight notes on the clarinet where pitch problems most commonly occur and reveal alternate fingerings that may help correct the problems. These alternate fingerings by no means represent all the possible solutions. (See Appendix A for additional fingering charts and names of books that cover clarinet fingerings more comprehensively.)

The alternate fingerings presented in the following sections usually work best on notes you hold longer. They're less practical for playing fast technical passages, because they tend to be somewhat awkward.

Correcting problem notes below the staff

Several notes below the staff are known troublemakers. The following list identifies the most likely culprits and provides alternate fingerings for playing these same notes in tune:

- ✔ **Low A:** Low A tends to play sharp. Lower this note to pitch by stiffening the finger over the lowest tone hole and resting it on the rod that holds the ring keys, as shown in Figure 15-6. This is called shading the tone.

- ✔ **Low B:** Low B tends to play sharp, especially if played *pp* (pianissimo, or very softly). Use the chromatic fingering or shade the note downward the same way you do for low A. Playing very softly on any note can cause the pitch to go sharp on the clarinet because of the added pressure on the reed.

- ✔ **Low D:** Low D tends to be sharp, especially at soft dynamic levels. Add the right-hand low B/E key or close the sixth tone hole, as shown in Figure 15-6.

Play low A, low B, and low D using the alternate fingerings shown in Figure 15-6.

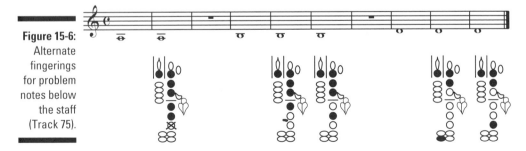

Figure 15-6: Alternate fingerings for problem notes below the staff (Track 75).

Correcting problem notes in the staff

Even notes in the staff can cause trouble. The following list identifies the most common problem notes in the staff and provides alternate fingerings for playing these notes in tune:

- ✔ **E2:** First-line E (E2) tends to be flat. Raise the note to pitch by adding the C♯ – G♯ key. If it plays very flat, add the first trill key on the upper joint.

- ✔ **F2:** First-space F (F2) tends to be flat. Raise this note by adding the first trill key on the upper joint.

- ✔ **Open G:** Open G tends to be flat. Raise this note by opening the first trill key on the upper joint.

- ✔ **Throat tones:** All the throat tones tend to be a loose mix of sharp and flat. Take special care to choose a clarinet that plays the throat tones in tune or slightly sharp, not flat. See Chapter 13 for special fingerings for throat tones.

- ✔ **C2:** C2 tends to be sharp. Have your technician lower the lowest pad on the instrument slightly.

Play E2, F2, and G2 using the alternate fingerings shown in Figure 15-7.

Figure 15-7:
Alternate fingerings for problem notes in the staff (Track 76).

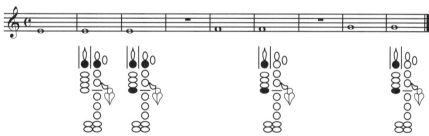

Correcting problem notes above the staff

You may encounter problem notes above the staff, too. The following list identifies the most common problem notes above the staff and provides alternate fingerings for playing these notes in tune:

- ✔ **C3:** C3 tends to be sharp. Use your fingers to close the tone holes on the lower joint.

- ✔ **C3♯:** C3♯ tends to be sharp. Never play this note with the low A♭/G♯ pinky down.

- ✔ **F4:** F4 tends to be flat. Add the fork key on the lower joint to bring it up to pitch. Many experienced players use this fingering whenever possible.

Play C, C♯, and F using the alternate fingerings shown in Figure 15-8.

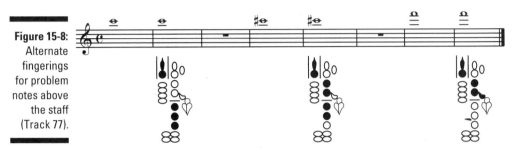

Figure 15-8:
Alternate fingerings for problem notes above the staff (Track 77).

Tackling Bigger Tuning Problems

You've tried everything and can't seem to fix a nagging out-of-tune note. Now what? Consult a more experienced player first. If that person can't figure it out, your clarinet may be experiencing a more serious issue.

In some cases, you have to pull out the barrel so far that you create a large gap in the bore (inside the clarinet), called a *Lacuna,* that can cause other tuning problems. Where the gap is located, the bore hole is wider. This can also occur between the mouthpiece and the barrel if you pull out the mouthpiece more than a thirty-second of an inch.

If you really need to pull out the barrel or mouthpiece that far to tune your clarinet, you may be able to fill the gap (Lacuna) with a tuning ring that fits inside the top or bottom of the barrel. The tuning ring serves a dual purpose:

✔ The tuning ring fills the Lacuna so that the bore hole is a uniform diameter where the parts of the instrument have been pulled apart.

✔ After you insert the tuning ring, you can push the two parts snug against the tuning ring, retaining the added length you need to be in tune while also strengthening the joint.

You can order tuning rings from Muncy Winds or Lomax Classic Mouthpieces. Some music stores also carry them.

For really out-of-tune notes, your last resort is to take your clarinet to the clarinet doctor, a technician. However, fixing badly out-of-tune notes usually requires the craftsmanship of an artisan technician. Here are the names of four artisan technicians to start you on your search: Morrie Backun (Backun Musical Services), Phil Muncy (Muncy Winds), Tom Ridenour, and Brannen Woodwinds.

Chapter 16

Heading to the Practice Studio

In This Chapter

▶ Establishing a productive practice routine

▶ Reinforcing what you've learned with exercises and etudes

▶ Discovering strategies for playing tough passages

*P*ractice makes perfect, right? Well, not necessarily. Unproductive practice can be worse than no practice. If you practice the wrong technique, you develop bad habits that are tough to shake. If you focus exclusively on improving your technique, you miss out on exercises designed to improve your tone and your ability to play difficult passages. And if your practice sessions are all work and no play, you can become a very dull player — worse, you may lose interest in playing altogether.

In this chapter, I explain how to make your practice sessions more productive and enjoyable. You discover how to block out some quality time, structure your practice sessions to get more out of them, play in front of a small audience to raise the bar, and have some fun so you learn how to relax and retain your joy of playing. I also introduce you to collections of exercises and *etudes* (short compositions more for practice than performance) and to other resources that can make your practice sessions more productive. And I reveal a few additional practice strategies for improving your technique.

Building a Solid Foundation for Practice

Practice is essential to improvement, especially when you're just starting to play any woodwind instrument, because it's such a physical activity. With practice, you not only improve your ability to read music and master essential techniques, but you also strengthen the muscles and develop the physical coordination to play well.

Fortunately, practice needn't equate with drudgery. By blocking out some quality time, roughing out a practice schedule, pacing yourself, and taking time to play just for the fun of it, you make practice sessions more enjoyable, productive, and rewarding. In the following sections, I show you how to develop practice routines — and occasionally break them — for optimum results.

The secret to productive practice is to be a talented turtle: patient and persistent.

Blocking out some quality time

Life can get pretty hectic. You probably go to school or have a job — or both. You have friends and family who need you, meals to eat, TV shows and movies to watch, places to go, books to read, Facebook, texting, and a whole slew of other demands on your time, focus, and energy. With so much going on, clarinet practice can fall through the cracks, so make it a priority. Set aside a block of time to spend with your clarinet, according to the following guidelines:

- ✔ At least 30 minutes a day.
- ✔ Five to six days a week. Although practicing every day is ideal, taking a day off won't hurt you.

As with most things worthy of our time, quality time is more important than quantity. Dedicating a half-hour to a concentrated practice session is likely to produce better results than sort of practicing for an hour while watching *American Idol.*

Make a date with your clarinet, mark the dates and times on a calendar, and check off each date after your practice session. This holds you accountable and gives you a sense of accomplishment.

Structuring your practice sessions

Structuring your practice sessions improves your ability to improve in all areas of playing the clarinet:

- ✔ **Technique:** Working on fingering develops required finger strength and coordination.
- ✔ **Tone:** Focusing on embouchure and breathing develops endurance to play gracefully with full expression.

✔ **Problem solving:** Playing difficult passages enables you to identify problem areas and invest more practice time where it's really needed.

In the following sections, I provide guidance on how to work on all three of these key areas, followed by a seven-step practice routine that covers them all.

Runners don't just run around for an hour and call it practice. They typically follow a structured practice session. They may begin with some warm-up exercises followed by stretching, and then spend a portion of a training session working on speed. On alternate days, they may focus on developing strength or endurance.

Technique

When practicing technique, let your fingers do the walking. Technique exercises call for finger motion between individual notes and for playing groups of notes:

✔ Finger motion between individual notes requires strength and coordination. Rhythmic trill studies, as explained in Chapter 14, are best for this.

✔ The goal of practicing finger motion for groups of notes is to enable you to hear the note patterns in your head while feeling them in your fingers. Playing scales and arpeggios is most effective in getting a feel for various note patterns. (See "Scales and arpeggios," later in this chapter, for details.)

Tone

Working on tone is like engaging in endurance training. In addition to increasing your lung capacity, you develop techniques for inhaling, exhaling, and delivering air into the clarinet more efficiently. Breathing and embouchure control are key in improving tone and being able to produce the more expressive qualities in the music.

Following are two of the best exercises for toning up:

✔ Play very long tones, such as B2 in Figure 16-1. Incorporate crescendos and diminuendos into the long tones, to build control of your dynamic range, from the softest to the loudest volume levels you can play. Doing this requires much more muscle control, making time spent on the long tones more productive. With the metronome set at quarter note = 60, crescendo for eight beats and then diminuendo for eight beats.

✔ Play slow, beautiful pieces or etudes. (For more about etudes, see "Honing Your Skills and Technique with Exercises and Etudes," later in this chapter.)

Figure 16-1: Improve your tone by playing very long notes (Track 78).

Problem solving: Tackling difficult passages

Practice less of what you know and more of what you don't know or struggle with. This is a good strategy when mastering any skill or subject. For example, if you're better in English than in math, you may need to force yourself to spend more time studying math. Employ this strategy in your practice sessions by focusing more time on the most difficult passages.

Play through a piece and highlight the sections that trip you up. Count the difficult passages and then add them to your practice schedule, to focus on learning one or two per day.

Spend less time, not no time, on easier passages. At some point, you want to play the entire piece, and that means being able to play both the easy and the more difficult passages, transitioning smoothly between them.

Getting in the groove: A seven-step routine

The structure of each practice session and the amount of time you spend on technique, tone, new lines, and difficult passages is likely to vary, depending on your individual needs and whether you're working on general skill-building or preparing for a performance. However, having a basic routine in place provides structure to your practice sessions. You can establish a structured routine and then modify it as necessary so that you spend different amounts of time on each step as your needs change.

Here's a daily seven-step practice routine I recommend:

1. **Warm up with several long tones.**

   This warms up both you and your clarinet. Include crescendos and diminuendos in your long tones to develop control of your dynamics (see Figure 16-1).

2. **Play several trill or tremolo studies.**

   See Chapter 14 for trill and tremolo studies. Try to focus on the combinations of notes that cause coordination problems for you.

3. **Work on some mechanical exercises to integrate single skips into the context of short passages.**

   See "Mechanical exercises," later in this chapter, for more about mechanical exercises and resources for such exercises.

4. **Play scales and/or arpeggios.**

   See "Scales and arpeggios" for more about scales and arpeggios.

5. **Play some etudes or pieces you're working on.**

   See "Honing Your Skills and Technique with Exercises and Etudes," later in this chapter, for details. Also see "Additional Resources for Productive Practices," near the end of this chapter, for recommendations on additional collections of music suitable for practice sessions.

   Take a systematic approach to learning new music. If an etude has 12 lines of music, divide 12 lines by 5 practice sessions per week, to determine that you must learn a little more than 2 lines per session. In each practice session, review the lines you've already learned.

6. **If a performance is coming up, review all the difficult passages in each piece daily and play straight through each piece.**

   This builds the necessary endurance for the performance.

7. **End your session by playing pieces you love and don't necessarily want to play for others.**

   Just play for fun and for yourself.

As a ballpark figure, beginning and intermediate players should spend about 80 percent of each practice session on exercises and etudes, and the other 20 percent on ensemble and solo literature (music). Advanced players should spend about half their time on exercises and etudes, and the other half on ensemble music and solo literature.

Practicing with a tiny audience

Playing a musical instrument for your own edification is fine, but most musicians enjoy playing for others. If this is your goal in learning a particular piece, then at some point in the process of practicing it (before you perform it to a general audience), play it for a couple friends.

This is exactly how Broadway does it. Broadway musicals always play out of town before they open in New York City. This gives the performers a chance to iron out any wrinkles in the performance and polish it for the Big Apple.

Having some fun, too!

Except for the many guys who learn guitar just to pick up chicks, most people choose to play a musical instrument because it sounds like fun. Unfortunately, learning to play an instrument may sometimes feel more like work than play, leading many to abandon their instruments long before they get to the fun part.

Having some fun during practice is important for two reasons:

- ✔ **Fun keeps you going.** It reminds you why you picked up the clarinet in the first place.

- ✔ **Playing for fun is relaxing.** It enables you to *play* in every sense of the word and put your own personality and emotion into the music. Often musicians sound their best when they're being playful and playing a piece they really love.

End every practice session by playing a piece of music you love. To make this a no-pressure deal, choose a piece that you're *not* planning to play in a performance. Just play it for fun!

Honing Your Skills and Technique with Exercises and Etudes

The most efficient way to develop your clarinet-playing skills and technique is to play exercises and etudes:

- ✔ **Exercises:** Drills written primarily for developing skills through repetition

- ✔ **Etudes:** Short compositions for a solo instrument written more for practice than performance

Exercises and etudes are the staple of any clarinet player's practice sessions. Fortunately, plenty of them are available for the clarinet. In the following sections, I introduce you to the resources I've found most useful for my students and me.

Learning by rote with exercises

If you do something often enough, eventually you'll practically be able to do it in your sleep. That's the idea behind playing exercises written for the clarinet. By practicing a particular piece, passage, or technique repeatedly, you eventually memorize it to the point at which playing it becomes almost instinctive.

Your practice routine should include two types of exercises:

- ✔ **Mechanical:** For building finger dexterity, coordination, and strength

- ✔ **Scales and arpeggios:** For gaining comfort in playing all the notes in the full range of the clarinet and transitioning between notes

In the following sections, I introduce you to several popular and useful collections of exercises, scales, and arpeggios for use during your practice sessions.

Mechanical exercises

Mechanical exercises focus on particular fingerings alone and the context of the notes around them. Following are two of the most commonly used collections of *mechanical* (also referred to as *mechanism*) exercises:

- ✔ *Celebrated Method for the Clarinet,* by Hyacinthe Klose, published by Carl Fischer. Many clarinetists call this the "Bible of the Clarinet." It includes two large sections of "mechanism" exercises for developing raw technique. Figure 16-2 shows a sample exercise from the book, an excellent exercise for throat tones. If you buy only one clarinet method book, this is the one to get. It takes clarinet players from ground zero to advanced levels.

- ✔ *Vade Mecum du Clarinettiste,* by Paul Jeanjean, published by Leduc. This book contains many mechanism and articulation exercises, along with a long exercise for developing technique for notes played by the left hand. Figure 16-3 shows a sample exercise from the book; it's an excellent chromatic note-to-note study.

Both books are suitable for players of all levels.

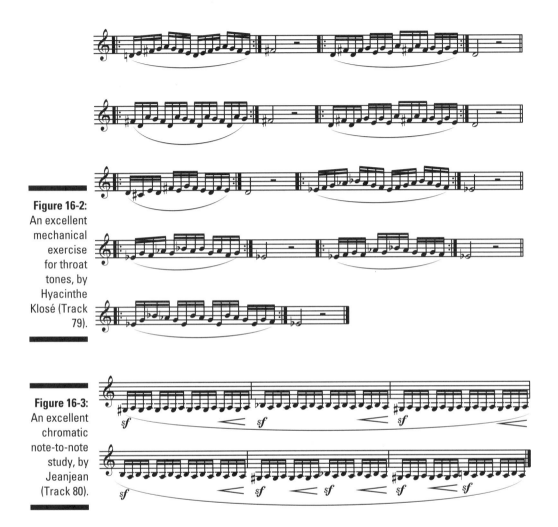

Figure 16-2: An excellent mechanical exercise for throat tones, by Hyacinthe Klosé (Track 79).

Figure 16-3: An excellent chromatic note-to-note study, by Jeanjean (Track 80).

Scales and arpeggios

Scales and arpeggios are the vocabulary of music. For the clarinet, they comprise about 300 different "words" used to produce all phrases in clarinet music:

✔ **Scales:** A scale is a series of notes varying in pitch according to a specific scheme and usually within an octave. Do-ra-mi-fa-so-la-ti-do is a scale. Scales also function as musical "glue," often filling the gaps between notes.

✔ **Arpeggios:** For many instruments, an arpeggio is a chord with the notes played separately in succession rather than simultaneously. On a clarinet, you can play only one note at a time, so you can't play bona fide "chords." Arpeggios enable you to practice harmonies on the clarinet and outline the harmonic progression of the music. Arpeggios are so similar to chords that an arpeggio is often referred to as "the arpeggiated version of a chord."

Following are four of the most commonly used collections of scales and arpeggios for the clarinet:

✔ *Rubank Clarinet Method,* by H. Voxman, published by Rubank Publications. This is the number one method book for beginning clarinetists. It contains scales and arpeggios that are well suited to beginners.

✔ *Clarinet Method, Volume III,* by Carl Baermann, published by Carl Fischer. This is an excellent book for upper-intermediate and advanced players. It contains scales, arpeggios, scales in thirds, and returning scale patterns in the full range of the clarinet, including the upper-altissimo notes to C4. Figure 16-4 shows one of the scales from this book.

✔ *Twenty Four Varied Scales and Exercises,* by J. B. Albert, published by Carl Fischer. This is an excellent choice for intermediate players. It presents all the arpeggios and scales in thirds in the normal clarinet range. Figure 16-5 shows a sample scale in thirds from the book.

✔ *Gammes et Exercises,* by Hamelin, published by Leduc. *Gammes* means "scales" in French. It's an excellent book for upper-level intermediate and advanced players. It contains short exercises that integrate the scales and arpeggios. The book is also excellent for learning the high notes on the clarinet. Figure 16-6 shows a sample of an exercise that combines arpeggios.

You may not be able to find these books at traditional booksellers, even Amazon.com; shop for them at music stores instead. Luyben Music of Kansas City (www.luyben.com) carries an excellent selection of books and sheet music for the clarinet.

Figure 16-4:
Scale as
written by
Baermannn
(Track 81).

Figure 16-5: Scale in thirds as written by Albert (Track 82).

Figure 16-6: Combined arpeggio as written by Hamelin (Track 83).

Gaining concentrated practice with etudes

An etude is a short composition, typically much longer than an exercise, written more for concentrated practice than performance. You play etudes for the same reason you pop a 500 mg vitamin C tablet instead of eating ten oranges a day: to get what you need as efficiently as possible. Instead of playing 20 or 30 pieces to experience and reinforce a particular concept or technique, you play a two-page etude that includes several repetitions of the concept or technique. Very good etudes are not boring to play or listen to. Many of them are fine pieces of music and may even be performed for the public.

Etudes play several important roles in your practice routine. They

- ✔ Reinforce concepts learned through exercises, such as the exercises sprinkled throughout this book
- ✔ Reinforce common patterns, including scales and arpeggios
- ✔ Help develop music reading skills
- ✔ Serve as a great way to build endurance

Most etude books combine study pieces that address technique, rhythmic issues, and melodic playing and have been written by composers who lived in European countries such as Germany, France, and Italy — places where the clarinet developed or where a great deal of music for the clarinet was written. Each etude genre has slightly different sounds and different styles, usually influenced by the clarinet tradition in that country.

Practice with a variety of etude books to acquaint yourself with different sounds and rhythms. Variety in etudes is the spice of life!

The following section introduces you to the most popularly used books that include excellent etude collections for beginners, followed by intermediate-level etude books grouped by country: Germany, France, Italy, and the United States. These are by no means the only countries where etudes have been written, but clarinetists from all around the world use these etude collections.

Etudes for beginners

The following books contain excellent collections of exercises and etudes for beginners and upper-level beginners:

- ✔ *Rubank Clarinet Method,* by H. Voxman, published by Rubank Publications. This is the number one method for beginning clarinetists. It contains exercises for learning chalumeau and clarion notes of the clarinet, as well as rhythm. It also contains short duets.

- ✔ *Rubank Intermediate Clarinet Method,* by H. Voxman, published by Rubank Publications. Even though the title includes the word "intermediate," this book works well for upper-level beginners. It is excellent for learning alternate fingerings, and it contains short duets as well.

Etudes from Germany/Austria

Etudes from Germany and Austria carry the sounds of Weber, Mozart, and Beethoven. Two collections from Germany stand out among the rest:

- ✔ *Clarinet Method Volumes I–III,* by Carl Baermann, published by Carl Fischer.

    The melodic etudes in Baermann's Volume II, one of which is shown in Figure 16-7, are among the most beautiful in etude literature.

- ✔ *416 Progressive Daily Studies for the Clarinet, Volumes I–IV,* by Kroepsch, published by Carl Fischer. These are highly technical etudes suitable for upper-level intermediate players. They combine arpeggios and scales.

Figure 16-7: Melodic etude from *Clarinet Method, Volume II* (Track 84).

Etudes from France

Composers from France have developed several excellent collections of etudes. The music in the Klosé and Rose books listed here sound like a mix of German and French music:

✔ *Clarinet Method,* by Hyacinthe Klosé, published by Carl Fischer.

The pattern etudes in the Klosé book, one of which is shown in Figure 16-8, are among the most helpful in the etude literature. If you buy only one method book, purchase the Complete Edition of the Klosé book. It is written to take clarinet players from ground zero to the advanced level. It contains mechanism exercises and exercises and etudes of all descriptions, as well as excellent duets.

✔ *Progressive and Melodic Etudes,* Books 1 and 2, by Paul Jeanjean, published by Leduc. These books were written by a clarinet professor at the Paris Conservatory closer to the twentieth century. They contain more modern sounds, in the sense that they don't sound like Beethoven. The melodies are highly influenced by French folk songs.

✔ *Forty Etudes* and *Thirty-Two Etudes,* by C. Rose, published by Carl Fischer. *Forty Etudes* comes in two volumes. Both books present a combination of upper intermediate level technical etudes and phrasing studies. *Thirty-Two Etudes* is one of the most popular books in the entire clarinet etude literature. It contains upper intermediate etudes and phrasing studies.

Figure 16-8:
A pattern etude from Klosé's *Clarinet Method* (Track 85).

Etudes from Italy

The following etude collections hailing from Italy deserve mention:

✔ *Clarinet Method,* by Lebanci, published by Ricordi. This is another complete method book, like the Klosé book. I mention it because it has some excellent duets and other melodic studies that sound slightly different from those included in the Klosé book.

✔ *Rhythmical Articulation,* by Bona, published by Schirmer and *Practical Study of the Scales,* by Stievenard, also published by Schirmer. These are the two best books for learning rhythm.

Etudes from the United States

The following two books from the United States are great for developing technique for all styles of music, including music written in the twentieth century. Both were written by Americans:

- *Hand-in-Hand with Hannon,* by Buddy Defranco, published by Hal Leonard. This book is excellent for jazz and classical players. It contains material on improvising, along with the Hannon piano exercises transcribed for the clarinet. (The Hannon piano exercises combine short groups of scales and arpeggios, much like players use when improvising modern jazz.)

- *Odd-Meter Etudes for All Instruments in the Treble Clef,* by Gates and Everette, published by Alfred Publishing. This is an excellent book for players trying to develop the ability to play mixed-meter, rhythmically complex twentieth-century music.

Sharpening Your Skills with Three More Practice Tips

Clarinet players and teachers constantly discover new ways of playing and teaching the clarinet, and they share their discoveries freely with the clarinet community. Over time, this has contributed significantly to enriching the art form and raising the bar for both players and composers.

In the following sections, I reveal three of my favorite tips specifically for practicing the clarinet, from three accomplished clarinet teachers and players.

Slowing down to get better faster

Famed clarinet player and teacher Mitchell Lurie used to say, "The fastest way to learn a piece of music is slow." Playing a passage slowly helps you see what is in the music and relate it to the scale and arpeggio patterns you already know.

Imagine driving down a mile of winding country road at 80 miles per hour. The entire time, all you'd be thinking about is keeping your car on the road and not smashing into a farmhouse or a wayward cow. At the end of the road, you'd remember little or nothing of what you saw — and probably didn't even notice. Drive the same road at 20 miles an hour, and you could talk for hours about all the fields you saw, the farmhouses, the crops and animals, and the architecture and colors.

When you're picking up a new song, slow down. Smell the roses. Take some time to absorb the details.

Practicing the opposite extreme

Robert Sprenkle, former oboe teacher at Eastman School of Music, described his approach to practice like this: "Practice is where you *eliminate* what you don't want and *reinforce* what you do want." This means exaggerating the opposite. If a note keeps coming out too short, practice playing it waaayyy too long. If it comes out too softly, practice it waaayyy too loud.

To gain some practice at exaggerating the extreme, play the passage shown in Figure 16-9. To be sure the eighth notes on the upbeat of a measure aren't too short, play them again with eighths and dotted quarters to get used to playing and hearing them as long notes. If you tend to perform a passage too softly when nervous, practice the same passage by playing it too loudly.

Figure 16-9: Exaggerate the opposite (Track 86).

Playing beat-to-beat for fast passages

One of the best ways to crank up your speed on a fast passage is to practice it using the beat-to-beat method developed by the late Leon Russianoff, a former clarinet teacher at the Juilliard School of Music. This system helps players develop speed in a passage by playing one group of notes at a time.

1. **Fire up your metronome so you can gauge your tempo.**

2. **Play from the sixteenth notes of each successive beat to the following beat, but turn the note on the following beat into a quarter note, as shown in Figure 16-10. Continue to do this for each successive beat in the bar that contains sixteenth notes, or other short (fast) note values.**

    This may sound complicated, but when you see it in music, as shown in the figure, it's pretty clear.

3. **Play the passage beat to beat faster and faster, keeping an eye on the metronome, until you're 20 points faster than the tempo for the piece. Then go back and play it at tempo, as written, instead of beat to beat.**

Whenever you need to learn a fast passage, practice it using this beat-to-beat method, and you'll quickly gain confidence in playing the passage fast.

Figure 16-10:
Practice playing fast passages with the beat-to-beat method (Track 87).

Additional Resources for Productive Practices

Practicing is fun and all, but it's all about preparing to play music that you love. The following list provides an outstanding array of solo collections from the clarinet repertory. Well-edited collections are the most economical way to obtain multiple pieces of sheet music. Luyben Music of Kansas City (www.luyben.com), which has the largest stock of clarinet music in the United States, provided the following list of collections. All the items listed here are in print as of the writing of this book:

- *Amazing Solos,* edited by Howard Harrison, published by Boosey and Hawkes. Good transcriptions of exciting and varied music for late-elementary level players.

- *Bravo Clarinet,* by Carol Barratt, published by Boosey and Hawkes. Easy, fun, and mostly all-original compositions.

- *Clarinet Collection,* with CD, by Hal Leonard. Volume 1 is easy to intermediate; volume 2 is intermediate. Both contain literature suitable for recitals or contests (from the Schirmer library).

- *Compositions for Clarinet,* with CD, by Graham Lyons, published by Useful Music. These original pieces for beginners combine the best of various styles of music, including folk, rock, boogie, dance, classical, romantic, and jazz.

- *Concert Repertoire for Clarinet,* by Harris and Johnson, published by Faber. Transcriptions and originals for late elementary to early intermediate players, from Baermann to Gershwin.

✔ *Contest and Concert Album Collection for B♭ Clarinet Solo* (CD available), edited by Himie Voxman, published by Hal Leonard. Includes clarinet solos and piano accompaniment. The accompaniment CD includes full performances by professional players and tracks with piano accompaniment.

✔ *Festival Performance Solos — Clarinet,* Volumes 1 and 2, published by Carl Fischer. Both volumes are for intermediate players and include many Langenus and Bellison arrangements.

✔ *First Repertoire for Clarinet,* edited by Paul Harris and Emma Johnson, published by Faber. Includes 16 easy to intermediate selections for clarinet and piano, from Bruch to Britten, Telemann to Alkan. It also features classics from shows and television, including Cole Porter's "Night and Day" and Barrington Pheloung's theme from *Inspector Morse.*

✔ *Music Through Time,* Volumes 1, 2, and 3, edited by Paul Harris, published by Oxford University Press. Selections designed to provide elementary, late elementary, and intermediate players with engaging material. Selections in each volume are arranged chronologically and include notes to help students relate the style of music to its period.

✔ *Rubank Book of Clarinet Solos,* edited by Himie Voxman, published by Hal Leonard. Collection includes 11 clarinet solos with accompaniment from the Rubank solo sheet music library.

✔ *Solo Pieces for the Beginning Clarinetist, Solo Pieces for the Intermediate Clarinetist,* and *Solo Pieces for the Advanced Clarinetist,* arranged by Norman M. Heim, published by Mel Bay Publications. Selections represent a variety of musical styles.

✔ *Solos for the Clarinet,* by Denise Schmidt, published by Carl Fischer. More than 20 original solos, from grade 2 to grade 5 on a difficulty scale of grades 1 to 8 (many from the Fischer out-of-print archives).

✔ *Solos for the Clarinet Player,* edited by Arthur H. Christmann, published by Hal Leonard Schirmer. Selections of classical music, mostly for the intermediate-level player, ranging in difficulty from medium to medium-difficult.

✔ *Style Workout,* by James Rae, published by Universal Edition. Elementary solos in classical, jazz, rock, and Latin styles.

When you're ready to take your clarinet playing to the next level, the following books may serve as perfect stepping stones:

✔ *The Bonade Legacy,* by Larry Guy, published by Rivernote Press. This book contains a revised version of Daniel Bonade's *Compendium for Clarinet,* as well as etudes and orchestral excerpts. Bonade was a legendary clarinet pedagogue and former first clarinetist of Philadelphia Orchestra. He was a major influence on present-day clarinet playing in the United States.

✔ *The Clarinet Doctor,* by Howard Klug, published by Woodwindiana Press. This book provides additional insight on clarinet playing from a highly effective clarinet teacher who is on the faculty of Indiana University.

✔ *Clarinet Fingerings,* by Thomas Ridenour. This is the go-to book to find all possible alternate fingerings for all possible notes in the clarinet's range.

✔ *Perfect a Reed . . . and Beyond: Reed Adjusting Method,* by Ben Armato, published by Reed Wizard. Ben Armato, former clarinetist of the Metropolitan Opera, has forgotten more about clarinet reeds than most people know. This book provides a detailed, systematic approach to reed working.

✔ *A Practical Approach to the Clarinet for Advanced Clarinetists, Revised Edition,* by David Etheridge, published by Woodwind Educators Press. This book presents a systematic approach to learning all the elements of clarinet playing that upper-level intermediate and advanced players need. It also includes more than 30 complete etudes from Rose, Cavallini, and Stark.

✔ *A Practical Approach to the Clarinet for Intermediate Clarinetists, Revised Edition,* by David Etheridge, published by Woodwind Educators Press. This book includes detailed explanations and illustrations of the basic elements of clarinet playing, as well as skill games and many exercises from Klosé and Baermann.

✔ *The Single Reed Adjustment Manual,* by Fred Ormand, published by Amilcare Publications. A well-written and systematic approach to reed working by one of the more influential clarinet pedagogues in the U.S.

Chapter 17

Refining Your Reeds

A clarinet player at any level is only as good as the reed she's using. You can have the best embouchure and breath support, skilled and nimble fingers, and superior technique, but if you have a worn-out, damaged, or sub-standard reed or one that's improperly adjusted for you and your clarinet, you're going to sound lousy. A high-quality reed in tip-top condition that's properly fitted enables you to tongue with ease, produce the full range of notes from lowest to highest with a beautiful sound, and play very loud or very soft with no compromise in tone.

Just looking at a reed, it doesn't seem so impressive, and that's part of the mystery. How can such an unassuming stick of wood wield so much influence over your ability to play your clarinet and produce quality sound? In this chapter, I answer that question and go way beyond to explain how you can diagnose problems with a reed when it plays poorly, tweak it a wee bit to make it respond better, and deal with the common problem of warped reeds.

When I use the term *adjust* or *tweak,* I'm talking about very, very small changes to the reed. Good reed workers count the grains of sawdust as they come off the reed. You'll be working in a world of ten thousandths of an inch — that's .0001 inch. The tip of a reed measures .0005 inch, so taking off .0001 inch is a 20 percent adjustment, which is pretty drastic.

Solving the Mystery of Reeds

Later in this chapter, you're going to be performing surgery on your reed. Before a lead doctor even thinks about passing the scalpel to an intern, that intern must pass at least one course in human anatomy (the parts of the body) and physiology (how those parts function separately and together as a whole). Consider this your crash course in reed anatomy and physiology.

Examining reed anatomy

Granted, a reed doesn't look like much, but through the eyes of a craftsman, the reed consists of numerous parts. Knowing the parts by more precise names than *thingamajig* and *whatchamacallit* is essential when selecting reeds for customization and doctoring those reeds.

As shown in Figure 17-1, the key parts of a reed include the tip, ears, heart, edges (sometimes called side rails), shoulders, stock, heel, and bottom. The actual cut of the reed is called the *vamp,* where you make most adjustments. (The *cut* is the part that tapers down toward the tip rail. It extends from the beginning of the first cut all the way to the tip of the reed.)

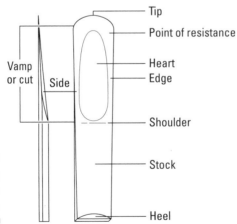

Figure 17-1: Parts of a reed.

Brushing up on reed physiology: Vibration

When you're playing the clarinet, all you need to know is that the reed vibrates. Performing surgery on a reed requires a deeper understanding.

Reeds vibrate in two modes simultaneously. As shown in Figures 17-2 and 17-3, the entire part of the reed over the facing moves up and down like a diving board, while the ears flap like the tips of a bird's wings.

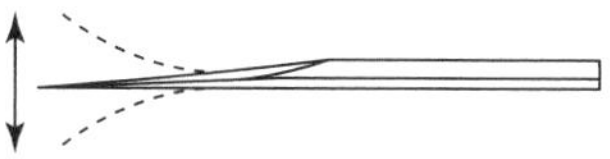

Figure 17-2:
The reed vibrates up and down like a diving board.

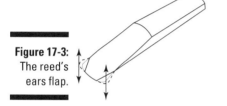

Figure 17-3:
The reed's ears flap.

This cool experiment enables you to witness this for yourself. You can burn an image on your brain that will help enormously in deciding which adjustments are necessary:

1. **Plug your ears. This is about to get loud and annoying.**

2. **Use an old reed that's a little on the soft side.**

   A soft reed vibrates with bigger, more noticeable swings and vibrates more easily than a harder reed.

3. **Stand in front of a mirror.**

4. **Hold the cork of the mouthpiece in your mouth.**

5. **Watch the reflection of the reed closely in the mirror while you suck air through the mouthpiece.**

   As you hear the horrendous sound of the reed vibrating, you have a ringside view of the reed as it vibrates up and down like a diving board.

6. **Suck harder.**

   If you suck air hard enough, you hear a high-pitched shriek and see the ears of the reed vibrating up and down.

Plato's master artisan

Plato believed in three modes of knowing, three modes of art, represented by the painter, the craftsman, and the rider (as in, the horseback rider). According to Plato, the painter is at the bottom of the heap (in terms of knowledge), because all he has to know is what a harness looks like. The craftsman is one step up, because he needs to know the function of the harness, its parts, and how the parts all fit and work together. Superior to both is the expert rider who knows how to *use* the harness to control his horse.

If you're a painter, you probably take issue with Plato's hierarchy, but it's useful in understand-ing the importance of knowing how a reed is structured and how it functions before you start adjusting and customizing reeds. By knowing what a reed looks like, the parts that comprise it, and how it works, you're much better able to make the required adjustments and foresee the probable effects of those adjustments.

As a clarinet player, you have an even bigger advantage. You're like the expert rider in Plato World because you know how to use the reed to adjust your sound. That knowledge, coupled with the knowledge and skills you acquire in this chapter, may just transform you into a master craftsman!

The point at which the reed begins to bend when it vibrates up and down over the mouthpiece facing is called the *fulcrum* (see Figure 17-4). It's sort of like the place where the diving board is anchored to the side of the pool. The fulcrum is also the point on the reed where the facing of the mouthpiece bends away from the reed. (I show you how to locate this point in Chapter 6 with the business card trick.)

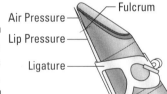

Figure 17-4: The reed's fulcrum.

 The thickness of the reed at the fulcrum is critical to its vibration. If the reed is too thin here, it collapses over the facing and can't vibrate. When working with reeds, mark the location of the fulcrum and keep your tools away from it (in almost all cases). Making this point too thin is like sawing a notch in the end of the diving board nearest the pool — not a nice thing to do to the divers.

 I make additional notations on my reeds. The first time I play a reed, I write the date on the bottom near the heel. I put stars on my really good reeds. I also keep a history on each reed of the adjustments I've made to it.

Recognizing the Necessity of Adjusting Even Good Reeds

Think of a reed as a car engine. Like a car engine, most reeds function to some degree, but a well-tuned, broken-in reed responds instantly when you give it the gas (fast air) and produces a superior sound throughout the clarinet's full range. When a reed is out of tune (balance), it may still be able to chug along, but you probably have to blow your brains out, and you may find it nearly impossible to play very softly or tongue with ease. You end up wrestling with the reed so much that you can't focus on the music.

Whether a reed is brand spankin' new or has a few miles on it, it probably needs a tune-up to optimize performance. Adjustments are often required to

- ✔ Correct minor imperfections in the reed itself.
- ✔ Minimize differences among reeds. Reeds are all slightly different and play slightly different, even if they come in the same box.
- ✔ Establish a better match with the mouthpiece. Regardless of how careful you are in choosing reeds that fit your mouthpiece, no reed fits perfectly right out of the box.
- ✔ Adapt the reed for your own physical characteristics, including your dental structure.

Reeds that are out of balance never play well, whether they're old or new. They just wear out as you play them.

Selecting the Most Talented Reeds to Tune Up

In Chapter 3, I offer guidance on choosing reeds. You'll be happy to hear that I'm not going to rehash all that now. This section is more about picking just the right reed out of a collection of reeds that you already have or are going to purchase.

When possible, buy your reeds by the box. They usually come ten to a box. Not only does this save you some money, but it also improves your chances of getting some reeds that are closest to playing well with minimal adjustment. Ben Armato, former clarinetist of the Metropolitan Opera Orchestra and one of the most knowledgeable reed workers in the country, refers to such reeds as "talented reeds." To identify the most talented reeds of the bunch, here's what you do:

1. **Using a soft lead pencil, number three or four reeds that you want to try so you can keep track of them as you run your tests.**

   Write on reeds only when they're dry, use a soft lead pencil so it doesn't dig into the cane, and write on the end of the reed that clamps to the mouthpiece — never the end that vibrates.

2. **Soak the reeds in a small glass of warm water for two minutes. A shot glass works well.**

   Cane more readily absorbs warm water. If you don't have ready access to warm water, soak the reeds in your mouth for a couple minutes. (After opening a box of reeds, store the unused reeds in a humidifier, as explained in Chapter 5.)

3. **Mount one of the reeds to your clarinet.**

   Chapter 5 shows how to clamp a reed to your mouthpiece using the ligature.

4. **Play the reed for two or three minutes, starting with the low notes.**

   You start with the low notes because they use the full diving board mode to limber up the reed. In short, you're breaking in the reed.

5. **Take the reed for a spin, playing the full range of the instrument at different dynamic levels, both slurring and tonguing, so you can determine whether the reed is capable of producing all the notes.**

   Don't expect the reed to sound great right away. You'll be testing the reeds over several days. The best reeds are usually slightly hard when you first try them. The reed that plays the worst on day one may play the best on day three.

6. **Remove the reed from the clarinet and place it back into the plastic container it came in.**

   As you test your other reeds, make sure you arrange the reeds (in their containers) in order from most to least talented, or vice versa. You may want to keep a written record (on paper) of how the reeds test — for example, Day One: 1–OK, 2–Good, 3–Bad, 4–Best, 5–Worst.

7. **Repeat Steps 2–5 to test the other reeds.**

8. **Mark with an S (for "too soft") any reeds that can't produce the highest notes you can play, and set them aside.**

   Reeds that can't play the upper register don't have enough resistance to make a good sound, let alone play the full range of clarinet.

9. **Repeat Steps 1–7 every day for three or four days until you feel comfortable choosing the most talented of the group.**

10. **Mark the least talented reeds on their bark with an S (for "too soft") or H (for "too hard").**

11. **Store each reed you're going to use in a humidified reed case.**

    Rico and Vandoren make excellent, inexpensive, humidified reed cases that are small enough to fit inside a clarinet case.

12. **Store your rejects in a humidified box and test them again in another season of the year.**

    A reed that plays poorly in the winter may play well in the summer, and vice versa, because of changes in temperature and humidity. Reeds are made of wood, so they swell in high humidity and become harder (more resistant). In low humidity, they dry out, shrink, and become softer.

Diagnosing a Reed's Shortcomings

Even the most talented reeds are never perfect right out of the box. In fact, a reed is rarely perfect even after its break-in period. Before you tweak a reed to perfection, identify areas for improvement.

Patience is key. Unless you absolutely need a reed for immediate performance, give every new reed some time to prove itself and reveal its shortcomings. You need to play a new reed for 15 minutes or so over a period of two or three days to make an accurate diagnosis. As cane absorbs moisture and then dries between playing sessions, it changes properties. Some reeds get softer; some get harder.

Before even wetting a reed that you're going to play test, mark the fulcrum area on the front and back of the reed with a soft lead pencil. Marks made on wet reeds are impossible to remove, and hard lead tends to scratch the reed. To locate and mark the fulcrum point, here's what you do:

1. **Attach the reed to the mouthpiece and set its proper position, as explained in Chapter 6, using the business card trick.**

2. **Gently slide that business card between the reed and the facing, and mark a line on the front of the reed where the card stops.**

3. **Slide a piece of notebook paper (thinner than the business card) between the reed and the facing, and mark the reed where the paper stops, as shown in Figure 17-5.**

The area between the two lines is the area you almost always want to avoid when removing cane from the reed. Remember the analogy of the diving board at the pool. Weakening the fulcrum area takes all the spring out of the reed.

4. **Mark the ears and heart (thicker center) of the reed, as shown in Figure 17-6.**

You mark the ears and heart now simply to keep track of where they are, for when you begin your adjustments.

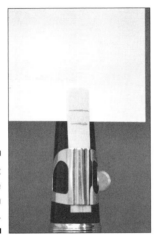

Figure 17-5:
Mark the fulcrum area.

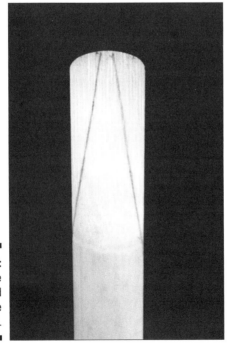

Figure 17-6:
Mark the ears and heart of the reed.

In the diagnostic process, your focus is on the following two areas of the reed:

- ✔ **Top of the fulcrum to the tip:** This is the area affected by air flow.

- ✔ **Back of the fulcrum to the beginning of the cut:** This area is affected by lip pressure.

As with tone, the basic parameters of a reed (above the fulcrum and below the fulcrum) are interdependent, but during the diagnosis, you must approach them one at a time, as presented in the following sections.

For best results in diagnosing problems in new reeds, spend time with new reeds at the end of your practice session. Judging a new reed is much easier when you can compare it to one of your playable reeds.

Testing the top of the fulcrum to the tip of the reed

The first order of business is to test the top of the fulcrum to the tip of the reed, the area affected by air flow. You actually test three distinct parts in this area: the heart, ears, and sides.

As you perform the diagnostic tests in the following sections, jot down the results so you have a full record to guide you later. Don't place any additional marks on the reed until you've completed the tests and confirmed your diagnosis. You mark the reed only after you've obtained all the test results.

Testing the heart

To test the strength of the heart area of the reed, play open G very softly and at normal volumes, and note the following:

- ✔ If the sound is fuzzy or lacking in clarinet warmth, the heart area of the reed is too hard. Make a note of it.

- ✔ If the reed plays too easily (you don't have to blow as hard as you usually do to produce the note), the heart is too soft. Set aside this reed for another season, if possible. If you must play a reed that's too soft, see "Adjusting overly soft reeds at the tip," near the end of this chapter.

- ✔ As Goldilocks can tell you, if it's neither too soft nor too hard, it's juuuuust right.

Testing the ears

No, this isn't a hearing test. Here you test the strength of the ears. You want to make sure both ears are balanced so that one doesn't wiggle (vibrate) more than the other. To test the strength of the ears, perform a dampening test, as follows:

1. **As you're playing, bend the right side of the reed into your lip, as shown in Figure 17-7.**

    This dampens the vibration on the right side of the reed so that only the left side can vibrate. In this step, you're simply setting a baseline for comparison purposes.

2. **While dampening vibration on one side of the reed, play an open G with a single puff of air.**

3. **Listen to the decay (diminuendo) of the ear opposite the side you dampened.**

    Steps 2 and 3 comprise what's commonly referred to as a "puff test."

4. **Repeat Steps 2 and 3 for the other side of the reed.**

5. **Note which ear stops vibrating the quickest.**

Figure 17-7:
Dampen
vibration on
one side of
the reed.

The ear that stops vibrating the quickest is the harder of the two ears and may need to be sanded or shaved down.

The ears must be exactly the same strength for the reed to close evenly on the tip rail. When the ears are out of balance, tonguing and playing very softly is difficult.

Testing the side rails from the fulcrum to the tip

To test the strength of the side rails of the reed in back of the tip, do the following:

1. **Play an open G very softly and note the quality of the sound.**

2. **Move the tip of the reed slightly to the left, as shown in Figure 17-8.**

3. **Play an open G very softly again, noting whether the sound quality is better.**

4. **Move the tip of the reed slightly to the right, as shown in Figure 17-9.**

5. **Play open G very softly again, noting whether the sound quality is better than it was in Step 1.**

If the reed sounded better after you moved the tip over, the side rail in back of the tip is hard on that side and may need some cane removed.

Figure 17-8:
Tip of reed
moved
slightly to
the left.

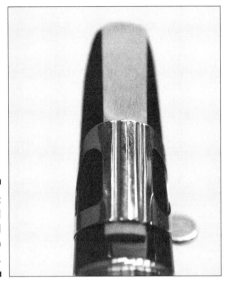

Figure 17-9:
Tip of reed moved slightly to the right.

Testing the back of the fulcrum to the beginning of the cut

After you have tested the area affected by air flow, as explained in the previous section, test the area affected by lip pressure — the back of the fulcrum to the beginning of the cut. You actually test two separate parts in this area: the shoulders and the heart at the back of the fulcrum.

Testing the shoulders

To test the strength of the shoulders (the side rails of the reed in back of the fulcrum), perform the following dampening test on both side rails:

1. **While dampening vibration on the right side of the reed, play a very soft, sustained (four beats) open G, listening for the hiss of air escaping under the reed.**

   - To dampen vibration on one side of the reed, bend that side of the reed into your lip, as shown back in Figure 17-7.

   - You must play the note softly enough to hear the hiss over the note.

2. **Note the loudness of the hiss.**

3. **Repeat Steps 1 and 2 for the left side of the reed.**

4. **If the hiss on either side of the reed is louder, make a note of it.**

The side of the reed that hisses the most is too hard and may need to be shaved down.

Another way to test the shoulders is to move the heel of the reed over to one side on the mouthpiece, play an open G, and then repeat the process for the opposite side. The side that sounded best with the heel of the reed moved over is the side that's too hard and may require adjustment.

Testing the heart at the back of the fulcrum

To check the strength of the heart in back of the fulcrum, perform the following test:

1. **Play B2 (B in the staff), and make a long, slow diminuendo, noting the following:**

   - The level of difficulty in producing the diminuendo.

   - The clarity of the sound.

2. **Move the ligature up almost above where the cut of the reed begins, as shown in Figure 17-10.**

3. **Play B2 again, just as you did in Step 1, noting the difficulty of producing it and the clarity of the sound.**

If producing the diminuendo is easier and the reed makes a clearer sound when the ligature is moved up, the back of the heart is too hard and you may need to remove cane from this area.

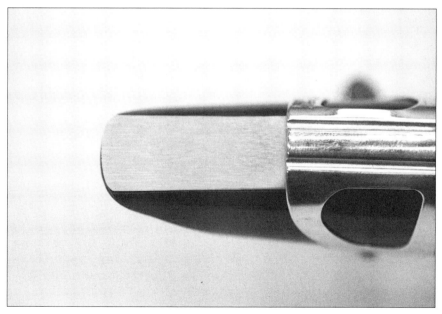

Figure 17-10:
Mouthpiece
with ligature
moved
way up.

Confirming or refining your diagnosis . . . before you grab that knife!

Reeds aren't cheap, and really talented reeds don't come along every day, so take a few minutes to confirm your diagnosis before you take a knife to that reed. The following tests change the way the reed vibrates without removing any cane from the reed. The results of these tests help you . . .

✔ Correct for minor discrepancies in the reed so you don't have to perform surgery.

✔ Question your diagnosis so you can retest the reed, to make sure it requires the adjustments you think it needs.

✔ Reinforce your diagnosis so you can proceed with more confidence.

You may not need to fix a reed by removing cane. Repositioning the reed may help correct minor defects in the reed.

Retesting the top of the fulcrum to the tip of the reed

The following sections provide tests to confirm or overturn your diagnosis of any problems with the reed in the area affected by air flow — the top of the fulcrum to the tip of the reed.

Retesting the heart

If you decided that the heart area is too hard, perform the following test to be sure:

1. **Move the reed down from the tip of the mouthpiece until a small portion of the mouthpiece's tip rail is showing, as in Figure 17-11.**

2. **Play open G very softly and at normal volumes, noting whether the reed is more or less resistant to your air.**

If the reed is less resistant to your air with the reed moved down, your initial diagnosis that the heart of the reed is too hard is correct. If the reed plays well mounted a little lower, you do not need to adjust it at this time. At a later date, you may want to remove a small amount of cane from the heart of the reed, but you can hold off for now.

Another way to recheck the hardness of the heart is to perform the following test:

1. **Gently roll a pencil over about half an inch of the tip area of the reed, as shown in Figure 17-12.**

2. **Play open G very softly and at normal volumes, noting whether the reed is more responsive and sounds better.**

If the reed responds and sounds better after rolling a pencil over the tip area of the reed, your initial diagnosis that the heart of the reed is too hard is correct. In this case, you need to remove a small amount of cane from the area in back of the fulcrum. See "Adjusting areas below the back of the fulcrum," later in this chapter, for details.

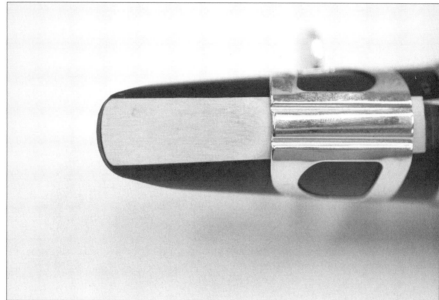

Figure 17-11: Lower the reed so that the tip rail is visible.

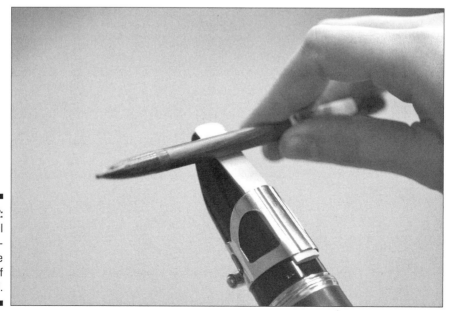

Figure 17-12: Roll a pencil over a half-inch of the tip area of the reed.

If your initial diagnosis is that the reed is too soft, recheck it by performing the following test:

1. **With the reed mounted in its normal position, play a few notes, including some high notes, noting the quality of the sound and the reed response for the high notes.**

2. **Move the reed so its tip extends slightly beyond the tip rail of the mouthpiece.**

3. **Play the same notes you played in Step 1, noting the quality of the sound and the reed response for the high notes.**

If the sound is less buzzy and the reed response for the high notes is better (high notes are easier to play) with the reed moved up, your initial diagnosis that the heart of the reed is too soft is correct. If the reed plays fine mounted a little higher, no adjustment is needed at this time. If it is still too soft, taking about 1/64 inch off the tip should do the trick. See "Adjusting overly soft reeds at the tip," later in this chapter, for details.

Retesting the ears

If you diagnosed a difference in the hardness of the two ears, check your diagnosis by performing the following test:

1. **Play a few notes, noting the reed response and the lightness or darkness of the sound.**

2. **Bend just the corner of the tip of the reed you identified as being too hard down a little on the mouthpiece table, as shown in Figure 17-13.**

3. **Play the same few notes you played in Step 1, noting the reed response and the lightness or darkness of the sound.**

If the reed responds better and the sound is darker, your initial diagnosis of that particular corner of the reed being too hard is correct. You must adjust the ear you diagnosed as being too hard during your initial tests.

If you decided that one of the ears was too soft, bend it upward slightly and retest. If the reed makes a fuller sound, you were correct. If one of the ears is too soft, try removing a tiny amount of cane from the harder ear, as explained in "Taking a little off the ears," later in this chapter. If that's not enough, take a very small amount of cane off the tip, as explained in "Adjusting overly soft reeds at the tip," later in this chapter.

Figure 17-13:
Bend the
corner tip
of the reed
down on the
mouthpiece
table.

Retesting the side rails from the fulcrum to the tip

If you diagnosed the side rails in back of the tip as too hard, confirm or refute that diagnosis by performing the following test:

1. **Play a few notes, including some high notes, noting the clarity of the sound and the reed response for the high notes.**

2. **Using a pencil eraser, gently push down on the reed about ¾ inch back from the tip, as shown in Figure 17-14, and release.**

3. **Play the same notes you played in Step 1, noting the clarity of the sound and the reed response for the high notes.**

If the reed sounds clearer and is more responsive after pressing down on it with the eraser, your initial diagnosis is correct. You must adjust the side rails in back of the tip, as explained in the section "Adjusting the side rails in back of the tip," later in this chapter.

Figure 17-14:
Gently push down on the reed with a pencil eraser.

Retesting the back of the fulcrum to the beginning of the cut

The following sections provide tests to confirm or overturn your diagnosis of any problems with the reed in the area affected by lip pressure — the back of the heart and lower shoulders (areas below the fulcrum).

Retesting the lower shoulders

If your initial test results indicate that the reed is too thick along the back of the shoulders, recheck the diagnosis by performing the following test:

1. **Play a very soft, sustained (four beats) open G, listening for the hiss of air escaping under the reed.**

2. **Gently roll a pencil down the reed over the fulcrum area of the reed.**

3. **Repeat Step 1, listing for the hiss.**

If the reed sounds less hissy and better, your initial diagnosis is correct; you need to remove cane from along the back of the shoulders.

Retesting the heart at the back of the fulcrum

If your initial test results indicate that the reed is too thick at the back of the heart, recheck the diagnosis by performing the following test:

1. **Play B2 (B in the staff) and make a long, slow diminuendo, noting the clarity of the sound and listening for any hiss.**

2. **With your thumb, gently press the middle of the back of the reed below the fulcrum down into the window of the mouthpiece, as shown in Figure 17-15.**

3. **Repeat Step 1, noting the clarity of the sound and listening for any hiss.**

If the reed is less hissy and the sound is clearer, your initial diagnosis is correct; you need to shave some cane off the back of the heart.

Figure 17-15:
Gently press
the reed
down into
the win-
dow of the
mouthpiece.

Marking adjustments on your reed

Before a plastic surgeon steps into the surgical room, he takes a felt-tip marker and outlines the areas to adjust. Do the same to your reed. Make sure it's dry, and then use a soft lead pencil to mark the areas that require adjustment, using the results of your tests as your guide. Figure 17-16 shows areas on a reed marked for adjustment.

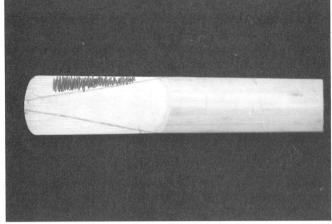

Figure 17-16:
Mark the areas that require correction.

Adjusting Your Reed: Scalpel, Please

You've diagnosed one or more problems with your talented reed and confirmed your diagnosis. The prognosis is good, but you've decided that the reed requires more than some minor repositioning on the mouthpiece. It needs surgery. You're now ready to gather your surgical instruments and start making some intelligent adjustments to your talented reed.

As you proceed, follow precautions, gather your tools, and make your adjustments, as explained next.

A tailor doesn't tear out the seams of the legs when adjusting the cuffs. Good reed workers have the attitude that the reed in question is 95 percent right in the first place. Inexperienced reed workers often touch too much of the reed and destroy the measurements of the parts that were right in the first place.

Following a few simple precautions

Before you pick up that scalpel, read and follow these precautions and expert advice:

- ✔ Be careful with the tools. Some tools may be sharp.
- ✔ Go slowly. You can always remove more cane, but you can't reattach it. Most adjustments require making only one or two strokes of sandpaper, or removing a sliver of wood with a reed knife.

✔ Make only one correction at a time. If you make more than one adjustment at a time, you never know which one actually helped.

✔ Test your reed after every single adjustment.

Using the ligature to clamp the reed to the mouthpiece to test it after every tiny adjustment is a hassle. You may use your hands to "clamp" the reed in place, if you're very careful not to let it shift out of proper position during the test. Also keep in mind that reeds act slightly less resistant when secured to the mouthpiece with the thumb. When you're done making adjustments, do a final check with the ligature.

✔ Just as a doctor does, keep a record of your work. As you make adjustments, mark what you've done on the flat side of the reed above the brand name. Also write the date on the reed when you started playing it, to help you remember just how long you have been playing it.

Patience is crucial. If you're in a hurry, you're more likely to overcorrect and ruin a talented reed.

Gathering essential tools and materials

Before you perform reed surgery, you need to outfit your operating room. Fortunately, most of the tools are inexpensive and available in the home or at the local hardware store. Here's what you need:

✔ **Soft lead drawing pencil:** Soft lead works best because it doesn't score the reed.

✔ **Reed plaque:** You can purchase a bona fide reed plaque or just cut a piece of Plexiglas measuring ½ by 3½ inches.

✔ **Flat glass surface:** This can be a piece of plate glass measuring 8-by-8 inches, or you can purchase it as part of the Ridenour ATG Reed System.

✔ **Reed knife:** A reed knife looks like a straight-edge razor, which old-time barbers used to use to shave their customers. Good reed knives are made from high quality steel and usually cost around sixty dollars. This should be a once-in-a-lifetime purchase and is well worth the money. A pocket knife with a sharp straight blade may be a suitable substitute. A utility knife is a poor substitute: A reed knife is made of better steel and has a better handle, for more precise control.

Reed knives are made for both righties and lefties, so make sure you get a knife designed for your cutting hand.

✔ **Sandpaper:** Use wet-or-dry sandpaper #350, #400, and #600. Sandpaper works best near the tip of the reed. (The higher the number, the finer the sandpaper.)

- **Reed rush:** Sometimes referred to as Dutch rush, reed rush is an abrasive reed material for making small adjustments to reeds. Some players use it instead of sandpaper and sometimes instead of a reed knife (when making adjustments to the back of the fulcrum). You can purchase reed rush from Muncy Winds or pick it yourself along a stream bank . . . assuming that you have access to a stream bank and can identify Dutch rush.

- **Ridenour ATG System:** This system comes with a flat glass surface and a sanding block tool. Along with the Armato tool, this kit will save you hours. I also refer to this as the "Ridenour tool." The Ridenour tool is good for just about everything except making adjustments to the back of the fulcrum, so you still need reed rush or a reed knife.

That's really all you need, and everything on the list is fairly affordable. The Ridenour tool costs around forty dollars and is worth every penny. A couple additional tools are great to have if you can afford them:

- **Armato Perfecta Reed Measuring Tool:** This tool costs about $225 and is great for measuring the precise thickness of reeds.

- **Armato Reed Wizard:** This tool makes highly accurate minor adjustments to any part of the reed. Selling for about $200, it might sound pricy, but is worth every penny. If you're in a school band, ask your director to purchase one for your clarinet section to share.

Unless you've gained some experience adjusting reeds, I recommend against using a reed clipper, a cross between nail clippers and a guillotine. You clamp the reed in place and then pull a lever to bring the blade down and slice a sliver off the tip of the reed. If you're not careful, you can do a lot of damage with one of these.

Adjusting areas above the fulcrum

Look for the adjustment marks you made in areas above the fulcrum. If you see any, skip to the section for that specific area next and follow the instructions to make the necessary adjustment.

Performing minor heart surgery

Use your Ridenour tool to make the reed act softer in the upper heart area. Move the tool against the grain in three or four strokes from the tip of the reed back toward the heal to the upper fulcrum mark. See Figure 17-17.

If you don't have a Ridenour tool handy, use a piece of #400 sandpaper in the same manner.

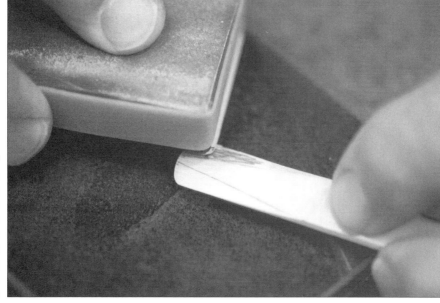

Figure 17-17:
Use a
Ridenour
tool to make
adjustments
to the heart
area above
the fulcrum.

Taking a little off the ears

If one ear is harder than the other, pretend you're a barber whose customer
has asked you to "take a little off the ears." To make one of the ears slightly
softer, place the Armato Reed Wizard cutter about ¼ inch back from the tip of
the reed, as shown in Figure 17-18, and push the tool gently toward the tip of
the reed.

Figure 17-18:
Using the
Armato
Reed
Wizard.

You can perform the same operation with your Ridenour tool. Move the tool against the grain *only once* across the corner of the reed that needs adjustment.

Adjusting the side rails in back of the tip

If one of the side rails in back of the tip needs adjusting, here's what you do:

1. **Place a business card, in portrait orientation, on your glass work surface or the glass of your Ridenour tool. (See Figure 17-19.)**

2. **Tape three sides of the business card to the glass, keeping the side nearest you open.**

3. **Slide the tip of the reed under the business card and up to the second fulcrum mark on the reed.**

4. **Brush your Ridenour tool against the grain in three or four strokes from the edge of the business card to the fulcrum of the reed.**

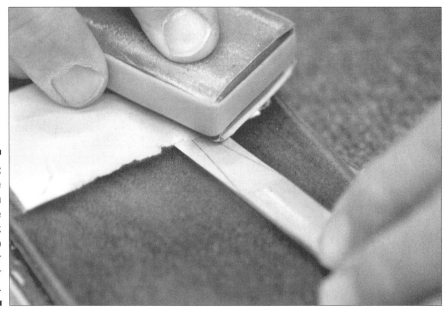

Figure 17-19:
Remove cane from the side rail in back of the tip using your Ridenour tool.

If you don't have a Ridenour tool, use reed rush or a reed knife to remove cane from this area of the reed.

When using reed rush, hold the reed in your hand so you can feel the pressure on the reed. This helps prevent you from taking off too much material at one time.

Adjusting areas below the back of the fulcrum

Inspect the reed for any adjustment marks in areas below the back of the fulcrum. If adjustment marks are present, skip to the section for that specific area next and follow the instructions to make the necessary adjustment.

Adjusting the lower heart area

To make the reed softer in the area from the back of the fulcrum to the beginning of the cut, use a reed knife or reed rush to remove a tiny amount of cane from the lower heart area, as shown in Figure 17-20. If you're using a reed knife, scrape very gently with the grain to remove only a small amount of the tops of the fibers (xylems) of the reed. The xylems act like the ribs of an umbrella. If you break a rib, the umbrella collapses, so you don't want to cut too deeply into the xylems.

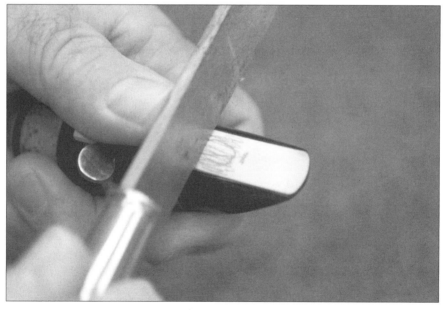

Figure 17-20:
Remove reed from the lower heart area.

Adjusting the lower shoulders at the back of the side rails

To make the reed softer in the area marked at the bottom of the shoulders, use a reed knife or reed rush to remove a tiny amount of cane from this area, as shown in Figure 17-21.

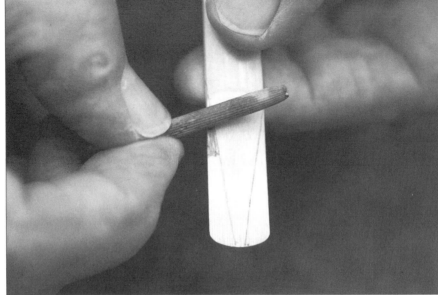

Figure 17-21:
Remove
cane from
the lower
shoulders
at the back
of the side
rails.

Adjusting overly soft reeds at the tip

When a reed is too soft, the best option usually is to set aside the reed for another season. If you really need to play the reed or you've already tried that approach and the reed is still too soft, remove some cane from the very tip of the reed. You have two options for doing this:

✔ Use a reed clipper to clip a very small amount of cane from the tip (no more than ¹⁄₆₄ inch), as shown in Figure 17-22.

Figure 17-22:
Clip a tiny
amount of
cane from
the tip of the
reed.

✔ Sand the tip with #600 sandpaper. Hold the sandpaper perpendicular to the reed and make two slight passes of the sandpaper over the very tip of the reed, as shown in Figure 17-23. (Do not use reed rush.)

Figure 17-23: Touch the very center of the tip of the reed with sandpaper.

After clipping or sanding the tip, retest the ears, as explained in "Testing the ears," earlier in this chapter. By removing a tiny bit of cane from one of the ears, you can usually bring the tip back in balance.

Revitalizing old, warped reeds

To function as a perfect spring, a reed must be absolutely flat on the bottom. If you play any reed for more than a week, chances are good that it'll become warped, even if you store it in a humidified box or reed case. The bark below the cut traps moisture, and the reed retains some moisture and swells up a little where it's supposed to be flat, becoming slightly round instead. To test for warping, perform the following steps:

1. **Draw lines on the flat side of the reed, across the grain, as shown in Figure 17-24.**

2. **Place a sheet of #350 sandpaper on a flat surface, abrasive side up.**

3. **Keeping the very tip of the reed off the sandpaper, lightly rub the marked surface against the sandpaper.**

   If the centers of the lines disappear, the reed is warped. If the lines sand off uniformly, the reed isn't warped badly enough to require adjustment.

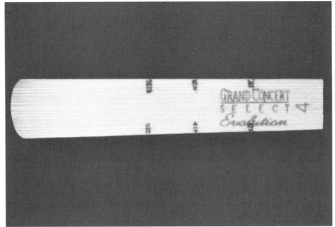

Figure 17-24:
Mark lines on the underside (bottom) of the reed.

To correct warping, here's what you do:

1. **Place a small sheet of #350 sandpaper on your glass work surface.**

2. **Place a piece of double-stick tape on the bark side of the reed.**

   The tape keeps the reed from slipping under your fingers as you rub the flat side of the reed against the sandpaper.

3. **Draw two small circles on the reed where your fingers will press down on it, as shown.**

4. **Set the reed flat side down on the sandpaper, keeping the area of the reed above the fulcrum off the sandpaper.**

   Keep the area of the reed above the fulcrum off the sandpaper so you don't remove cane from the tip.

   Don't take cane off the reed near the very tip or above the fulcrum, and don't completely remove the pencil marks. This ensures that you don't remove cane from critical areas and don't remove too much cane overall.

5. **Place the tips of your index and middle finger on the circles you drew on the back of the reed, as shown in Figure 17-25.**

6. **Gently press down to keep the reed flat while rubbing the reed on the sandpaper in a small figure-eight pattern, keeping the reed tip off the sandpaper.**

   Remove a very small amount of cane from the underside. You don't have to remove all the lines you drew on the reed to test for warping; remove only enough cane to make that surface flat.

Figure 17-25:
Gently press
down and
sand a little
cane off the
flat side of
the reed.

With warping, an ounce of prevention is often a pound of cure. Keeping your reeds hydrated helps you avoid most warping issues. When you're not using a reed, store it in a humidified box or reed case. Soaking the reed for a few minutes in warm water may also help and is sometimes useful in correcting very minor warping. In arid regions such as Arizona, warping is more prevalent.

Chapter 18

Gaining Expertise and Exposure through the Clarinet Community

*A*lthough making music is often a private and personal pursuit, it's also very family and community oriented. In fact, developing your skills and playing with other musicians, along with sharing your talents and your joy of playing with others via live performances and recordings, may be the most fun and rewarding aspect of playing an instrument. All these experiences contribute immensely to improving your skills and technique.

This chapter opens the doors to the bigger world of music, to expose you to other people who can help you take your clarinet playing to the next level and make it more enjoyable and rewarding. Here you discover how to find a teacher to give you expert feedback and guidance to correct weakness and build on your strengths. I encourage you to join an ensemble, such as a band or orchestra, to connect with other musicians and challenge yourself to do your best. I introduce you to the possibilities of connecting with a duet buddy or piano accompanist to further develop your skills. Finally, I share some performance tips to help you make the most of your stage time.

With the guidance in this chapter and your willingness to get involved in your local (and perhaps national and international) music communities, you can begin to expand your network and more fully enjoy the clarinet and the bigger world of music.

Teaming Up with a Teacher

With a good clarinet teacher, you can achieve your clarinet-playing goals much more quickly than if you try to fly solo. Experienced teachers have been there and done that. They know what works and what's simply a waste of time. They know the pathways to learning and the steps you need to take along the way. Systematic instruction on the clarinet steers you clear of many of the blind alleys that lead away from your goals.

A good teacher offers several additional perks by assisting you in the following areas:

- ✔ **Setting reasonable expectations:** When players first start playing the clarinet (or any instrument, except maybe the kazoo), they often become frustrated or discouraged because they expect too much too soon. Players also become discouraged by setting their expectations too low and then wondering why they're not progressing faster. A teacher can help manage your expectations and maintain an appropriate pace.

- ✔ **Keeping you motivated:** A good teacher is like a trainer at the gym. A teacher keeps you on track, gives you something to practice for, and, to some degree holds you accountable, especially if you're the type of person who likes to please others (which most people are, to varying degrees). A good teacher also encourages you when necessary and may become one of your biggest fans.

- ✔ **Providing trustworthy technical support:** Your teacher can assist you in choosing the right clarinet for you, purchasing it at a reasonable price, selecting reeds and other equipment and accessories, adjusting your reeds as necessary, and keeping your instrument in tip-top shape.

- ✔ **Introducing you to performance opportunities:** Most clarinet teachers are well connected in the musical community. Your teacher can likely put you in touch with other musicians and, when you're ready, introduce you to performance opportunities in local ensembles or contests.

Your teacher may even serve as your first accompanist or duet buddy!

Sizing up qualities and qualifications

Before you start shaking the bushes for a suitable clarinet teacher, draw up a shopping list of the essential qualities and qualifications you're looking for in a teacher. A qualified teacher who's a good fit for you meets the following minimum requirements:

✔ **Experienced or even specialized in teaching the clarinet:** Someone who focuses on teaching piano or violin and dabbles in teaching the clarinet may not be the best choice, especially if you're playing at a higher level. You may end up knowing more than your teacher!

✔ **Experienced or even specialized in teaching clarinet players at your level of experience:** Some outstanding beginning-level teachers are unable to teach intermediate or advanced techniques. Teachers who deal with more advanced students may not have the patience to work with beginners.

✔ **Just plain experienced:** A person who has taught for many years typically knows the materials and learning strategies better than a novice teacher. However, a good teacher can be any age. So can a lousy one.

✔ **Plays the clarinet, preferably in performances:** A musician who performs on the clarinet has a better perspective of what you really need to know to play at that level.

✔ **Solid track record:** You can tell a great deal about a teacher by measuring the progress and accomplishments of the students.

Knowing where to look

You don't exactly notice clarinet teachers walking around. Their names and faces aren't plastered on billboards. They may not even hang out a shingle or have a listing in the Yellow Pages. You might think they're an endangered species. However, digging up some names of good prospects isn't difficult. Here's a list of resources to start tapping for references:

✔ **Local colleges or universities:** Contact the clarinet instructor in the school's music department, and let her know the type of clarinet teacher you're looking for. These instructors are the most familiar with the clarinet scene in your area and can recommend former or current students who give lessons.

✔ **Local high schools:** Most high schools, especially the larger ones, have a band director. Contact the band director and let him know the type of clarinet teacher you're looking for. If he can't or won't recommend a particular individual, he can probably give you a list of people he recommends for students in the band.

✔ **Local music store:** Contact the owner of a local music store. Music store owners and managers are usually well aware of the qualified clarinet teachers in their town. The store may even have a message board where teachers can post their business cards or flyers.

Checking recommendations and references

To determine whether a teacher meets your minimum requirements, interview two or three candidates and ask the following questions:

- ✔ **What percentage of your teaching is devoted to clarinet, as compared to other instruments?** The higher the percentage, the better, but look for a teacher who devotes at least 60 percent of her time to teaching the clarinet. Someone who teaches mostly clarinet and some saxophone is usually better than someone who teaches all woodwinds.

- ✔ **Which level do you enjoy teaching the most?** If you're just starting out, the answer you want to hear is "Beginner" or "Elementary level."

- ✔ **How long have you been teaching the clarinet?** Generally, the more years the better, but look for someone who has been teaching the clarinet for at least a couple years.

- ✔ **Do you play clarinet in any ensembles?** The right answer here is "Yes." You may want to follow up with a question of where and when the teacher plays so you can catch the next performance.

- ✔ **How much do you charge?** Unless money is no object, find out how much the person charges per lesson and the length of each lesson. Prices vary greatly, but by interviewing a few candidates, you can quickly determine a reasonable price range.

Before you leave (or the candidate leaves), obtain the names and phone numbers of a few of the teacher's current and former students who have been (or had been) with the teacher for more than six months. Contact a couple of them to obtain student perspectives on the teacher. Consider asking the following questions:

- ✔ **How long have you been a student of so-and-so?** Knowing how long the student has been with the teacher helps you assess other answers about the progress the student has made.

- ✔ **Do you feel you've made sufficient progress under so-and-so?** If the student feels she has made good progress, the teacher is doing a sufficient job of teaching or managing expectations — preferably both. A possible red flag is the student expressing frustration or discouragement.

- ✔ **During your time with so-and-so, did he really address your playing issues by helping you identify them and providing systematic solutions?** A creative teacher can use either etudes or solos to address each individual student's needs.

✔ **What are some of your clarinet-playing accomplishments while studying under so-and-so?** You want to know whether any of the teacher's students sit (or sat) at the top of school bands, whether they were named to area honor groups or all-state bands, whether they went on to play in college or major in music (or played just for fun), or whether any are accomplished clarinet professionals.

Playing Well with Others in an Ensemble

When you finally feel ready to take the stage and perform before a live audience, you may be inclined to start small and work your way up. The better strategy is to start big and work your way down. As a member of an ensemble (group), you're likely to feel less pressure than when you're playing alone or with only piano accompaniment, when all eyes are on you and all ears tuned into your clarinet.

Playing in larger ensembles provides some additional benefits as well:

✔ You pick up many important music-making skills that you can carry over to smaller ensembles, such as clarinet choirs, quartets, trios, and duets.

✔ You practice teamwork as you contribute to the group sound.

✔ You learn to play in tune.

✔ On top of it all, you develop friendships with others who share your enthusiasm for music.

In the following sections, I describe the types of larger ensembles you may want to explore. Of course, availability of such ensembles depends a great deal on where you live and the opportunities in your community.

Considering a school band or orchestra

School music programs offer budding musicians excellent opportunities to get started in music and provide the support early learners need to stick with it long enough to reap the benefits. If you're in junior high, high school, or college (many colleges have bands for non-music majors), consider joining the band and taking private music lessons to optimize your progress. (Some elementary schools also have excellent music programs.) If you're a parent and your child's school has a music program, subtly encourage your child to get involved.

Venezuela and "The System"

Rumor has it that Venezuela is producing some of the most talented young classical musicians in the world. Actually, it's more than just a rumor. *60 Minutes* broadcast a segment on it back in 2008. (Google "60 minutes system" to find the link for the page on which you can watch the segment.)

Venezuela's national music program is referred to as *El Sistema* in Spanish, which translates as "The System." It began 35 years ago with 11 students and an amateur musician by the name of José Antonio Abreu, who believed classical music could cure the societal ills of family disintegration, poverty, and crime.

During the writing of this book, more than 300,000 Venezuelan children, most from run-down neighborhoods, are enrolled in The System and are involved in any number of ensembles and choirs throughout the country.

And it's working. Wherever The System is in place, communities see a noticeable decline in crime and drug use. Music teaches discipline, exercises the brain cells, and provides students with something more valuable and meaningful in their lives than most of what pop culture provides.

A great way to encourage children to get involved in music without being too pushy about it is to take them to performances, where they can see and hear musicians in action. Many communities have ensembles that play for free or charge next to nothing for admission.

School music programs deliver valuable benefits for the school as well as the individuals involved. Consider the following facts:

> **Fact:** According to Dr. James Catterall, UCLA, a ten-year study indicates that teens who play an instrument are less likely to have discipline problems.

> **Fact:** According to Steven M. Demorest and Steven Morrison in their article "Does Music Make You Smarter?" *(Music Educators Journal)*, SAT scores showed incremental increases for every year of music study.

Exploring new horizons for older players

After graduating high school or college, the challenges of finding suitable music programs and venues to develop your skills and discover opportunities to perform increase dramatically. Fortunately, community and even national organizations have developed to provide these opportunities for older players.

One notable national organization is the New Horizons International Music Association (NHIMA). For the past 30 years, NHIMA has been providing wonderful opportunities to adults who want to learn to play the clarinet and also play in a band or jazz band. During the writing of this book, NHIMA bands counted well over a hundred, and the movement is growing rapidly.

Initially started for adults over age 50, NHIMA bands are now accepting younger adult players as well. Approximately 80 percent of NHIMA members start with no musical experience. The other 15 to 20 percent of members played an instrument in their school music program.

Members attend a weekly instructional session and a band rehearsal. For more information, and to find out whether NHIMA is active in your area, visit its website at `www.newhorizonsmusic.org`.

Whether you're an aging teenager, you just received your AARP card, or you've joined the ranks of the septuagenarians (or have even more life experience), don't be afraid to join an ensemble. According to the American Music Conference (`www.amc-music.com`), only 31 percent of teenagers and adults in a 2000 survey who don't play an instrument feel they're too old to start learning. I have one word for those folks: "Nonsense!" Many famous clarinetists, including Sabine Meyer, began playing the clarinet in their early teens, but many others started much later, after establishing successful careers in fields completely unrelated to music.

Checking out the local fare: Community concert bands and orchestras

Many communities refuse to sit idly by twiddling their collective thumbs in anticipation of a national movement coming to their town or *The Music Man* rolling into town to spark some interest. These communities take the initiative themselves.

Your community may have its own band or orchestra, and you simply don't know it yet. To find out, head over to the Association of Concert Bands Website, at `www.acbands.org`, and click the Community Music Lists link for a list of registered community concert bands, along with contact information for each. Last I checked, the list contained the names and contact information for 1,618 community bands and orchestras across the United States.

If your city or town doesn't have one or two, check some nearby towns and cities.

Joining the choir . . . the clarinet choir

This may sound a bit cliquish, but some communities have ensembles exclusively for clarinetists, called *clarinet choirs*. These ensembles consist of all members of the clarinet family, from contra to E flat soprano. Clarinet choirs typically have a large repertory and create a fabulous sound. Clarinet choirs are common in Europe, and the idea is catching on in the United States.

In the U.S., clarinet choirs are usually an outgrowth of community bands or New Horizons music groups, so you can find out about them through these local organizations. In Europe, clarinet choirs are typically associated with community music schools, which they call *conservatories*.

Auditioning for ensembles

School and community bands are usually come-one-come-all affairs — you don't need to audition to land a spot in the band. For smaller ensembles, such as orchestras, which use only four clarinets, you may need to audition.

If you're required to audition, the keys to success are preparation and practice. Orchestras usually have a standard list of pieces you must perform. Ask your teacher (or someone from the orchestra, if you don't have a teacher) for the list. If you take lessons, your teacher can help you prepare.

If you're requested to play a piece of your choice for an audition, choose a piece you've played for others many times. This is likely to make you more comfortable so that your playing is a true reflection of your talent and ability.

Thinking Smaller: Duet Buddies and Accompanists

Pairing up with a piano or another clarinet adds an extra dimension to your sound — and additional challenges. You and your cohorts must collaborate, rehearse, and learn to play together as a unit. The benefits are significant, in terms of both the richness of the collaborative sound and the details you pick up from one another.

In the following sections, I introduce you to more limited music collaborations, including duets, trios, quartets, and piano accompaniment. I also offer guidance on how to find fellow musicians to play with and make your collaborations more productive.

Finding duet buddies for duets, trios, and quartets

Teaming up with a fellow clarinetist to form a duet is a wonderful way to learn any instrument, including the clarinet. You and your duet buddy not only learn how to play together, but you also have the opportunity to share what you've both learned and discovered on your own. Furthermore, you hold one another accountable, challenging each other to bring your A game.

Your first duet buddy is likely to be your teacher. Most good teachers play duets with their students on a regular basis. If you play in a band or orchestra, you'll find duet buddies there as well. Other small ensemble opportunities, including trios and quartets, tend to grow out of your association with fellow clarinetists.

When playing a duet, remember that the two parts are equally important; neither should predominate over the other. Playing as equals not only makes the music sound better, but it also makes the experience more fun and preserves valuable friendships.

Finding pianists for accompaniment

Most of the solo sheet music written for the clarinet includes music for piano accompaniment. In other words, when you choose to fly solo, you're going to need a co-pilot on piano.

Most of the good accompanists are busy, so finding one that has openings can be quite a challenge. As with finding a duet buddy, start with your teacher, who may play piano or at least is likely to know good accompanists in your area. You can also check the usual places for good leads: music stores, music departments in local colleges and universities, high school band directors, and any other musicians you happen to know.

To be politically correct and show respect for your fellow musician, drop the term *accompanist*. Instead, refer to her as a *collaborator*. Your collaborator is an equal partner. Just as a stereo can't have a woofer without a tweeter, a good clarinet soloist needs an equally talented collaborator on piano. In addition to sharing the stage equally, this makes your association much more fun and rewarding. Think of the pianist as another duet buddy, a fellow clarinetist.

A little etiquette goes a long way with pianists. Most of the good ones are busy, so be prepared for rehearsals. One smart thing to do is listen to recordings of the piece(s) you're going to play before your first rehearsal.

Also, it is important to know that some pianists charge for accompanying, so do inquire about the financial arrangements when you ask them to play for you.

Overcoming Performance Anxiety

One of the joys of the world is music, and that joy is meant to be shared. As that old philosophical question goes, if a clarinet plays in the forest and nobody is around to hear it, did it really make a sound? When you feel ready, I strongly encourage you to perform in front of a live audience. The preparation required for a live performance is one of the best motivations to practice, and the applause of an appreciative audience provides the encouragement to stick with it.

If you're a little nervous about stepping on stage, you're not alone. Most performers, from rank beginners to the most seasoned pros, experience at least a little performance anxiety. This anxiety is perfectly natural and usually stems from a desire to do well in front of others. Assuming that you're well prepared, the fear of not doing well in front of others becomes a non-issue. The real issue, then, becomes simply not being accustomed to the performance environment.

One of the keys to overcoming performance anxiety is to make performance in front of audiences a part of your environment. Frequently play for small groups of people — friends, wives, mothers, and others — especially with a piece you've never performed.

Even the pros rehearse

Rehearsing in front of a small group of people before you give a live performance is something almost all performers do. For example, theater groups do dress rehearsals before opening night.

Accomplished musicians do the same. Eugene List, piano professor emeritus at the Eastman School of Music, was contracted to perform the "Grieg Piano Concerto" for the reopening of the Eastman Theater. Even though it was to be his eight hundredth performance of the piece, he still assembled his students and played it for them before his first rehearsal with the orchestra.

Regardless of how many times you've practiced your piece, playing in front of others is an entirely new way of experiencing that music. One way to overcome the jitters and build confidence is to play in front of a smaller audience first.

Part IV
The Part of Tens

"Does anyone else feel the clarinet and cello part is a bit too appasionato?"

In this part . . .

*E*very *For Dummies* book includes a Part of Tens — chapters containing ten bite-sized, easily digestible tips, tricks, or insights designed to improve your success and enhance your life — and keep you mildly entertained.

In this part, I offer ten inside tips on how to improve your technique and name ten A-listers of the clarinet world — ten must-hear clarinetists past and present.

Chapter 19

Ten Insider Secrets to Great Clarinet Playing

In This Chapter

▶ Improving breath support, embouchure, and tonguing

▶ Producing fast air by hissing like a snake

▶ Playing in tune, on pitch, and with a rhythmic pulse

▶ Developing faster fingering with sneaky fingers

Regardless of how experienced they are, clarinet players at every level, from beginner to advanced, struggle with the same basic problems and must constantly return to the basics to fine-tune their technique and improve their tone.

This chapter reveals the ten insider secrets to great clarinet playing that you must constantly remind yourself to do. While they may appear to be merely mechanical, they actually have a significant effect on your ability to produce beautiful music with your clarinet. Understanding the importance of these ten items and addressing them every day saves you significant time and effort in achieving your clarinet-playing goals, in addition to making you and your clarinet sound a whole lot better.

Straighten Your Back

Good posture is the foundation for good breathing. I once asked Stanley Hasty, my clarinet teacher at the Eastman School of Music, what he thought was the most essential factor in playing the clarinet. His answer: "Keep a straight back."

Never forget that the clarinet is a member of the wood*wind* family — like a sailboat, those notes aren't going anywhere when the air is still. You can practice for hours playing difficult passages and finger all your notes to perfection, but if you don't deliver fast air, those notes won't respond. Sit or stand up straight to maximize your lung capacity and get any kinks out of your airway.

To improve your clarinet playing posture, at least twice a week, practice while standing. When sitting, make sure the top of the music stand is at eye level.

Expand and Control Your Breathing

World-renowned clarinet player and teacher Mitchell Lurie once said, "If you want a bigger sound, take a bigger breath." Air speed is key, but so is air volume. Only with sufficient air volume can you

- ✔ Produce a full sound that reaches out to an audience.
- ✔ Match the volume of the other musicians around you.

- ✔ Improve the fullness of the sound and the response of the notes.

Following are some tips to improve your deep breathing:

- ✔ Perform the Arnold Jacob breathing exercise as described in Chapter 6.
- ✔ Remember to breathe through the corners of your mouth, not through your nose.
- ✔ Try to fill your stomach with air from the bottom up. Trying to breathe into the stomach encourages abdominal breathing — a must for wind players.

Air control through controlled breathing affects the beauty of the sound. You can't expect to use a full tank of air for a four-beat note and sound beautiful. Use too much air at one time, and you lose focus and control. Follow one of these two rules of thumb, depending on your level of play:

- ✔ **Beginners:** Try to play at least 12 beats in one breath.
- ✔ **Intermediate to advanced:** Try to play complete phrases in one breath.

Work Your Chops

"Chops" is music lingo for "embouchure," and good chops is what you need to achieve response of the full range of the clarinet, smooth skips between notes, and impeccable articulation. Reeds and mouthpieces are designed for good embouchure. Cooperate by maintaining good embouchure, and your mouthpiece and reed reward you by making your job easier and producing quality sound. Use poor embouchure, and your mouthpiece and reed punish you, making you work harder to produce any sound at all.

If you don't take enough mouthpiece in your mouth, you need to use a very hard reed to prevent it from closing on the facing, instead of vibrating as it should. Playing a reed that's too hard causes difficulties in making color and dynamic changes as well as in producing a clear sound and clean beginnings of notes. To get your embouchure right, keep four things in mind:

- **Rotate your jaw forward when you play.** Your upper teeth should be about ¼ inch down from the tip of the mouthpiece, while your lower teeth are about ¾ inch down from the tip of the mouthpiece and slightly covered by the lower lip.

- **Smile with the bottom lip pressed tight against your teeth to form a very narrow ledge on which the reed rests.** Say "mu" as in the beginning of the word "music."

- **Frown with your upper lip.** Say "vuum."

- **Visualize a business card under the reed to ensure you have enough reed vibrating inside your mouth.** See Chapter 6.

Tongue the Tip of the Reed to the Tip Rail

Clear attacks are absolutely essential for good rhythm and good ensemble playing. If your fellow band members can't tell exactly where your notes begin, they're going to have a tough time playing with you, so attack those notes with your tongue. Many of the finest clarinetists don't have *dragon tongues* (clarinet lingo used to describe a very fast tongue), but they do have crystal clear articulation.

Both the tongue and the reed are movable objects. The tip rail is the immovable object. Envision the tip rail in your mind's eye and use your tongue to move the reed toward it, as discussed in Chapter 9.

Tongue Fast with the Letter "D": Duh!

At the top of the worry list for many players is concern that they won't be able to tongue fast enough to keep up with the composer's tempo. The key here is to keep the tongue relaxed and trade in your tongue syllable "T-hee" for a faster tongue syllable — "Deh," "Dah," or "Duh."

Articulation has two speed settings: slow and fast. Slow articulation calls for very short staccato notes and guitar-style articulation. "T-hee" works fine for the slow style. Fast style is for tongued sixteenth notes at very fast tempos. Distinct D's produce plenty of space between notes at fast tempos while keeping the tongue muscle relaxed. For more about fast tonguing, see Chapter 14.

Fatigue is an enemy of fast tonguing. Don't overwork or strain the tongue by pressing it too hard against the reed. A light touch of the tongue can stop the reed vibration without tiring out your tongue.

Arch That Tongue: Hiss Like a Snake

Correct tongue position is essential for producing fast air, and fast air is essential for doing the following:

- ✔ Getting the reed to respond when playing the highest notes
- ✔ Producing overtones for a rich, beautiful sound

Create a wind tunnel, as explained in Chapter 11. Aim the air toward the bridge of your nose, hiss like a snake, and sculpt your cheeks inward against your teeth as you do when you whistle. Correct tongue position aims the air stream upward so the air strikes the reed in a perpendicular direction (like making the letter "T"), thus applying the greatest possible force with minimal effort. Another way to think of this is to imagine a target drawn on the top half-inch of the reed, and aim your air at the bull's-eye.

You can control the color of your sound by slightly altering your tongue position. Raise the tip of your tongue to speed up the air and produce a more brilliant sound. Lower the tip of your tongue to slow down the air and take some of the color out of the sound, when desired.

Grasping the nuances of the tongue position is difficult, because you can't really see what's going on inside a clarinet player's mouth when she's playing. Experiment by slightly adjusting the arch of your tongue to produce faster and slower air until you get a better feel for it.

Check Your Rhythmic Pulse

Playing with good rhythmic pulse adds energy to fast passages, making them much more engaging for listeners. To play with a rhythmic pulse, focus equally on the downbeats and the upbeats:

- ✔ **Downbeats:** Downbeats correspond to the rhythmic pulse of the music. This is what we dance or tap our toe to and what we feel during each measure. To play with pulse, accent the downbeats with a faster pulse of air as you play them. Feeling the pulses in this manner adds energy and pizzazz to your playing and increases your rhythmic accuracy. This also facilitates finger coordination, because motion is timed off rhythmic movement, as discussed in Chapter 14. It has been said that music is either a song or a dance. For songs you don't accent the pulse as much as you do when playing fast, dance-like passages.

- ✔ **Upbeats:** Upbeats are between the downbeats. If you're tapping your toe to the music, your toe is off the floor during the upbeat. Just like a clock, every tick has a tock. When you're learning a passage, accenting the upbeats is just as important as accenting the downbeats. Practice playing the piece at a slow tempo, accenting both the downbeats and the upbeats. This helps you internalize the upbeats, so you can *feel* them when you're playing at a fast tempo even though you're playing too fast to accent them. The increased breath support you use while building them into passages keeps them full and rich when you perform them.

Music is either a dance (more pulse) or a song (less pulse).

Develop Sneaky Fingers

To play very fast passages, your fingers must be quick and nimble to move from one fingering to another. Remind yourself of Elsa Verdehr's advice, given in Chapter 14: "Have sneaky fingers." Sneaky fingers begin with proper hand and finger position, as explained in Chapter 7:

- ✔ Top of right thumb under the thumb rest at the knuckle to support the clarinet
- ✔ Left thumbprint, at the two o'clock position, pressed against the tone hole at the back of the clarinet
- ✔ Fingers arched in a natural curvature to form C's over the tone holes
- ✔ Fingers moving at the knuckles only, not wiggling wildly

Play in Tune and on Pitch — Always

Top singers and musicians are always in tune or on pitch. Listeners expect it. This is the baseline requirement you must meet just to be considered a satisfactory player. Everything above and beyond this point is what separates the great players from the good ones. To play in tune and on pitch, attend to the following:

- ✔ Keep your clarinet in tune, as explained in Chapter 15. This applies to practice and before and during a performance. Good intonation and excellent tone are intertwined. One helps the other.

- ✔ Great tone is a function of amplitude, pitch, color, and focus. Produce ribbons of sound, as explained in Chapter 11.

Making minor adjustments in pitch with alternate fingerings also goes a long way toward helping you stay in tune during a piece, as explained in Chapter 15.

Exaggerate the Opposites During Practice

Proper practice makes you comfortable enough with your music to play it with confidence and conviction. One of the best approaches to gaining confidence is to exaggerate the opposites during your practice sessions:

- ✔ Practice slow to learn a piece faster. By making your first trip through the piece a slow one, you're better able to see what's there much more easily.

- ✔ If a note in a run barely comes out, play it too long during practice.

- ✔ If a note in a run sounds too weak, play it too loud when practicing.

See Chapter 16 for additional guidance and tips on how to practice more productively.

Chapter 20

Ten (Plus) Clarinetists
You Gotta Hear

*I*n Chapter 20 I give you ten secrets to great clarinet playing. Number 11 on that list would be to listen to as many CDs of outstanding clarinet players as possible. If you know what to listen for, a CD can be the equivalent of ten music lessons.

This chapter introduces you to a limited selection of outstanding clarinetists who represent various facets of clarinet playing, from tone to style. With so many wonderful clarinetists around the world, I could easily triple this list.

These players (and numerous others, including Grammy winner Larry Combs, principal clarinetist of the Chicago Symphony) are gems in their own respect, and any attempt to compare them would be like determining which diamond you like best on a particular day. I suggest you listen to and enjoy each of them to tune your inner ear to some of the greatest clarinet sounds the world of music has to offer.

Alessandro Carbonare

Italian clarinetist Alessandro Carbonare is one of Europe's most prominent soloists and orchestral performers. He also plays chamber music with the Quintetto Bibiena. He is presently Principal Clarinetist of Orchestra di Santa Cecilia in Rome, Italy. His earlier positions include: Co-principal of the Lyon Opera Orchestra (he joined at age 21) and Principal of Orchestre National de France. He has also played principal clarinet with Berlin Philharmonic.

Carbonare is known for his breathtaking performances of pieces by the masters, as well as more contemporary music. His playing represents clarinet sound at its best and he has a wonderful sense of artistry. I recommend the following recordings:

Rota: Concerto for Cello No. 2, Concerto for Strings, Clarinet Trio
Label: Concerto

Weber: Concertos for Clarinet
Label: Arts Musci

Eddie Daniels

Eddie Daniels is a Grammy-winning American jazz clarinetist who has performed and recorded all over the world, frequently appearing on television as a soloist and as a collaborator with other leading jazz figures. He has toured and recorded extensively with a variety of bands, small groups, and orchestras; has an impressive background as a classical musician; and holds degrees from Juilliard.

Daniels initially gained fame as a saxophone soloist with Thad Jones, but has concentrated on the clarinet since the early 1980s. He currently tours as a jazz soloist and leader of his own jazz groups.

As Buddy Defranco carried jazz clarinet playing to a new level beyond that of his swing predecessors, Eddie Daniels has shared Defranco's mantle as an outstanding innovator and leader in the field. His improvisation is wonderfully imaginative, and he has the brilliant technique and tonal control to carry out his ideas. To sample the sound of Eddie Daniels, I recommend the following:

Swing Low Sweet Clarinet
Label: Shanachie

Five Seasons (A crossover album)
Label: Shanachie

Crossing the Line, with Larry Combs (Principal Clarinet, Chicago Symphony)
Label: Summit (Classical)

A Duet of One
Label: Ipo Recordings

Buddy Defranco

Following in a long line of clarinet greats, including Artie Shaw, Benny Goodman, and Woody Herman, is Buddy Defranco, one of America's preeminent jazz clarinetists. Defranco has built a lengthy and legendary career as a jazz soloist and leader of a variety of small groups and bands. His discography includes hundreds of albums, and he has mentored many players on the Who's Who list of jazz greats.

Defranco began his impressive career as a member of swing bands, including the Tommy Dorsey Orchestra. He gained fame as one of the first bebop clarinetists and played with many famous small groups, including the Count Basie Septet. Bebop jazz transcended the styles of the earlier swing band players and is much more technically demanding. He also served as bandleader for the Glenn Miller Orchestra from 1966 to 1974. At the age of 87, he continues to maintain an active performance schedule at music festivals and in Carnegie Hall Concerts in New York City. Defranco is always a joy to hear, but I especially recommend listening to the two following CDs:

> *Like Someone in Love*
> Label: Progressive Records
>
> *Hark: Buddy Defranco Meets the Oscar Peterson Quartet*
> Label: Ojc

Stanley Drucker

Stanley Drucker is an American clarinetist who has had a remarkable career as an orchestral performer, soloist, and chamber music performer. Drucker performed with New York Philharmonic for 61 years (retiring in 2009). He joined the orchestra in 1948 and shortly thereafter won the position of Principal Clarinet. Drucker gained fame not only as an orchestral player, but through landmark solo performances and recordings of extremely technically difficult concertos by Nielsen and Corigliano (a concerto written specifically for him). Prior to joining the New York Philharmonic at a very early age, he played with the Indianapolis Symphony Orchestra and served a short while as Principal Clarinet with the Buffalo Philharmonic Orchestra.

Over his impressive career, Drucker has raised the bar for clarinetists around the world through his technical virtuosity and artistry. He never fails to bring a sense of life and freshness to the music that he performs. Following are a few of Drucker's most notable recordings:

Nielsen: Concertos, Hindemith, Bernstein, New York Philharmonic
Label: Sony

Corigliano: Concerto for Clarinet, Drucker/New York Philharmonic
Label: New World Records

New York Legends-Stanley Drucker Principal Clarinet
Label: Cala Records

Giora Feidman

Giora Feidman is an internationally know Klezmer clarinetist, originally from Buenos Aires, Argentina, but now from Israel. He has had an extensive career as a soloist and recording artist, including solos on the soundtrack of *Schindler's List.*

He began his career as an orchestral clarinetist and first performed with the Israel Philharmonic. He was the youngest clarinetist ever to perform with this orchestra and was a member for 20 years. Feidman has also performed with the Berlin Symphony Orchestra and numerous other orchestras and chamber ensembles.

Mention Klezmer clarinet and the name Giora Feidman comes up. He epitomizes this style of Jewish clarinet playing. His playing reaches to the depths of the listener's soul. For a small sampling of Feidman's work, check out the following CDs:

The Magic of Klezmer
Label: Delos

Prokofiev: Piano Concertos 2 and 4 Etc., with Israel Philharmonic Orchestra and Juilliard String Quartet
Label: Sony

Jon Manasse

Clarinetist Jon Manasse is an internationally known American soloist, chamber music player, and recording artist. He also performs regularly with the American Ballet Theatre and the New York City Ballet, and has performed as Principal Clarinetist of the Metropolitan Opera Orchestra and numerous festival orchestras and chamber music festival ensembles.

Along with Carbonare and Morales, Manasse represents a younger generation of players who have taken classical clarinet playing to new heights. A consummate performer, he exhibits flawless playing that incorporates one of the most dramatic, dynamic ranges to be heard on the clarinet. He is capable of playing very expressively at just a whisper. I recommend the following recordings:

> *Mozart, Spohr: Clarinet Concertos/Manasse, Schwarz*, with the Seattle Symphony
> Label: Harmonia Mundi

> *Brahms: Sonatas, Op. 120 No. 1 and 2/Manasse, Nakamatsu*
> Label: Harmonia Mundi

Paul Meyer

Paul Meyer is one of France's best known contemporary clarinet soloists, chamber music players, and recording artists. In his early years, after graduating from the Paris Conservatory, he won numerous Young Artists competitions. He has collaborated with many notable performers and conductors and has performed around the world. He has also served as conductor of the Seoul Philharmonic Orchestra and the Copenhagen Philharmonic Orchestra.

Paul Meyer represents the very best of French clarinet playing with an impeccable sound and amazing technique. His recordings always sparkle, as is evidenced in the following recordings:

> *French Clarinet Art/Paul Meyer, Eric Le Sage*
> Label: Denon Records

> *20th Century Music for Unaccompanied Clarinet/Paul Meyer*
> Label: Denon Records

> *Messien: Quartet for the End of Time/Shaham, Meyer, Et Al*
> Label: Deutsche Grammophon

> *Saint-Saëns: Le Carnival Des Animaux, Septour-fantasie*
> Label: EMI Classics

Sabine Meyer

German-born clarinetist Sabine Meyer is a world renowned soloist and chamber music player. She presently resides in Lübeck, Germany, and shares a professorship at the Musikhochschule Lübeck with her clarinetist husband, Reiner Wehle. She has recorded extensively and has appeared with most major orchestras around the world, including the Chicago Symphony Orchestra, the London Philharmonic Orchestra, the Toronto Symphony, and the Vienna Philharmonic and Berlin Philharmonic.

Meyer began her career as an orchestral clarinetist as a member of the Bayerischer Rundfunk Symphony and then joined the Berlin Philharmonic, which at that time was conducted by Herbert von Karajan. She has carried clarinet playing to new heights with a blend of wonderful clarinet tone and thoughtful and sensitive musicianship combined with dazzling technique. Her recordings never disappoint:

Mozart Clarinet Concerto, Debussy Premiere Rapsodie, with Claudio Abbado and Berlin Philharmonic
Label: EMI Classics

Brahms Clarinet Quintet with Alban Berg Quartett
Label: EMI Classics

A Night at the Opera Orchester der Oper Zurich
Label: EMI Classics

Ricardo Morales

Ricardo Morales, Principal Clarinetist of the Philadelphia Orchestra, is a native of San Juan, Puerto Rico. He also has an active career as a soloist, chamber music player, and recording artist. Prior to assuming his present position, Morales was Principal Clarinetist of the Metropolitan Opera Orchestra for 11 years, winning the position at the age of 23.

Morales has soloed with the Philadelphia Orchestra, the Chicago Symphony, and orchestras around the world. He also appears at numerous summer music festivals.

Morales consistently produces breathtaking performances. His playing combines extraordinary technique with an uncanny sense of phrasing, using his massive dark sound to bring it all off.

French Portraits/Ricardo Morales, Michael Chertok
Label: Boston Records

Brahms: Piano Trios Vol 1/Kalichstein Loredo Robinson Trio
Label: Koch International Classics

Contrasts-Bartok: Violin Works/Wood, Riley, Morales
Label: Endeavour Classics

Paulo Sergio Santos

Paulo Sergio Santos is from San Palo, Brazil. He has had an extensive career as an orchestral player, a studio recording artist, and a soloist on popular Brazilian music. He blends a solid background of classical training with a passion and talent for playing popular music. Santos is the Eddie Daniels of South America.

Santos's first important orchestral position was as Principal Clarinetist of the Orquestra Sinfonica do Teatro Municipal do Rio de Janeiro. He has recorded with all the major popular Brazilian artists of note.

Santos is an excellent representative of the wonderful clarinet playing traditions of South America. No one can tongue faster or for longer than Paulo Sergio Santos does when he plays Brazilian *choros* (popular folk-like Brazilian music). He deserves a place among the world's finest clarinet players.

> *Bach in Brazil/Camerata Brasil*
> Label: EMI Classics
>
> *Saudade Do Cordao* with Guinga
> Label: Boscoito Fino (Brazil)
>
> *Café Brazil*
> Label: Teldec

Richard Stoltzman

Two-time Grammy-winning American clarinetist Richard Stoltzman maintains a highly successful career as a soloist, chamber music player, and recording artist.

Unlike many of his peers, who are primarily orchestral clarinetists, Stoltzman has chosen to forge a career as a soloist and recording artist and has released almost 40 albums. He first gained success at the Marlboro Music Festival, where he performed for ten years. He also became a fixture at the Mostly Mozart Festival in New York. Stoltzman has performed concertos with over 100 orchestras around the world, frequently performing with the New York Philharmonic and Atlanta Symphonies.

Stoltzman is one of the best known and most flexible clarinet soloists. He has recorded in all media and genres, from classical to jazz and chamber music to concertos, with major orchestras. His incorporation of wide vibrato into clarinet tone has made him one of the most instantly recognizable recording clarinetists. He has an uncanny ability to pick up (tune in on) the composer's style.

Finzi: Clarinet Concerto, Bagatelles, etc., with Guildhall String Ensemble
Label: RCA Red Seal

Amber Waves-American Music
Label: RCA Victor Red Seal

Aria/Richard Stoltzman, with Slovak Philharmonic and the Kalman Opperman Clarinet Choir
Label: RCA Red Seal

Brahms: Sonatas for Clarinet/Stoltzman, Goode
Label: RCA Gold Seal

Beethoven, Brahms, Mozart: Trios for Piano, Clarinet, Cello/Richard Stoltzman, Emanuel Ax and Yo Yo Ma
Label: Sony

Part V
Appendixes

The 5th Wave   By Rich Tennant

"And this is supossed to help you flutter tongue?"

In this part . . .

The Part of Tens usually signals the end of the book — when the curtain falls, the applause trails off, and the audience and musicians head for the exits. In this book, however, I decided to include an encore — a couple extras at no additional cost.

In this part, I provide fingering charts you can use as quick reference tools, along with a list of what you can expect to find on the CD. Ahhh, the CD. I had almost forgotten — a second encore!

Appendix A

Fingering Charts

The charts on the next couple of pages show you the proper fingering for all of the notes you can play on the clarinet.

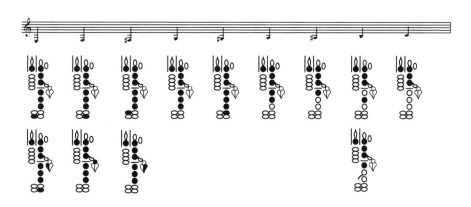

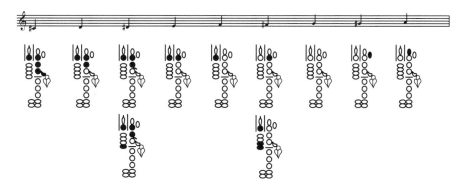

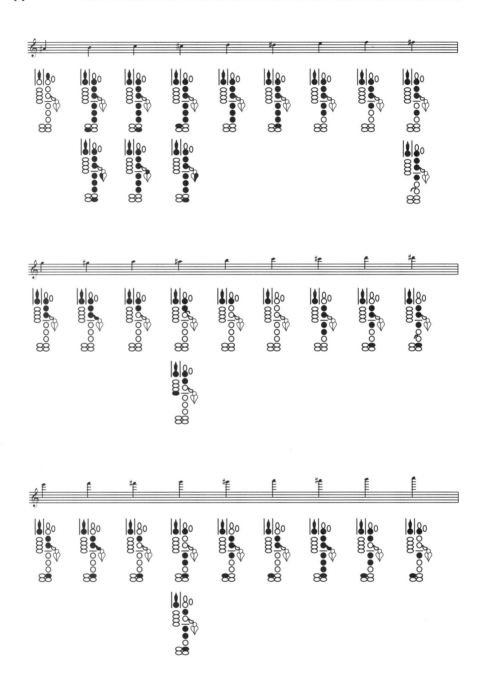

Appendix B

About the CD

The CD that accompanies this book contains 87 tracks. Each of these tracks presents musical examples that you can listen to and practice as much as you need to in order to improve your clarinet playing.

A fun way to use *Clarinet For Dummies* is to scan the chapters for the On the CD icon. In every instance, the text flagged by this icon refers to a musical example that not only appears as written music but also is presented as an audio track on the book's CD. When you see an example that seems interesting, skip to the corresponding track on the CD and give it a listen.

Relating the Text to the CD

Throughout the book, the text contains musical examples in the form of figures that you can play and practice over and over again. If a piece of music appears on the CD, the CD's track number is listed in the caption. Just use the track-skip buttons on your CD player to move to whatever track you want to listen to.

System Requirements

For many of you, all you're going to do is pop the CD in your CD player and skip around to the tracks you want to hear and play along with. Others may want to load the CD onto a computer.

Audio CD players

The CD included with this book will work just fine in any standard CD player. Just pop it in and press play or use the track-skip buttons to jump to whatever tracks you want to explore.

Computer CD-ROM drives

If you have a computer, you can insert the CD into your CD drive to access all the CD tracks. Make sure your computer meets the minimum system requirements shown here:

- ✔ A computer running Microsoft Windows or Mac OS
- ✔ Software capable of playing MP3s and CD audio (such as iTunes or Windows Media Player)
- ✔ A sound card (almost all computers these days have the built-in ability to play sound)
- ✔ A CD-ROM drive

The Tracks on the CD

The following table lists all 87 tracks on the CD along with the corresponding figure numbers from the chapters in the book.

Track Number	Figure number
1	Figure 6-1
2	Figure 6-2
3	Figures 7-11 through 7-13
4	Figures 7-14 and 7-15
5	Figures 7-16 through 7-18
6	Figures 7-23 through 7-29
7	Figures 8-1 through 8-5
8	Figures 8-6 through 8-9
9	Figure 8-10
10	Figures 8-13 through 8-18
11	Figure 8-19
12	Figures 8-20 through 8-22
13	Figures 8-23 through 8-28
14	Figures 8-29 through 8-37
15	Figure 9-1

Track Number	Figure number
16	Figures 9-2 through 9-6
17	Figure 9-8
18	Figure 9-9
19	Figure 9-10
20	Figure 9-12
21	Figure 9-14
22	Figure 9-15
23	Figure 9-16
24	Figure 9-17
25	Figure 9-18
26	Figure 9-19
27	Figure 9-20
28	Figure 9-21
29	Figure 9-22
30	Figure 9-23
31	Figure 9-24
32	Figures 10-1 through 10-3
33	Figures 10-5 and 10-6
34	Figure 10-7
35	Figure 10-8
36	Figure 10-9
37	Figure 10-10
38	Figure 11-3
39	Figure 11-7
40	Figure 11-8
41	Figure 11-9
42	Figure 11-10
43	Figures 11-11 through 11-13
44	Figure 11-14
45	Figure 11-15
46	Figures 12-3 and 12-4
47	Figure 12-5
48	Figure 12-6

(continued)

(continued)

Track Number	Figure number
49	Figure 12-7
50	Figure 12-8
51	Figure 12-9
52	Figure 12-10
53	Figures 13-1 through 13-3
54	Figure 13-5
55	Figure 13-6
56	Figure 13-7
57	Figure 13-8
58	Figure 13-9
59	Figure 13-10
60	Figure 13-11
61	Figure 13-12
62	Figure 13-13
63	Figure 13-14
64	Figure 14-1
65	Figure 14-2
66	Figure 14-3
67	Figure 14-4
68	Figure 14-5
69	Figure 14-6
70	Figure 14-7
71	Figures 14-8 and 14-9
72	Figure 15-3
73	Figure 15-4
74	Figure 15-5
75	Figure 15-6
76	Figure 15-7
77	Figure 15-8
78	Figure 16-1
79	Figure 16-2

Track Number	Figure number
80	Figure 16-3
81	Figure 16-4
82	Figure 16-5
83	Figure 16-6
84	Figure 16-7
85	Figure 16-8
86	Figure 16-9
87	Figure 16-10

Troubleshooting

If you have trouble with the CD, please call the Wiley Product Technical Support phone number at 800-762-2974. Outside the United States, call 1-317-572-3994. You can also contact Wiley Product Technical Support at `http://support.wiley.com`. John Wiley & Sons will provide technical support only for installation and other general quality control items. For technical support on the applications themselves, consult the program's vendor or author.

Index

• *♪* •

• N •

• O •